D1483927

P R O
Frank Beard
on the Golf Tour

PRO

Frank Beard
on the Golf Tour

Edited by Dick Schaap

The World Publishing Company
New York and Cleveland

A Maddick Manuscripts Book
Published by Maddick Manuscripts Inc.
345 East 56th Street, New York, New York 10022

Distributed by The World Publishing Company
2231 West 110th Street, Cleveland, Ohio 44102

Distributed simultaneously in Canada by
Nelson, Foster & Scott Ltd.

First Printing—1970

Copyright © 1970 by Frank Beard and
Dick Schaap

Library of Congress Catalog Card
Number: 77-115806

Printed in the United States of America

·

WORLD PUBLISHING
TIMES MIRROR

to RALPH, SR.

and RALPH, JR.

**Who Deserve Far More
Than Life Has Given Them**

Contents

Editor's Note

Frank Beard lives golf. When Frank was a teen-ager in Louisville, he played in the snow, chasing a red ball through drifts and slush. Sometimes, as he tried to master the game, he played as many as seventy-two holes in a single day, from sunup until past sundown, till his hands were raw, punishing himself for each shot he failed to execute perfectly.

Today, at the age of thirty, nothing in the world gives Frank Beard more pleasure than the game of golf. And yet nothing in the world frustrates him more.

Pro is, to a great extent, a story of frustration, which makes it the story of every golfer who ever lived, from Ben Hogan to Spiro T. Agnew. But it is also the story of one particular individual, one human being, whose livelihood depends on his ability to hit a round ball with a long stick and whose moods, whether he wants them to or not, reflect that ability.

Pro is a spontaneous story, an immediate story, told day by day.

Each night on the golf tour, Frank Beard spoke into a tape recorder his impressions of the preceding twenty-four hours while they were still fresh, before they could be tempered or polished. It is sprinkled with contradictions, with petulance, with opinions that sway and shift, as would be the diary of any man who lives under pressure and honestly reports his emotions and his experiences each day.

If Frank Beard sometimes loses his patience with caddies, with courses, with the demands of a nomad's life, even with the rain and the wind, he is not really angry with *them*, with those variables that can range, in each area, from magnificent to miserable. He is angry with himself. No caddy is a godsend when Frank shoots a 76; no hole is a completely fair test when he double-bogeys it. Conversely, when he shoots a 68, each caddy seems quicker and more intelligent, each fairway more lush, each green more true; when he runs off a string of birdies, there are no villains. In other words, he is human.

As I received each tape from Frank Beard and edited and organized his diary, never modifying his reports to accommodate ensuing developments, I was fascinated by the way his spirits soared and sank in direct relationship to his play. If he had never mentioned a daily score, I could have guessed, strictly from his remarks and his tone, within a stroke or two.

I wasn't particularly surprised; in an earlier book, *Instant Replay: The Green Bay Diary of Jerry Kramer,* Kramer's words provided an equally sensitive key to his own and his team's fluctuating fortunes. Kramer's world sometimes battered him physically; Beard's battered him mentally.

I found fascinating, too, the emphasis in Beard's account on money earned, down to the penny—an emphasis imposed by the nature of his game. Professional golf is the one sport in the world, outside Wall Street, in which until 1970 golfers were officially ranked by the amount of money they earned, as they still are unofficially but publicly; it can determine their eligibility for both tournaments and honors. (The basis for official ranking has now been changed to a point system.) Quite naturally the subject of earnings frequently invades the golfer's mind.

Ultimately Frank Beard's story is one of triumph, of victory over his own frustrations. Then, when the drives are long and straight, when the irons hold their lines, when the putts are falling, the world of professional golf looks to Frank Beard, one of its most gifted and articulate practitioners, once more like the best of all possible worlds.

DICK SCHAAP

New York City
March, 1970

INTRODUCTION

One of the Pros

I'm not Arnold Palmer. I'm not Jack Nicklaus. I'm not one of the handful of superstars on the professional golf tour. I don't fly my own jet from tournament to tournament. I don't have my own equipment company. I don't have any fan clubs, and when I walk down the fairways, unless I'm playing with Arnie or Jack or Billy Casper or somebody like that, I don't usually have much of a gallery to bother me.

I'm a professional golfer—and a good one, I think—but I'm just not one of the glamour boys. I don't dress up like a circus—like Doug Sanders. I try to wear nice clothes, but with my belly, even a pair of fifty-dollar slacks doesn't always look too sharp. I don't have any special flair. My wife and I were very friendly with the late Tony Lema, who used to send buckets of champagne to the press each time he won a tournament, and my wife has suggested that each time I win a tournament I ought to plug my home state and send the press buckets of Kentucky Fried Chicken. It's a nice idea, but I keep remembering that the press called Lema "Champagne Tony." You know what they'd call me.

Nobody would get very fat on my shipments of chicken. I haven't won a tournament in a year and a half, not since the 1967 Indianapolis "500" Festival, my third victory of that year. But I don't want anyone to waste any sympathy on me. Last year I became the first man in golfing history to earn more than $100,000 in prize money without winning a single tournament. I finished second three times and I placed among the top fifteen in nineteen tournaments, more often than any other golfer, including Palmer, Nicklaus, and Casper. The heart of my game is consistency.

Right now, a few months short of my thirtieth birthday, I should be approaching the peak of my game. I'm looking forward to the 1969 tour. I hate the traveling life, but I love to play golf, and I'd love to make this my biggest year. I'd especially like to win one of the major titles—the United States Open or the Masters. Those are the titles you keep for life, that nobody ever forgets, that lift you up near the superstars.

I've got a shot at those titles this year, maybe as good a shot as I'll ever have. I tied for fifth in the Masters last year, my best finish yet at Augusta, and we're playing the Open this year at Champions Golf Club in Houston, where I won the Houston Champions International in 1967 and finished seventh in 1968. Those are good courses for my kind of game.

I'd love to be able to explain in this diary how I won the Masters or how I won the Open or how I became one of the superstars of the pro tour. But, realistically, the odds are against me. I'll be satisfied if I can show what it's like to be a fairly typical touring professional golfer, one of 250 who sets out each year with clubs and hopes, one of the minority who manages to earn more on the tour then he spends. I want to express my own feelings, my own opinions, and I'm not going to promise that they're the same as anyone else's.

The tour's not what most people seem to think. It's not all sunshine and pretty girls and cheering crowds. (In my case, anyway, the cheers of the crowd are drowned out by the sounds of crying children. Whenever I can, I travel by car with my wife, Pat, and our children—Danny, who is two, and Randi, one—and we live in motel rooms and eat in cafeterias.) It's a life without roots. It's a potentially rewarding life, but also a frustrating life. There's no real opponent except your own stupid mental and physical mistakes.

I'm going to try to show the rewards and the frustrations, the stars and the hangers-on, and, if all goes well, if I can avoid dumb mistakes, if I can putt the way I know how, then I'm going to show exactly what it's like to win a professional golf tournament.

FRANK BEARD
Louisville, Kentucky
January 1, 1969

Frank Beard's Professional Record

1962–1968

YEAR	EVENTS	1ST	2ND	3RD	TOP 15
1962	5	0	0	0	1
1963	32	1	0	0	7
1964	33	0	0	1	10
1965	33	1	0	2	10
1966	32	1	1	0	17
1967	33	3	0	1	13
1968	32	0	3	0	19
Totals	200	6	4	4	77

AVERAGE SCORE	OFFICIAL MONEY	UNOFFICIAL MONEY*	TOTAL MONEY
72.50	$ 270.00	$ ———	$ 270.00
72.00	17,938.38	201.47	18,139.85
71.50	21,079.61	1,848.99	22,928.60
71.58	40,377.96	12,419.78	52,797.74
71.18	66,041.23	4,196.17	70,237.40
71.30	105,778.87	4,666.30	110,445.17
70.66	98,209.43	3,777.41	101,986.84
71.36	349,695.48	27,110.12	376,805.60

* Includes money won in pro-ams and in unofficial tournaments such as the Bing Crosby National Professional-Amateur and the Bob Hope Desert Classic.

1

Is California
Necessary?

TOURNAMENT	SITE	PURSE	DATES
Southern California Open*	Los Coyotes Country Club, Buena Park, California	$ 30,000	Jan. 4–Jan. 5
Los Angeles Open	Rancho Park Golf Club, Los Angeles	100,000	Jan. 9–Jan. 12
Kaiser International Open	Silverado Country Club, Napa, California	135,000	Jan. 16–Jan. 19
Bing Crosby National Pro-Am*	Three different courses, Pebble Beach, California	125,000	Jan. 23–Jan. 26
Andy Williams–San Diego Open	Torrey Pines Golf Club, San Diego	150,000	Jan. 30–Feb. 2

* Unofficial tournament

January 3 / Buena Park, California   Pro drove me and the family to the Louisville airport this morning. Pro is my father, Ralph Beard, Sr., who's a teaching golf professional and who's given me the only lessons I've ever had. Everyone calls him Pro. I do; my wife, Pat, does; my son, Danny, does; and when my daughter, Randi, learns to talk, she'll call him Pro, too.

Pro lives and dies with my performances on the golf course. He's the biggest sports fan in the world, and he's raised children who share his enthusiasm. My brother, Ralph, Jr.—technically, he's my half-brother, but we're as close as brothers can be—was an All-American basketball player at the University of Kentucky.

My father never pushed me into golf. When I was a kid, I played baseball with a passion. I could hit the ball pretty good. I was going to be a center-fielder in the big leagues someday; then, when I found out my arm wasn't exactly like Mickey Mantle's, I was going to be a second baseman. One day, when I was twelve, we were playing Little League baseball and we cut practice short, and one of my teammates asked me to play golf. I'd never hit a golf ball till then. I went out and shot 116. Of course, I must've cheated a little to get that score. Everyone cheats when they first start playing golf; a lot of people don't ever stop.

For six months, I played golf left-handed—my natural way—and my father didn't say much one way or the other. Then, when I began playing almost every day, he said, "I see you're taking this seriously. If you are, I'm going to help you." Right away, he changed me over to playing right-handed—for two reasons.

First, there's a golf theory, never really proven, that left-handers should play right-handed, and vice versa, because a golfer's leading side should be his strong side, and a right-handed golfer's leading side is his left side. The fact that Ben Hogan, the greatest golfer ever, was a natural left-hander gives some support to this theory. But, by the same token, Arnold Palmer and Jack Nicklaus are both natural right-handers, and I can't imagine either of them playing better left-handed.

Second, my father felt that it'd be much easier for him to instruct me. "I'm right-handed myself," he said, "and I see you as a right-handed player. If you play left-handed, I'll have to change all my thinking." I've played right-handed ever since.

We decided just three days ago that we were going to go to California today. I've been worrying about getting myself—and my golf—in shape. The last tournament of 1968 was the Cajun Classic in Louisiana late in November, and I played only two rounds of golf in December. When I came home from the Cajun, I just took it easy for a couple of weeks and didn't even think about golf. I didn't want to hear a word about the game.

Then I decided I'd take a week off in December and fly down to Florida and play some golf there. But I got all tied up—mostly making a series of instructional golf films for a local TV station, with the hope that eventually we'd syndicate them to other cities—and, before I knew it, the 1969 tour was just about on me.

Three days ago, Bill Boone, a Louisville attorney who acts as my business agent, called me and asked me if I wanted to play in the Southern California Open this weekend. It isn't a lot of money, but I figured I could use the competition. I asked Patty if she could get ready to leave in three days, and she said sure. In the past, we've driven out to California, and I've worked out at Palm Springs for a few days, but I decided this year I wasn't going to lose a week of my life driving to and from California. I decided I was going to fly with Patty and the kids. She's almost seven months pregnant; she's been pregnant most of the time since we got married three years ago.

After I talked to Patty, I called Bill Boone back and told him to enter me at Southern Cal. Then I went out and played golf. It was so cold it was ridiculous, sixteen degrees above zero, but I needed the work, so I wrapped myself up in a few sweaters and a jacket, carried my hand-warmer, and just barely managed to survive. Father Jack Jones, a priest who seems to spend more time on the tee than he does in the pulpit, and I won about twenty dollars from Pee Wee Reese, the ex-baseball player, and another fellow.

The next two days, I got my affairs in order. I arranged for a neighbor to keep an eye on my house, went to the bank and to the travel agency, watched the New Year's Day football games on TV, said good-bye to a few friends, finished up the instructional films, got a flu shot, and packed up. I've got a very modest wardrobe compared to some of the guys on tour. I'm taking twelve pairs of slacks with me, six sweaters, fourteen golf shirts, two pairs of street shoes, and two pairs of golf shoes. I get my shoes free from Foot-Joy, and my shirts, sweaters, underwear, and socks free from Munsingwear. Foot-Joy doesn't pay me—or any other golfer, as far as I know—to wear their shoes; they just give me as many pairs of shoes as I need for myself and my family. Munsingwear does pay me a yearly salary to wear their products, plus bonuses for winning tournaments and for finishing among the leading money-winners. They give me clothes for my family, too. Only three or four guys on the tour have sponsors who give them slacks. I don't; you've got to have a slim waistline for that. I pay about forty or fifty dollars a pair, and I use up about a dozen pair a year.

My most lucrative contract's with Hillerich & Bradsby, the equipment manufacturer I represent. H & B's a Kentucky company—they make the Louisville Slugger baseball bats, as well as Power-Bilt golf clubs—and they've always treated me very well. Even when I was an amateur, they gave me golf clubs. They paid me $1,500 my rookie year on the tour, and the salary's gone up almost every year since then. One of the things I like best about representing H & B is that, because they don't manufacture golf balls, I'm free to use any ball I want. I use Titleists. Titleist doesn't pay anyone, but gives its ball away free to any pro who'll use it. The guys who have contracts with Wilson and Spalding and other companies that make pro-quality balls have to use their company's ball, but most of the rest of us use Titleists. It's the best ball.

When we got up this morning, the kids were both running a fever. Randi's was up to 103, and Patty and I were worried. But we had to go. We had no choice. We gave Randi some baby aspirin and some juice and the fever went down, but when we boarded the plane, her fever shot up to 105. We gave her some more aspirin, and by the time the plane landed in Memphis, only an hour away from Louisville, the fever was broken. Even though we waited two hours to take off in Memphis, she seemed all right the rest of the way to Los Angeles.

In Los Angeles, some fellow from the Southern California Open committee picked us up and drove like a lunatic down to Buena Park, where the tournament's being played. He kept turning around and talking, and I didn't think we'd ever get here alive.

Somehow, we made it, but because of the delay in Memphis, I got to the course too late to practice. I took the courtesy car the tournament committee provided for me, checked the family into a motel, ate dinner, then went to a local driving range for a workout. I figured I'd be all alone at the range, but when I walked around a little hedge to start hitting, there was Lee Trevino, the United States Open champion in 1968, flanked by a few of his fans, Lee's Fleas. Lee's a Mexican-American, a real extrovert with a wild sense of humor. He's one of the characters of the tour, always playing to the galleries, not just for show, but because he likes to. But he's dedicated to the game. If he weren't, he wouldn't be out at a driving range the night before a little tournament.

"Hey, Beard," Lee said. "You trying to steal my thunder? I thought I had this place cornered."

We're not particularly close—Lee's not much for hanging around the motels, and I've never seen him in one of our bridge games—but I honestly like him. I enjoy watching him bubble over. We said hello and wished each other a Happy New Year. Then I hit shots for about an hour and a half. I was kind of surprised what good shape I was in. My muscles were more supple than I thought they'd be, and my hands weren't as sore as I expected them to be. Mainly, I was just trying to loosen up. I guess golfers aren't really athletes, not the way football and basketball players are, and we don't go through any regimented conditioning program. It always takes me the first two weeks of the tour to work out the winter kinks. I can't do it any quicker than that, and sometimes it takes longer. I just start off not expecting to play well for at least two weeks.

I was thinking last fall about skipping the first month of the tour this year and, instead, going to Florida and working on my game there. I always play terribly in California, partly because my timing is off and partly because I putt horribly on California greens. I lived in Texas till I was sixteen, then in Louisville, then went to the University of Florida, and in all those places, the greens are Bermuda grass. In California, the greens are bent grass, which means, generally, a faster putting surface than I'm used to. I'm a good putter most of the time—in fact, I was named the All-American putter in 1967—but in California I'm an atrocious putter. I don't mean I'm just relatively bad. I'm really bad. The thing about tournament golf is that you can win fairly good money provided either you're hitting the ball very well or you're putting very well; if you're doing both very well, you win tournaments, big money. I don't do either well out here.

Yet I can't help coming back. In the four major tournaments on the coast—before we move to the desert courses for three weeks—we're playing for a total of $510,000 in prize money, not even counting pro am money. I just can't pass that up. I've got to try for that money. Even if I play badly, which I usually do, I can still make expense money. Yet last year, I didn't even make expenses; in the four coast tournaments, I missed the cut twice and didn't win a dime, tied for twenty-ninth once and tied for thirty-eighth once.

I must really be a dummy coming out here again. Maybe, down deep, I can't resist the challenge. Maybe, one year, I'm going to have a good California. Maybe.

January 4   "Hello, Frank. Boy, you look fat."
Everyone was picking on my belly today. I suppose I am getting fat. I'm up to 195 pounds, which doesn't spread out too well on

my six-foot body. I promise myself I'm going to go on a diet. To-morrow.

I went out to Los Coyotes Country Club around nine o'clock this morning. I wasn't teeing off until 11:15, but I wanted to spend a little time on the practice tee. First thing I did was put out some fishlines about getting an automobile. I've got a car from the tourna-ment committee for the two days here, but I need one for the whole six or seven weeks out west. I could rent one, but it'd cost seven, maybe eight hundred dollars, and I don't see any sense in spending the money if I don't have to. I've been trying to pull every deal I know to get a free car. I'd be happy to pose for publicity pictures in return for the use of a car. I'm just going to drive it for a few thousand miles and then turn it back in. So far, I haven't had any luck. I sure as hell hope I don't wind up renting one. That's a lot of money just for driving around.

I asked Charlie Sifford, who's from Los Angeles, if he knew any-one who could help me. Charlie's the first Negro to make it on the tour, the first one to win an official tournament, and he was a little upset this morning because an article in the paper had him accusing the people at the Masters of discrimination. He said he hadn't been quoted accurately.

Charlie probably was misquoted. The whole situation with him and the Masters is kind of strange. He's played in every big tourna-ment except that one, but he can't really claim he's being dis-criminated against because he's never qualified for the Masters. In fact, no Negro has ever qualified for the Masters. The Masters is by invitation only, but in order to get an invitation, you must qualify. There are a bunch of different ways you can qualify—if you place among the top sixteen in the U.S. Open, for instance, or among the top eight in the Professional Golfers Association championship— but qualifying just means that you're eligible for an invitation, not that you get one automatically. Of course, I've never heard of an eligible player not receiving an invitation. There've been rumors that if a Negro ever qualifies, he won't get an invitation, and I imagine that's what disturbs Charlie. There've been other rumors that if a Negro qualifies, they'll just call off the tournament. But the people at the Masters have said that if a Negro qualifies, he will re-ceive an invitation; I just hope it's Charlie.

I played today with Bob Lunn, one of the best young players

to come along in a long time, a kind of quiet boy who's built like Nicklaus and hits the ball like Nicklaus, and with a boy who's an assistant pro at the club here. The assistant pro was out of it before he even got started. He's a typical example of the local pros who get into tournament competition. They find it's a whole different game, tournament golf. They play their home course well, well enough to qualify for the tournament, but when the chips are down, they just can't seem to perform. I suppose that's why they're working in a club shop instead of playing the tour.

I started off surprisingly well. I holed two fifteen-footers for birdies and went three-under after four holes. Then I three-putted a couple of holes, my usual California style. I scrambled back to four-under, then lost my concentration, bogeyed a couple more holes, and birdied the eighteenth for a 69. I'm not up with the leaders—Lunn shot a 66 and there were a pair of 65s—but I'm tickled pink. I wasn't even sure I was going to make the cut, the shape I'm in. I couldn't believe I'd hit the ball as well as I had. This tournament doesn't mean anything—it's only thirty-six holes, and it's not an official tour event—but still I'm getting a little excited. You'd think after seven years on the tour, I wouldn't get excited.

I drove back to the motel with Charlie Coody, a Texan who's one of my closest friends on the tour. He'd shot a 74, which meant he didn't qualify for the final round tomorrow, but he wasn't down in the dumps. Charlie wasn't counting on doing too well.

Charlie and I get along very well, and I love him to death, but he's like an old grandmother at times. He's so slow getting ready in the morning. He's so slow doing everything. He's so meticulous. He keeps records on everything he does in golf. He keeps every one of his scores, the number of greens he hit, the number of greens he missed, fairways hit, fairways missed, number of putts, number of one-putts and three-putts, chip-ins, bunker shots up and down, bunker shots missed, out-of-bounds, penalty strokes, everything you can imagine.

Charlie may record every conceivable statistic, but I don't think it helps him a lick. He came up to me last year and said, "Frank, you know I made more money last year than I ever made, but I took more putts than I ever took before. I can't figure it out."

"What are you talking about, Charlie?" I said. "You have all those charts. Don't you analyze them?"

"Can't figure it out," he said. "I made more money, but I had more putts. You'd think it'd be fewer putts."

"Charlie," I said, "did you ever stop to think that you hit more greens last year, that you had less chips?"

"Never thought of that," said Charlie.

He keeps track of his money the same way. I'm not a big spender, not by far, but Charlie really pinches his pennies. He writes down every cent he spends, and I remember one time last year he got all upset because his records didn't balance. He was missing one penny, honest to God, one penny short. And he turned to his wife, Lynette, and wanted to know exactly where that one penny went.

Lynette didn't have the slightest idea. She was so mad at him, she just said, "I put it in the gum machine for a piece of gum." I just about died laughing. I suppose old Charlie put it down in his records: one penny for a piece of gum.

I'm not much of a party boy myself, but I do enjoy a beer or a Scotch or two now and then. Charlie doesn't like to party at all. After a round, he wants to eat dinner, go back to his room, bring his records up to date, and then watch television till he goes to bed. He likes to go to bed precisely twelve hours before he's going to tee off. If he's got a 9:12 A.M. tee time, he tries to go to bed at 9:12 P.M.

Charlie really splurged tonight. He took his wife and his two kids and I took my wife and my two kids and we had a big night out at Shakey's Pizza Parlor. Best pizza I ever tasted.

Damn, I got to go on that diet tomorrow.

January 5 / Santa Monica   I guess I know what Doug Sanders goes through now. I was taking a lot of razzing today about a pretty girl who followed me on the course yesterday. She was a real knockout, but she wasn't following me just for my good looks. She's an old friend of mine and Patty's, and she came out yesterday with her boyfriend, Chuck Cottier, the baseball player.

I got a kick out of meeting Cottier. I'm still awed when I meet baseball players and basketball players and football players, real athletes. Chuck's never been a star, just a solid ballplayer, but I've watched his career pretty closely. He decided he wanted to follow a local pro he knows for a few holes, so while he did, his girl followed me. She was really something to look at. A lot of people looked at her.

Today I was getting the evil eye from all the golf wives around the course. They're like any other group of girls, I suppose; they love to have something to gossip about. I was getting a different kind of evil eye from the other pros. "Old Beard's turning over a new leaf," they were saying.

I don't have a reputation for being one of the playboys on the tour. We've got some pretty good ones—Doug Sanders will admit he's the all-time champion, if you ask him, and Ray Floyd's got to be a contender—but even though I played the tour for three years as a bachelor, I wasn't much for running around. I wasn't a saint. I just wasn't any good at meeting girls. I met Patty on a blind date that Tony Lema arranged. The Lemas and Patty lived in the same apartment house in Dallas, and the first time I saw Patty, at Tony's place, she watched television and didn't pay any attention to me at all. I was used to that.

You can't believe how naïve I was. There was a girl on the tour several years ago who was a real camp follower, a genuine nymphomaniac. Everybody knew about her except me. We were playing a tournament in Palm Springs, and as I finished my last round and came off the eighteenth green, she walked up to me, said hello, and told me she was a friend of one of the other guys. "I hear you're a bachelor," she said, "and you don't have anybody traveling with you, and I was wondering if you'd give me a ride to Phoenix." I was all ready to leave for Phoenix, so, without even thinking, I said, "C'mon, let's go."

It was just a four- or five-hour drive to Phoenix, and on the way, she made kind of a pass at me. She reached over and gave me a kiss on the cheek, but I didn't think anything of it. I just thought she was being funny. I didn't even wonder why she wanted to go to Phoenix. When we got to the outskirts of Phoenix, she said, "You know, I don't have any place to stay in Phoenix."

I really followed up on that lead. "Most of the golfers are staying at the Ramada Inn," I said. "Maybe you can get a room there."

We pulled up at the Ramada Inn and I went in and asked at the desk and found out they had a room available. The girl checked in, and I checked in, and I played the real chivalrous gentleman and carried her bags to her room, the sort of thing anybody would do for any female.

She immediately opened up a suitcase, took out a bottle of wine, and asked me if I'd like some. I said I'd have a glass. I didn't have any ulterior motive. I just like wine. About that time, she let me know she was going to make love to me.

"See you later," I said.

I walked out of her room. I suppose the fact that I had a pretty religious upbringing had something to do with it. Maybe the fact that she was very ugly had something to do with it, too. But it didn't seem to bother too many of the other guys. I mean, she really played the tour. And a few weeks later, she got up a list rating all the golfers she knew as to who were the best lovers and who were the worst, and the list got circulated around.

And there was old Beard, rated right at the bottom of the list.

I don't think it was fair. I shouldn't have been on the list. I never even held her hand.

On the putting green today, when the pros weren't kidding me about the girl, they were talking about my weight again. Bob Rosburg, the former PGA champion and a good needler, said he couldn't get over how fat I am. I can't take any more of that. I'm absolutely starting my diet tomorrow.

I kept asking around about a car to use out here. "Anybody makes as much money as you do ought to buy a car in every city," Al Geiberger, another former PGA champion, told me. Al was only kidding, but I'm not. I don't like to spend seven hundred dollars if I don't have to. I don't like to spend five dollars if I don't have to.

I got paired with Billy Casper and Harry Toscano today; we all had 69s the first round. Harry's a young boy, strong as a bull, hits the ball nine miles, but he's been out on the tour a couple of years now and he hasn't done a thing. He's one of the group people call the rabbits, the guys who don't have the security of being in an exempt category. You become exempt if you finish among the top sixty money-winners for a calendar year or if you win a tournament; that means you automatically qualify for every tournament (except the Open, the Masters, and the PGA) the following year. If you're not an exempt player, you can qualify in one of two ways: either by making the cut the previous week—you make the cut by placing among the top seventy plus ties after the first two rounds of a tournament—or by qualifying in a special competition on the Monday before the tournament. You really have to hustle if you're not exempt, but if you're one of the young boys, like Harry, who hasn't really shown one way or the other whether he can make it on the tour, you've got to take the gamble.

I gave up a long time ago trying to predict which individuals would succeed and which wouldn't. I'd have bet my life on some who fell flat on their faces—Frank Wharton's a good example—and I've laughed at others who made it big. If anybody had told me five years ago that George Archer would become a $100,000-a-year golfer, I'd have told him he was crazy.

Billy Casper is simply the finest golfer alive today, ahead of Nicklaus, Palmer, everybody. He's an absolute perfectionist—a beautiful putter, a good thinker. He does everything well.

On the first tee, Cas was his usual pseudo-jovial self. He used to be a pretty drab fellow, but somebody got hold of him and told him if he was ever going to be a great personality in the sports world, he'd have to shape up. So now he throws out corny lines to the crowd and tries to pretend he's a comedian. It just isn't like Billy at all. He's really a serious, mature type, but I guess that isn't a very profitable image.

Cas didn't play well today, not by his standards. He had a 71; Toscano and I both shot 70, which ought to put us somewhere in the top ten. Bobby Lunn, the twenty-three-year-old boy I played with yesterday, shot 69 today and won the tournament. I guess we'll be hearing his name a lot this year. Last year, he missed the cut in eight of his first twelve tournaments, when he was still a rabbit, then came on stronger than a garlic milk shake to win over $100,000. He won two tournaments in a row in the middle of the year.

As soon as I finished, one of the men from the tournament committee drove me up to Santa Monica, less than an hour from Buena Park. I'd packed up the car in the morning and sent my family ahead with Charlie Coody and his family. Poor Charlie volunteered to take both families to Disneyland today—those four kids must've driven him out of his mind—then to meet me at the motel in Santa Monica.

We've got a nice setup here in Santa Monica. It's nothing fancy, but it's on the beach and it's reasonable and it's only about fifteen minutes from the Rancho Park Golf Club in West Los Angeles, where we're playing the L.A. Open this week. We've got a little kitchen with a dining area, a small living room with a double bed in it, and a separate bedroom for the children. The children's room is really just a large closet, but at least they're by themselves. Usually, in a motel, we get one room for the whole family, and it's pure bedlam.

I had to go to the supermarket for groceries tonight, and I realized I didn't have any cash. Bob Murphy, the rookie of the year on the tour last year, is staying in the unit right next to ours, sharing it with two other young fellows—Bunky Henry and Jim Grant—and when I heard he was going shopping, I borrowed one hundred dollars from him and went with him. While we were in the store, Charlie Coody came in and said he'd run out of cash, too, so I loaned him twenty-five dollars. We're kind of one big happy family on the tour, staying in the same places, shopping in the same stores, living the same lives. Tomorrow, Charlie and I'll cash checks, and he'll pay me back and I'll pay Bob.

After dinner, Jimmy Colbert and Steve Reid, two regulars in our touring bridge game, stopped by to say hello. Jimmy's very, very serious about his golf—I think if he'd loosen up a little and have a few laughs he'd be a better player—and we started talking about putting. I gave him a little lesson on the living-room rug. That's the way it is on tour; we try to help each other when we can. The only guy I worry about beating me is me.

I went to bed early, with two things on my mind: first, that damn diet, and second, I've got to find myself a car.

January 6   I started my diet this morning, just grapefruit, bacon, and eggs; no bread, no sugar. I've got to stick to it. I want to lose at least fifteen pounds and get under 180. I've got to demonstrate some self-discipline or they'll start calling me Porky Beard.

In the morning paper, I saw that I finished in a tie for sixth in the Southern Cal Open and won eight hundred dollars. That made me feel a little better. I covered the plane fare for me and the family.

I made a few phone calls about getting a car and got a few leads, but nothing definite. About 9:30, Charlie Coody drove me out to the course. I'd seen a few of my friends at Buena Park, but everyone's here, and I must've spent half an hour wishing people Happy New Year, all of us acting like we hadn't seen each other in years. It's only been about six weeks since the 1968 tour ended.

Charlie and I arranged a practice game with Steve Reid and Jimmy Colbert, and then I went through the normal procedure. I paid the standard fifty-dollar registration fee, picked up my admission badge and my parking sticker and a badge for Patty and half a dozen extras. Then I found the Titleist man and he gave me my usual weekly quota of three dozen free golf balls and three free golf gloves. I got my locker assignment, took my clubs, and went out to select a caddy.

Some of the pros have regular caddies they use most of the time, but I don't. I prefer to use a local boy, especially a high-school or college student, if they're available. I like to stay away from the traveling caddies, the few dozen who follow the tour, moving from tournament to tournament the same way the golfers do. Of course, some of them are good, hard workers, but I feel they're the exceptions. I just don't want to get involved with the touring caddies. It's not that they're bad caddies. They're good. But they think they're too good. They want too much money.

They want to get paid at a minimum what they call "ten-and-three." That's ten dollars a day and three percent of your winnings. I feel that's just too much money. Last year I averaged about three thousand dollars a tournament in prize money. In a normal tournament, you'll use a caddy for six days, Tuesday through Sunday, and that means he wants $150 for working about thirty hours. That also means if you win a tournament and collect an average first prize of twenty-five thousand dollars, the caddy expects $810, more than twenty-five dollars an hour. It's not worth it to me. It's the easiest possible work. I don't expect the caddy to tell me what club to hit; if I don't know my own game better than he does, I ought to be in a different business. I don't expect him to read the greens for me; I trust myself first. Once in a great while, you find a caddy who really helps you, but the majority are just bag-toters. The better

ones carry your bag and clean your clubs after each shot and clean
your ball on the green and obey the rules, and that's it. I don't want
to pay as much as twenty-five dollars an hour for that.

Whenever I use a touring caddy, I don't make any agreement
with him in advance; I pay him what I think he's worth. The touring
caddies know the way I figure, they know I don't pay well by their
standards, so generally they stay away from me, I stay away from
them, and we're both happy.

But I did use a touring caddy, a fellow named Johnny, in the
Cajun Classic, the last tournament of 1968. He caddied for me for
five days, and I think I won about eight hundred dollars, so, at
ten-and-three, that'd be seventy-four dollars. I gave him a hundred.
I felt he was worth that much to me.

Today, when I came out of the locker room, Johnny stepped up
and grabbed my bag. They must keep hoping that old Beard'll
soften up someday. Johnny and I went down to the practice tee, and
I bought a big bucket of balls for a dollar—sometimes we get them
free, sometimes we pay for them, depending on how the local pro
feels about it—and hit the ball pretty good, better than I'd expected.

I noticed right away that Johnny'd been drinking, which is not
unusual among the touring caddies. I could smell it on his breath,
and he was yakking ten times more and faster than I'd ever heard
him. "Well, this is a good way to start the year off," I thought.
Johnny's talking about how well he knows the course, how much he's
going to help me, how we're going to finish first, how we should've
won the Cajun, the kind of talk you usually get on Sunday when
the caddy's pushing for an extra tip. And this is only Monday.

On the first tee, Coody and I set up our match with Reid and
Colbert, a little two-dollar Nassau, two dollars on the front nine,
two dollars on the back nine, two dollars on the overall score. It's not
cutthroat stakes, just a little incentive to keep us serious. I made a
side bet, a two-dollar Nassau, with Jim Colbert.

We teed off and immediately started walking off the course,
getting our yardages. We pick a landmark for each hole, something
stationary, like a sprinkler head in the fairway or a distinctive tree,
and walk off the distances from the mark to the front of the green,
the middle of the green, and the back of the green. On a par-four
hole, for instance, the distances from the mark may be 140, 150, and
160 yards. No matter where you drive your ball the next day, you

can walk off the distance to your landmark and figure out exactly how far you are from the pin. We all carried pencils today and wrote the distances down on our scorecards. Some guys use little books. I've used the back of credit cards. All you need is enough space to give one line to each of the eighteen holes.

Charlie was carrying his scorecard from 1967, the last time we played here, and every now and then he'd let out a little moan. "They chopped down two of my trees and one of my fat little bushes," he said. He saves all his yardages, of course. I throw mine away after a tournament. I know that even if I save it, I'm still going to measure the course again next year. Courses do change.

Getting the yardages is one of the most important things we do all week. When I'm doing it, I'm serious to the point of being rude. I don't want anyone talking to me. Almost every pro gets his own yardages, but a few guys have caddies they feel they can rely on. Those are the guys who really lean on their caddies, the guys who pay as much as fifteen dollars a day and four and five percent of their winnings. I think it's just plain laziness to have the caddy measure the distances. You've got to walk to the green anyway, so you might as well count off the paces.

About the fourth tee today, Johnny, my caddy, was yakking away, and Steve Reid had had a little trouble on the first three holes, and Steve's a little on the volatile side—more than a little, actually—and I thought he was going to hit Johnny. I don't know why I didn't drop him right at the beginning and get a different caddy. "Listen, Johnny," I said, "you better slow down right now. Just take care of me and leave Steve and the others alone." Johnny got the message. He hushed up the rest of the day.

During the round, Steve and Charlie and Jimmy and I didn't do too much talking, except about the bowl games and pro football and the bets that looked good to us. Jimmy's our resident football expert. He played a little quarterback at Kansas State University. After college, he went into the insurance business, then turned golf pro in 1965, when he was twenty-four. In 1967, his second full year on the tour, Jimmy finished among the top sixty money-winners and was exempt from qualifying all last year. But he just fell apart in 1968. Even being exempt, he didn't finish among the top hundred money-winners. He lost his exempt status, and this year he's got to fight to get it back.

Jimmy told me today he's made a New Year's resolution not to take too many lessons this year. In the past, he's always been asking people for advice, and he's gotten so involved in mechanics he hasn't played his own game. We're glad to give each other advice, but sometimes, trying to be helpful, we just confuse each other.

I'd like to be able to give some good advice to Steve Reid, but the only one who can help him is himself. I've never met anyone who wants more desperately to be successful on the pro tour. Steve wants to win so badly he builds up unbearable pressure on himself, then gets angry when he makes a mistake and loses his concentration. He's a few years older than me—a Californian who lives in St. Louis now—but he didn't start playing the tour much until 1965, when he was twenty-nine. Steve had been a club pro for almost ten years before that; he has three children who are deaf, and it must've taken a lot of courage to give up a regular job and gamble on the tour. He hasn't come close to breaking the top sixty money-winners yet, but last year he won the Azalea Open—a tournament held the same week as the Tournament of Champions, when most of the big boys were in Las Vegas—and that gave him a one-year exemption, through the Azalea this year. I'm praying that that cushion, that freedom from having to qualify each week, will take some of the pressure off Steve and let him play the way he's capable of playing. Mechanically, he's an outstanding golfer. His problem is controlling his emotions. I'd like to see Steve do well because I know how much it means to him; I swear he'd cut off an arm if somebody promised him that'd make him a winning professional golfer.

Steve and Jimmy won the front nine today, one-up, so Charlie and I pressed on the back nine. I was really aching. The Southern Cal Open kind of pooped me out. "Charlie, I don't know if I can make it through this nine," I said. "I'm in bad shape. I'm ready to quit."

"C'mon," Charlie said. "We got to get our yardages."

We finally won the back nine, two-up, which meant that we each won four dollars. I won four dollars, too, on my side bet with Jimmy. Not a bad day.

Afterward, I sat my caddy down in the locker room and told him, "Johnny, I don't like many of the fellows that travel, but I like you. We get along fine. You're a good caddy. We'll do all right together, but I'm out here to make a living, the same as you are, and I can't if you're going to be drinking. Whatever you do tonight or any other night is your own business, but for the time we're working together, I don't want to smell anything on your breath."

He apologized and said it wouldn't happen again. I believe him. I don't think he'll be coming out bleary-eyed or half-looped tomorrow. I gave him twenty dollars in advance, to help him pay his rent.

I was too tired to practice after the round, so I just went home; ate a little steak, a little salad, and a little green beans; played bridge with Jimmy and Steve; gave them back the money I'd won on the course; and went to sleep. I did have one fall from grace. Right before I went to bed, I drank a Pepsi.

January 7   I had a terrible night last night. I woke up at three o'clock with my worst earache in ten years. Patty gave me some aspirin and put a hot towel on it, but it kept me up most of the night. I couldn't have gotten more than three hours of sleep.

I went to the course early, before nine o'clock, and when I came out of the locker room, ready to practice, Johnny, my caddy, was nowhere in sight. I carried my own clubs to the practice tee, no big deal, and while I was hitting, a fellow came up to me, a pro, and said hello and started talking. I just tuned out.

He is one of a certain type of golfer on the tour that I can't stand. These guys are like the rabbits, in that they have to qualify each week, but the difference is that the rabbits haven't proved what they can do or what they can't do. These guys have definitely proved what they can't do: they can't play on the tour.

There are some 250 golfers on the tour. The dedicated fan might be able to name forty or fifty of them. He hasn't even heard of the others. Almost every tournament has a starting field of 144. Of that number, maybe 120 qualified by being among the top sixty money-winners or by winning a tournament during the previous year or by making the cut the previous week or by getting a special exemption (the host pro, for instance). That leaves about twenty-five places for roughly 130 guys who try to qualify on Monday.

Perhaps a third of the guys trying to qualify are rookies. Each year about sixty graduates of the PGA school in Florida earn Approved Tournament Player cards. This means that they've shown they have the financial backing to go on the tour—either they or their sponsors are willing and able to put up $250-a-week expense money for at least six months—that they've got the proper character to play the tour, that they've passed written exams, and that they've performed well in a 144-hole qualifying competition.

To make room for the rookies, about sixty guys a year drop off the tour. Most of them drop off voluntarily—they run out of money or they realize they're not going to make it—but some have their ATP cards lifted by the PGA. These are the ones on the bottom of the money list, the worst players, the ones who obviously don't belong on the tour.

Aside from the rookies, a large percentage of the other guys trying to qualify each Monday don't belong on the tour. They don't have a chance in hell of winning anything. They should be weeded out, but under the present PGA rules, there's no way to do it. Once you've been an assistant pro at a club for a certain length of time (even if you've never entered a tournament) or once you've played on the tour a certain length of time and entered a certain number of tournaments (even if you've never won a penny), you become a Class A member of the PGA. And once you're a Class A member, you're eligible to try to qualify for any tournament. The PGA now has almost six thousand Class A members, so, theoretically, six thousand pros could try to qualify every Monday for maybe twenty-five spots. Of course, most of them have too much sense to show up.

This fellow who came up to me today is a Class A pro—he earned his membership working in a pro shop—and he's out on the tour full time. He can't hit his butt, but he's one of the 250 touring pros, and he's out to lord it over all the millions of other golfers in the United States. He's always telling people he's a touring pro, and he's always trying to buddy up to Palmer and Nicklaus and the other stars, and he's living in a fantasy world. He's a lot worse than a rabbit; if he's got half a brain, he knows he's never going to make it.

Most guys like this—and there are quite a few of them—are living off sponsors, men who pay their way on the tour. Most sponsors are pretty gullible, probably high-handicap golfers themselves. They like the idea of sponsoring a guy on tour; they think it's like owning a racehorse. They get to know Joe Local Pro in their home town. He's been playing the same golf course since he was five years old—most local courses are pretty simple layouts, with no sand traps to amount to anything—and Old Joe Local can go around it blindfolded. He goes out with some members one day and shoots a 69—par probably ought to be 66—and the members can't break 100. They think 69 is a great score. Monday morning, they read that Arnold Palmer won a tournament, and his last three rounds were 70-71-70, and they say, "Now, wait a minute. Old Joe shot 69 the other day. If he'd been out there with Arnie, he'd have won that tournament." They get a little money together and send Old Joe out on the tour, and, of course, he does nothing. But he comes home at the end of the year with the wildest stories you ever heard about why he didn't do well. "Poor Old Joe had all the bad breaks," the sponsors say. And they hand him some more money.

I don't know how these pros can justify what they're doing, even to themselves. A couple of them still think they're going to make it— maybe they've been playing five years, and the best year they ever had they won twelve thousand dollars, which doesn't even cover expenses—but most of them know they're living a lie. It's just high-class-bum living. They must be a pretty sad lot.

Charlie Coody and I gave Steve Reid and Jimmy Colbert a rematch today, and my caddy finally showed up as I was on my way to the first tee. I was ready to fire him, but he told me he had a helluva time getting to the course, and I guess I believe him. Public transportation in this town is miserable. At least Johnny didn't smell of whiskey today.

I had a pretty good round, a stroke or two under par, and Charlie and I picked up a little change again. After the round, I went to hit some balls on the range, and a physicist from Washington, D.C., came up to me. He'd talked to me at the Southern Cal Open and told me he'd invented a new club he wanted me to see. I told him to bring the club up to the L.A. Open, and he showed up with it today, a putter, one of the most bizarre-looking things I've ever seen. The shaft is angled normally, but the putter head is reversed, so, instead of facing away from you, it's facing back at your feet. I told the fellow it wasn't for me. I told him it felt all right mechanically, but it wouldn't sell because of its appearance. The putters people buy are the simplest, the most basic kind. I held the club, but I didn't hit any balls with it. It'd be just my luck to take it over to the putting green and knock in a long one with this guy's putter.

It could be pure luck, but he'd bug me from here to next Tuesday, saying, "Why don't you like my putter? Look what you did with it." The best reason for not trying it is that if I did, I'd be giving him a false glimmer of hope. If it's not for me, I won't try it.

I'm still trying to come up with a free car, but my leads have all fallen through. The situation's desperate now. Unless there's a miracle tomorrow, I'm going to have to rent a car. I'd hate to spend that money.

I'm amazed by the way my game's coming along. I'm hitting the ball better these two days than I have in a long time, even in mid-season. It's the first time I've ever hit the ball this well this time of year. I don't know what it means. If I pick up a big check here, I could say I was overcoming California, or I could say I was lucky. A victory could propel me to a fantastic year—first prize is twenty thousand dollars—but anything less than that, down to nothing at all, won't affect me too much one way or the other.

Still I can't help feeling that if everything keeps going right, if I can stick to my diet, if I don't have any problems with the family —we got word tonight that Patty's mother is very sick, and she's been bedridden seventeen years with multiple sclerosis—then maybe this is my year. "Honey," I told Patty tonight while she fixed dinner, "I'm almost scared I'm hitting the ball so good."

January 8   Today was good old pro-am day, and as usual, I asked for an early tee time. I ask for early tee times every pro-am day so that I can get finished and spend most of the day with my family or doing chores.

The pro-ams are the lifeblood of the golf tour. The entry fees the amateurs pay cover a large share of the purse money each week. Without the pro-ams, we'd be making a lot less money, and so would the charities that benefit from almost every major pro tournament.

Still, it's always a trying day for me. Most of the amateurs are good fellows, the kind I'd love to spend time with. But if I had a choice, I'd rather play bridge with them or have a drink with them than be on the golf course with them. On the course in a pro-am, they just can't relax and be themselves. They're often tense, understandably; they don't want to embarrass themselves or the pro they're playing with. I'm sure the same thing would happen to me if I went into their offices one day a week and tried to help them conduct their businesses.

I had an 8:04 tee time this morning, so I got up at 5:30, came outside at six in a damp, dark fog, and went to a diner for a leisurely diet breakfast of grapefruit, bacon, and eggs.

A little after seven, I stepped on the practice tee. The practice tee has two distinct functions: you can use it to practice—one club or every club—or you can use it to warm up. I use it mostly to warm up. I hit the wedge a few times, then a middle iron, then a long iron, then a fairway wood, then the driver, from the shortest club to the longest, gradually stretching the muscles. Today, when I finished with the irons and picked up my four-wood, Phil Rodgers, hitting next to me, yelled, "Hey, Beard, you can't be fat and hit the four-wood." Rodgers, a real clown, was needling me two ways. First, he used to be a butterball, and he's been on a diet and lost about twenty-five pounds, and he's looking very svelte, especially next to me. Second, I do have trouble with my fairway woods. Every pro's got trouble with some part of his game—if he didn't, he'd win every week—and my sore spots are my fairway woods and my bunker shots.

After I finished on the practice tee, I met my three amateur partners. I didn't tell them, but I suspect I'm the worst pro-am player in the world. With a random draw, I'm sure I get my share of good amateurs, but my teams almost never do well. It's probably my lack of ability to inspire my partners—I'm usually dragging myself on pro-am day—my failure to draw from them a better-than-average performance, which is what you need to win in a pro-am. If the amateurs just play to their handicaps, you don't win a thing.

I don't know how you get the amateurs fired up, whether you talk to them or lecture them or whip them or what. Big George Bayer gets down on his hands and knees, lines up each putt for his amateurs, gives lessons all the way around the course, does everything but beg his partners, and ends up with a very good pro-am record. Little Gardner Dickinson seems to inspire his teams, too. I can't do it. It's just not my game. Another thing that hurts my pro-am teams is that I'm not an erratic player; I won't get a lot of birdies and a lot of bogeys. My usual round is fourteen pars and four other holes that determine whether or not I had a good day. If three or four of the other holes are birdies, I score well; if three or four of the other holes are bogeys, I score badly. I'm steady, not inspirational.

I just struggle through the pro-ams and whatever money I win, which is not very much, I almost always win on my own ball. They pay prizes two ways for pro-ams—the top fifteen positions for the individual pros and the top five teams. When I win any money in the team competition, it's a rare day.

My partners today were pretty likable fellows, happy to be playing in a pro-am, fun to talk with, and serious about their golf. One of them kind of amused me. He's a standard type I call Joe Pro-Am. He's a successful businessman, but he's so wrapped up in golf he's prouder of the rounds he's played with Nicklaus and Palmer than of any business deals he ever swung.

This particular fellow today said he'd gone out to dinner with Nicklaus once after they'd played together, and Jack had talked to him for four whole hours about THEORY. He said that Jack Nicklaus had paid him a very high compliment, that Jack had said he knew more about the golf swing than anyone Jack had ever met. I'm sure Jack said it to be nice. But this poor fellow is now absolutely convinced he really knows the golf swing, and now he's going to learn every phase of the game inside out, and all it's going to do, I'm afraid, is worsen his plight. He probably does know more about the golf swing than I do, but all it does is mix him up. I'm playing pro golf, and he's got a ten-handicap. I hear the same story just about every week.

There was another fellow along today who's not quite an every-week kind. He's the fellow who caddies for his buddy in the pro-am and has tricky little ways of letting the pro know that he knows more about the game than his buddy does. He makes little comments that let me know he's being a martyr, hinting, "I really should be playing with you, Frank, but I'm giving my buddy a break." In fact, he probably couldn't break an egg. But he's dressed to the hilt and he's playing his role. I guess these people get to believing their own little fantasies.

The pro-am players, of course, fall into three separate categories —the low, the high, and the middle handicappers. I didn't have a low handicapper playing with me today. Surprisingly, he's generally the toughest kind to play with. He's the A player, between a scratch and a five-handicap, and he has only two goals.

First, and foremost, he wants to beat the pro. That's all he cares about, not about the team or anything else. Second, if he can't beat the pro, he wants to keep his own score (which doesn't mean a thing in a pro-am) and impress the pro with occasional totals. He'll say things like "Boy, I'm playing pretty good today. I'm only two over par." I suppose I can understand him; I'd love to be able to say I beat Charles Goren at bridge. But when the low handicapper tells his friends he was only two strokes behind Arnold Palmer or was two strokes ahead of Frank Beard, he doesn't mention that he was hitting from up front by the ladies' tee and was getting a lot of putts conceded to him and was in a non-pressure situation. It's like me saying I beat Goren without mentioning that he gave me two aces to start each hand.

The one I feel sorry for is the very high handicapper. He gets eighteen pops, the maximum allowed in a pro-am, and he ought to get about fifty. He's been paid into the tournament, either by his company or by himself—it costs anywhere from about one hundred to upwards of one thousand dollars to play in a pro-am —and he's got to play. He's never obnoxious. He's always a wonderful little fellow, but he can't hit his butt. There's no way he can help the team and, three holes after he's teed off, he's wishing he'd never seen a golf club. He's embarrassed. He can't help himself, and, as much as you'd like to, you can't help him. It'd take a year just to help him with one thing.

The middle handicapper, an eight to a fourteen, is usually the fellow who can help you win. He's a pretty good player, he's been in pro-ams, he knows what it takes to win, and he's a hustler. It's generally the middle handicapper and I who make up the team. The high handicapper and the low handicapper rarely help.

I had two middle handicappers playing with me today, and we didn't do too badly. We finished twelve under par, 59, which won't win anything, but it's respectable. I had an unusual round for me, only ten pars, three bogeys, and five birdies for a 69, which ought to win me a little money in the individual pro event. I took only twenty-three putts today, but that didn't really encourage me. I still can't get over my block about California greens. I made four putts from more than thirty feet today, the gagger type, the long, seagoing type, but I missed three little putts, less than six feet, which I should have made. Basically, I didn't putt well. Those long ones are at least part luck, and they don't elate me nearly as much as the missed short ones depress me. Some guys on the tour would be happy with a day like mine, but I'm not. Most of the guys are chronic criers about their putting. Billy Casper sometimes thinks he's the worst putter on the tour, and he's one of the two or three best. I'm one of the very few guys who'll admit he can putt. When I say I've putted badly, I have—compared to the way I should putt. Somebody might say to me, "Frank, I'd like to have your bad days," and I'll tell him, "You can have them. I don't want them." I might like to have his bad days in the bunker.

At the end of the round today, I got a phone call from Bill Boone, my attorney in Louisville, who said he thinks he'll be able to set up a car for me. He'll know for sure one way or the other tomorrow.

I hustled away from the course and back to the motel and began thinking ahead to the opening round tomorrow, the first official round of competition of the 1969 professional tour. I'm absolutely dreading it, for one reason and one reason only: I'm playing with Arnold Palmer.

I dread every round I play with Palmer, Nicklaus, Casper, and possibly Gary Player, but playing with Palmer is far and away the worst. It's got nothing to do with Arnie personally. Arnie's easy to play with—he concentrates, he doesn't say much, he's fast, he always knows whose shot it is—but Arnie's Army is impossible. They run and stampede to see Arnie. They knock you down. They know nothing about golf etiquette. They have no regard for anyone who's playing with Palmer. They're not real golf fans. They're what I call the center-field-bleacher types. They're just looking for some place to go. They look at the paper and they say, "Hey, Arnie's in town, let's go see him, let's go see Arnie." They don't understand the game at all. They wouldn't appreciate it if he did the greatest thing in the world. They don't even care if Arnie hits one good shot all day. If he pees in the fairway, they're happy.

January 9   I was up at 5:30 again today, off for another early tee time. At breakfast, reading the paper, I saw that my 69 won me $187.50 in the individual part of the pro-am yesterday. Every little bit helps.

I played with Dow Finsterwald today and with Arnold Palmer and Arnie's Army. We teed off early, around eight o'clock, so the gallery wasn't too bad at the beginning.

Arnie's a strange guy. He's one of the greatest golfers of all time, of course, and he seems to be pretty outgoing with the fans and the press, but he keeps to himself when it comes to the players. I never see Arnie away from the course, never see him or Nicklaus or Casper. They live in their own world, and their world has very little to do with mine. They don't play bridge with the other pros. They don't hang around the motels. I know the name of everybody's wife and kids, but I'd bet Arnie doesn't even know how many children I've got or whether they're boys or girls.

Arnie's reached a special status with us, and he knows it. I don't mean he demands that you bow down to him, but you have to let him know, one way or another, that you know he's Arnold Palmer.

Dow Finsterwald's a great golfer and a good friend to me. He's helped me ever since I came on tour. He got me a contract with a shirt company, and he used to give me tips on my game whenever I needed them. Dow doesn't play the tour regularly anymore, but for five years, from 1956 through 1960, he was the most consistent money-winner on the tour.

We had a little delay on the first tee, and while we waited, Arnie and Dow and I talked about one of our fellow pros who's been accused of cheating. Golf's a funny game. It's probably the easiest sport in the world to cheat at; it probably puts the greatest emphasis on a man's integrity. We call penalties on ourselves for the tiniest infractions, things like accidentally moving a ball or grounding a club in a hazard, things that nobody else could spot. I'd trust my fellow pros, just about every single one of them, in almost any conceivable situation. We've got to retain that kind of atmosphere. I don't know whether the accusations against this particular player are true or not, but if they are, he should be punished to the hilt. He was trying to take money out of the pockets of the rest of us. My brother Ralph was suspended for life from professional basketball, and he didn't do anything nearly as bad as cheating. He was accused of shaving points, and he never even did that. He did agree to do it once—to win by less than the point spread—but the other team got a big lead and Kentucky never did catch up. Ralph never thought about losing a game on purpose. He was a young kid who didn't realize the seriousness of what he was doing, and he got suspended for life.

I started off real well today. After a par on the first hole, I hit a big, big drive on the second hole, a 464-yard par-four. I knew I couldn't reach the green with my two-iron, but I really didn't want to use my four-wood. Here it was, just the second hole of the official 1969 tour, and I had to pull out the worst club in my bag. Well, I thought, I might as well get to it. I whipped that four-wood out and stayed down with it, and when I looked up, the ball was flying right for the flag. I never hit a better four-wood in my life. The ball came to rest about six feet from the pin, and I knocked it in for a birdie.

The next hole, a 208-yard par-three, I hit a great three-iron about three feet from the hole and made that one for a bird. I was two-under after three holes, and most people come through those holes one over par. I figured I had the world by the tail. I was walking around like I was on stage, like the cock of the walk. And I lost my concentration.

Next thing I knew, I put a drive over in the trees on an easy birdie hole. I was still thinking about my two great birdies and I hooked, and all I could do was pitch out and pitch up on the green and take two putts for a bogey. I parred the next four holes, but I had to adjust my game. I realized I was hooking. I'd been hooking earlier on the practice tee.

Pro golfers are human—we're not machines—and we wake up different every day. I woke up today and I was a hooker. One of the finest lessons I ever got in my life I got from Doug Ford when I joined the tour. Doug had already won about twenty tournaments by then, and he said when you go out on the practice tee to warm up, you're going to hit the ball a certain way, hook it or fade it or hit it straight, and that's the way you're going to be hitting it all day long. If you don't allow for it, you'll be in trouble. I started playing for the hook after the fourth hole today.

I came to the ninth hole still one-under, and, by then, the gallery had built up. It was getting unruly, cutting across the fairway, practically shoving the golfers, running from each green to the next tee as soon as Arnie putted out. I hit a good drive on the ninth, and Arnie hit a tremendous one.

Then I hit as good a second shot as I could, to the front edge of the green on this 504-yard par-five. Arnie hit his second off to the right, and the ball bounced through the crowd, past the green, and under a fence into a chipping practice area.

We had to wait ten minutes till a PGA official could be found to rule on whether Arnie was out of bounds or whether he got a free lift. I was really irritated. I didn't want to lose my momentum, but I just had to sit and wait.

Finally, the official showed up and ruled a free lift for Arnie, and then Arnie played a fair chip shot through the crowd to the back fringe of the green. He was just a few inches off the green, maybe twenty-five feet from the hole, and he stepped up with a putter and stroked the ball right into the cup. It was a fantastic shot, with a great element of luck, and the crowd started screaming and hollering as if he had brought someone back from the dead.

Meanwhile, before the ruling, I'd hit an excellent chip shot within two and a half or three feet of the cup, and all I'd gotten was a couple of pitter-patters that sounded as though my mother and father were following me around and giving me a little hand. It wasn't Arnie's fault—he can't help it if the crowd acts like he's God—but I was so upset after the long wait for the ruling that I stepped up and missed my little putt and had to settle for a par. The crowd didn't care. They'd already gone stomping off to the next tee.

On the tenth hole, I blew another short one; I three-putted for a bogey. Arnie had a little putt for a birdie right after I missed my par, and he missed, too, which almost killed the gallery. I wasn't hoping for Arnie to miss. I used to feel that way when I started on tour, hoping my playing partners would miss putts, but I learned not to pay any attention to what my partners did. Now, I only worry about one man and one line in the statistics—Frank Beard and his four rounds. That's the only thing that's going to determine how I finish.

When I'm playing with Arnie, I never want to see him miss because I know that if he gets in trouble, the crowd'll start pulling against me. As far as they're concerned, it's a head-to-head match, the kid against the king. The crowds remember me beating Arnie twice on long putts in 1967, both times on national television. The first time was in the Tournament of Champions in Las Vegas, and

I came to the final hole needing a par to tie Palmer for first place, a birdie to beat him. Arnie was already in the clubhouse, and I knocked in an eight-footer for a birdie and beat him.

Three weeks later, we came to the last hole of the last round of the Houston Champions International tied for the lead, playing head-to-head in the same threesome. We both reached the green in regulation, and he two-putted for a par. He was standing on the side of the green watching me, and I had a twenty-footer for a birdie, and I knocked that one in.

Of course, those putts were on Bermuda grass, and today I was playing on that California bent, and it's a world of difference. I missed putts of less than two feet on both the eleventh and the twelfth holes, took bogeys, and slipped two over par. I birdied the thirteenth, then parred in for a 72, not a bad score, but I should have had a great score the way I started. Arnie and Dow had 72s, too.

After the match, I signed a few autographs, hardly any at all compared to the crowd around Arnie. Some fellow had asked for my autograph in the middle of play and I'd told him to wait till later. I don't sign autographs during a round unless there's a long wait, like at a par-three, with two groups on the tee.

Except for missing those four straight short putts, I wasn't too upset with my round. I knew that if I could just shoot 70s the rest of the way, I'd pick up a good-sized check. I felt even better when a call came through from Bill Boone, telling me that he had arranged for a Los Angeles Buick dealer to give me a car for the entire West Coast swing. All I had to do in return was play in the Buick Open later in the year.

I went back to the motel feeling cheerful, picked up the car, played a little bridge, and was getting ready to eat dinner when the phone rang. Patty's dad was calling from Kansas City, her home town. He said that Patty's mother had caught pneumonia and it looked like she wasn't going to live through the night.

We just have to take off for Kansas City. There's nothing we can do about it. I called the tournament committee and withdrew, and we packed up all our suitcases and got the kids ready and tonight, at midnight, we're flying to Kansas City.

January 10 / Kansas City   Pat's mother, almost miraculously, is feeling a whole lot better today. I'm happy about that, yet at the same time, down deep, I'm worrying about my golf game. I'd laid off for so long, then I'd gone to California and worked hard on my game, and it was just starting to come around. Now I'm sitting in Kansas City for at least three days, and it's cold and snowy here, and I'll be right back where I started. My first concern's Pat's mother, of course, but I can't help thinking I've blown two weeks of preparation.

January 11   Pat's mother is coming along very nicely, and we've made tentative arrangements to rejoin the tour Monday. Steve Reid is going to drive our Buick from the Los Angeles airport to the next tournament up in Napa, north of San Francisco. We'll fly to San Francisco, then rent a car to get to Napa.

I hate not to be playing when there's a tournament going on. I can't stand to read the papers. It bugs me to see the scores, to see some guys winning a lot of money when I know I could be beating them and collecting the money myself. It doesn't make any difference whether I take a week off because of some unforeseen event, like this week, or whether I take a week off just to rest—it drives me crazy. I want the week to end as quickly as possible. I want to get back on the tour as fast as I can. I want to be back winning my share.

January 12   As much as I hate to, I looked at the papers this morning and saw that Charlie Sifford's leading the L.A. Open. I'm glad to see Charlie Cigar doing well. He's had to overcome a lot of problems, being the first Negro on the tour. He's a helluva golfer, but his performances are even more remarkable considering all the pressure he's been under.

The only good thing about being off the tour today is that I was able to watch the Super Bowl. The Jets really impressed me. Maybe if I grow a Fu Manchu, like Joe Namath, people'll notice me and recognize me. The way it is now, when I walk down the fairway, they say, "There goes what's-his-name."

January 13 / Napa   We said good-bye to Pat's mother, who's feeling much better, and flew to San Francisco this morning and rented a car. It rained all the way up to Napa, and when we got here, it was still raining and the course was closed. I'm chomping at the bit, wanting to get my game going again, and I couldn't even hit a practice ball today.

We've really got plush accommodations. This tournament is sponsored by Kaiser Aluminum—they've got a factory and offices in Napa—and they're very proud of their Silverado Country Club. The club has condominium apartments, and we've got a lovely setup, two bedrooms, a fireplace, and a kitchenette. I'm paying thirty-five dollars a day, which I couldn't afford every week, but it's worth it once in a while.

I played bridge this afternoon with Steve Reid, Jim Colbert, Harold Henning, and a few others. Harold Henning—"Harry the Horse"—is a South African, a solid player, and one of the eccentrics of the tour. Money means nothing to Harold. He loves to gamble, loves to spend. Most of the time, his family tours with him, and he always takes two motel rooms, one for his wife and children, one for himself. He thinks that's essential for him to be able to play well, and he's entitled to his opinion, but I think that's just plain wasting money. He calls his own room "The Bridge Room." He's the squire of the bridge players on tour, probably the best player we've got.

Harold was sort of strutting like a peacock today. He'd finished second at Los Angeles, losing a play-off to Charlie Sifford, and won $11,400. We kidded him about how well he'd played, but we didn't run up and slap him on the back or anything. We play too many tournaments each year to get excited about one second-place finish. (Charlie Coody and Steve Reid, incidentally, missed the cut in Los Angeles, and Jim Colbert finished way down the list; it wasn't a good week for my practice partners.)

After the bridge game, Patty and I went to the supermarket, and she just about bought out the store. Sometimes I feel we might as well not get a kitchenette we spend so much on groceries. Patty said I shouldn't worry, that we've got enough meat and vegetables to last all week. We bought grapefruit for my diet. I've only lost a little so far, but I feel I can get down to 175 in another month or two, which'll make me feel better and may help my game, too. I've gotten so heavy I feel bound up in my shoulders. I may not be turning properly.

In the supermarket, we met Jack Montgomery's wife, with her little son, and she was upset because she'd lost her car keys. We searched all around the supermarket and couldn't find them, so we drove the Montgomerys back to Silverado. Jack was there and he had an extra set of keys. I drove him back to the store to pick up his car. It was a typical tour incident, part of our family life. Jack's a good young golfer who's really beginning to come into his own. This is the first year he's been exempt from qualifying, and I expect to see him win a lot of money.

Patty cooked dinner tonight, and after we put the children to bed, I sat around and caught up on my mail and paid my bills. I have a neighbor in Louisville who forwards all my mail to me. With the kids asleep in the other bedroom, with Patty working in the kitchen, with the fire going in the fireplace, I really felt like I was at home. I guess, in a way, this is my home.

January 14   The sun was shining this morning, but the course was closed, still soaking from yesterday's rain. A couple of helicopters were whirling over the greens, drying out the grass, so while we waited for the course to open, we played bridge. Finally, at noon, they opened the course, and I went to the practice tee and hit some balls for the first time in almost a week. Considering the layoff, I hit the ball very well.

I found out we'll be playing two different courses, the north and the south, during the first two rounds of the tournament, because the weather here this time of year makes it impossible to tee off early in the morning. Once the cut reduces the field, we'll all play the same course for the last two rounds.

I teamed up today with Gene Littler and Phil Rodgers, a quiet Southern Californian and a loud one, and we were told we could play the north course, but not the greens. We got up an interesting game, a dollar for fairways and a dollar for sand traps. If you miss the fairway and the other two fellows hit it, you owe them each a dollar; if only one man hits the fairway, he collects a dollar from each of the others. Then we pick out a sand trap near the green, to give us roughly the proper distance to the pin, and aim at that trap. Again, if you hit it and the others miss, you collect a dollar from each. Phil kept kidding me about my weight as we played, and Gene helped me with my four-wood. Gene's a true student of the game, a real perfectionist, and he suggested that I grip the four-wood a bit firmer with my left hand. It seemed to help a little. It helped enough, anyway, so that I was three dollars ahead of Gene when we got to the sand trap on the ninth hole.

"Tell you what," Gene said. "I'll go double-or-nothing with you out of this trap. Whoever holes the shot wins."

Gene knows I'm a bad bunker player, and he's a good one, but I had him down three dollars, so I said, "Okay, but we'd better just play closest to the hole instead of holing out 'cause we're not going to hole out from this trap. We're twenty yards from the pin. We'd be wasting our time."

I hit first, and I hit probably the best bunker shot of my whole life. It looked like it was going right in the hole, but it stopped six inches short. I started dancing and giggling, and then Gene climbed in the trap and swung, and the ball took off and landed, on the fly, in the cup. Gene broke up laughing, and I felt kind of foolish, but it was worth three dollars to see that shot, it was so beautiful.

After nine holes, Gene and Phil decided they wanted to play nine on the south course. I'm playing the south anyway in the pro-am, so I let them go and played the back nine of the north course with Steve Reid, who wanted some advice on his game.

I must say I looked pretty good today, and I don't mean hitting the ball. I'm a pretty drab dresser—Patty's always on me to dress better—but today I put together blue slacks and a black shirt and a blue sweater, and young Marty Fleckman, one of the sharper dressers on the tour—he and his wife wear those Bonnie and Clyde outfits—told me I looked very good. In fact, Marty said I looked debonair. Nobody ever called me that before.

I'm happy with my caddy here. I've got a local boy named Pete, just out of high school, not one of the touring caddies. He hustles. He's polite, punctual, and pleasant, and he's always where I need him to clean my clubs and my ball and rake the traps.

I got a letter from Bill Boone today, and Bill's set up a few exhibitions for me this summer, one-day jobs, paying from $750 to $1,500 plus all expenses. Bill's also trying to set up a new golf-ball deal for me. I've got one now, with a man in Chicago, but I'm not too happy with it. The ball hasn't sold the way the man expected it would. I guess my name doesn't sell golf balls.

Now Bill's looking for a new deal, and I know I could make his job a lot easier if I won a tournament or two, if I got my name a little better known.

Patty and I played bridge tonight with Jack Montgomery and his wife. In this weather, I'm playing more bridge than golf.

January 15   Before the pro-am today, Miller Barber was standing next to me on the practice tee. Miller's a strange fellow; outside the fact that he went to the University of Arkansas, no one knows too much about his background. He goes around with Doug Sanders and Ray Floyd, the social set. His nickname on the tour is "The Mysterious Mr. X," which started when some of the fellows began noticing that they never saw Miller after dark.

Miller was having trouble with his swing, so he asked me to take a look at it. I watched him swing and I told him he was kind of going over the top of the ball and hitting a low duck hook. To correct it, he needed to move his body through the ball a little more. He tried my suggestion, and by the time I left the practice tee, he was hitting the ball pretty good.

I got my usual threesome in the pro-am, all nice fellows, but even with all their strokes, we barely played par golf. I wasn't making any birdies myself; my putting was as bad as ever in California.

I'm worrying about my putting. I'm worrying about my whole game. I'm a chronic worrier, and it seems like I always have to have something to worry about. Right now, my main concern is making the top sixty, finishing among the top sixty money-winners for 1969. You've got to be in the top sixty to make it worthwhile to play the tour. For one thing, if you're in the top sixty, you've earned at least thirty thousand dollars in prize money, which means you're doing better than breaking even. But more important, as long as you stay in the top sixty, you're exempt from qualifying during the following year. If you have to qualify each week, it's damned near impossible to make a living. There's just too much strain, too much uncertainty. You never get a chance to relax.

Most people'd think it's ridiculous for me to worry about making the top sixty. I've earned more than $100,000 each of the past two years, and you'd think I'd have no trouble, that it'd be as simple as falling off a log. It should be and it has been and it probably will be—I suppose I'll be laughing at my fears by the end of the year— but I still can't help wondering whether I'm heading for another good year, or a slump. I've seen too many players, brilliant players, have fantastic starts in their careers, have five or six years like I've had on the tour, then go into slumps lasting anywhere from one year to five.

Bob Goalby's a classic case. He was among the top fifteen money-winners from 1959 through 1962; then, suddenly, for the next three years, he wasn't even among the top forty. In 1964, he dropped out of the top sixty and had to start qualifying again. Bob ended his slump in 1966 and started three nice profitable years. I keep wondering if something like that is going to happen to me and, if it is, when it's going to happen. I can't afford a bad slump. I complain about the tour, but I know I don't want to go home and sell insurance or wind up in a pro shop. I much prefer what I'm doing, and I'm always afraid of losing what I've got.

Each year, once I clinch a place in the top sixty, I start having a helluva time. I have a few parties and I stop worrying and I don't practice too much, and I probably play better golf. But I can't start the year with that easygoing attitude. The tour's too tough. There are too many strong, hungry, talented rookies coming up each year, looking to take your place away from you. You have to prove yourself all over again. Your past doesn't count a bit.

My wife gets mad at me for worrying all the time, but I can't help it. I've got to make that first check of the year. I'd like to make it here at Napa—make one or two thousand dollars, just enough to reassure myself that I can still do it, that I can go on from here and collect that big money and get up in that top sixty—and then I'll feel a lot better.

January 16   Our locker room is a nervous place early in the morning. It isn't like a football locker room or a basketball locker room. No one's getting taped up or massaged, but you can feel tension. Somebody's always yelling, "What time is it?" and "When do I tee off?" and everybody's putting on their shoes and getting their golf balls and their gloves. There are jokes flying around, but they're nervous jokes made by nervous people. Golfers are nervous people.

I was extra nervous this morning because I felt like I was starting the year all over. Everybody else had a jump on me and I had to start catching up.

My playing partners were two of my favorites, Bob Rosburg, who's been on the tour for about fifteen years, and Tony Jacklin, who was a rookie last year. You have to know Rossy to appreciate him. He mixes cynicism with sharp sarcasm and a strong temper. Tony's a young Englishman, probably the best player ever to come out of England to play the American tour. He plays an American kind of game; he can hit the short wedge and he can hit his irons up in the air so that they'll hold the greens. In England, most of the players hit their irons low, punch it in, and run it up. Tony's a good-natured fellow, always telling jokes, and he's absolutely hooked on American television. He knows what time every show is on, and he watches everything he can.

I started off all right, parring the first three holes on the south course, the easier course here. Then, on the fourth, I three-putted for a bogey. On the sixth hole, I was still thinking about that stupid three-putt, about the way I always putt out here, and I pushed a three-iron on a par-three, hit a bad chip, and took another bogey. On the eighth hole, I three-putted again. I was three over par and heading for a horrendous score. I could've quit right there. I could've said the hell with it and just staggered home with a 75 or 76 or 77. But I talked to myself—I do that a lot on the course—and I said, "Hell, I'm going to whip this game if it kills me." So I birdied the ninth and the eleventh and would have birdied the eighteenth if I hadn't gone and three-putted again. I came in with a 73, one over par, and it could have been a lot worse, considering the way I started.

Rosburg really had it bad. Rossy hadn't played the south course at all in practice—he came in late—so, naturally, he didn't have his distances. Tony and I helped him out a little. We never told him what club to hit—we didn't tell him the right club *or* the wrong club—and we didn't give him exact distances, but if he seemed to be in a quandary about what to do on a particular hole, I'd say something like, "Bob, I've got 175 yards from that tree over there." He could either use my marker or ignore it, whichever he preferred. This is pretty common practice when a fellow pro hasn't seen the course.

Rossy was taking his caddy's advice, too, and he was using one of those professional touring caddies. Rossy's been around awhile, so he probably wasn't relying on the caddy too much. He was playing pretty good golf until he got to the eleventh, a long par-five with a creek running in front of the green. Where Bob hit his drive, there was no way he could get across the creek with his second shot. But his caddy started telling him he could make it. I wasn't going to butt in. I knew Rossy couldn't make it across with a rifle. Nobody could. But this big-time pro caddy, who wants fifteen dollars a day and five percent, talked Rossy into trying. He hit a Sunday punch with a three-wood and he landed right in the middle of the creek. Rossy turned to the caddy and started calling him every name he could think of. I didn't have too much sympathy for Rossy. He was just asking for trouble, looking for advice from the caddy. Rossy was screaming so loud, I think, because he realized how stupid he'd been to listen to the caddy. He took a double-bogey and ended up with a 75 and maybe lost his chance to qualify for the final rounds.

After we finished, I studied the scoreboard to try to figure out what score it's going to take to make the cut. I'm tied for about sixty-fifth with my 73, so it'll probably take about 146 to make the cut, another 73. It's never my objective just to make the cut—I want to win big prize money every week—but when you start off with a fairly poor round like I did today, you can't help figuring out your chances to be around for the last two rounds.

In the locker room, Arnold Palmer asked me where I'd gone last week after we'd played the first round together. I told him I'd flown to Kansas City because of Pat's mother's illness. "You're getting to be a real world traveler," Arnie said. "I've got a good jet plane I'll rent you any time you need one." He started laughing. "It's a lot cheaper than flying commercially," he said. "You really ought to get one." He kept on laughing. He's a real comedian, that Palmer—sometimes.

January 17   I felt like a rabbit this morning. All I could think was: "I've got to make the cut today, I've got to. If I don't, I'll start wondering whether I've lost my touch. I missed one tournament in Los Angeles and if I miss the cut here, everybody's going to have a head start on me. If I miss the cut, I'm going to begin to press."

We played the north course, the tougher course, today, and to make it worse, we started on the back nine, the tenth hole, one of the toughest holes we'll play all year—a long, narrow par-four. I hit a good drive, then hit a three-iron right at the flag. I could hardly believe the shot. It stopped two feet from the hole, and I had a birdie on a possible bogey hole. I felt like I had the whole day under control.

Even when I three-putted the next hole for a bogey, I just hitched up my britches, parred the third hole, then, on the fourth, sank a fifty-footer for a birdie, which really buoyed me up. I played great from there on.

Along the way, I caught something I'd been doing wrong. I'd been aiming too far to the right. Doug Ford and Doug Sanders had both told me I was doing this last year, and I'd straightened out. Now I was slipping back into the same bad habit. Right in the middle of the round, I made an adjustment. I don't like to do this, but sometimes you have to. I started aiming a little more toward the hole, left of where I'd been aiming, and it opened up my whole swing. It opened up my left side so I could move through the ball much better. I really began to hit my irons.

That wasn't the only bright spot for me. Everything I've been practicing—my short game, my bunker play, my fairway woods—paid off for me today. I don't think I hit a poor chip all day, and on one hole, when I pushed an iron shot into a trap, I had a tricky little sand shot, only about twenty feet, but up over the hump of the bunker, then straight downhill to the pin. I hit the shot perfectly, just nipped it out of the bunker, barely over the bank, and watched it run down about a foot and a half from the hole. It kept my hot round going. Later, on a long par-three, I had a little debate with myself whether to hit a two-iron or a four-wood. I knew in my heart it was a four-wood shot, but I've got no faith in my four-wood and I really wanted to hit the two-iron. I said the hell with it, I've got to hit the proper club, I'm a professional. So I hit the four-wood and blanked the flag out all the way to the pin and landed about eight feet from the hole. I got a birdie, and I never would have reached the green with a two-iron.

My whole game's coming around, except my putting. It was a little better today—I holed some long ones—but it wasn't what I'd like it to be. I'm still shaky on the short putts. I ended up with a 68, which moved me up into the top thirty, but if I'd been putting the way I can, I'd have shot 64 or 65 easily. Still I'm happy to be at 141. I've made the cut and I've regained a great deal of confidence. This may be a turning point in my California play.

One of those valuable professional touring caddies was acting up today. He was going around moaning that Charlie Sifford hadn't paid him enough at Los Angeles last week. He was complaining that he should've got three percent of Charlie's first-place money—six hundred out of twenty thousand dollars—plus one hundred dollars for toting the bag all week. He was crying, and I heard that Charlie gave him four hundred dollars, which is probably $350 more than he was worth. I doubt he helped Charlie at all. As long as Charlie's been around, nobody's going to help him much. He knows what club to use. He's from Los Angeles and he knows that Rancho Park course inside out. I guarantee that caddy did nothing but carry Charlie's clubs, and he thinks he deserves seven hundred dollars for the week.

Incidentally, Charlie missed the cut here today. He came in at

146, and it took 145 to make the cut. Dick Lotz, a youngster who won the Alameda Open, which was going on at the same time as the Los Angeles Open, also missed the cut today. It's just another indication of how stiff the competition is out here, how difficult it is to win money every week.

Old Mr. X—Miller Barber—is leading the tournament, after the lesson I gave him the other day. I don't know whether I helped him, but I do know he was hitting the ball poorly till I told him to work on his body action through the ball. I bumped into him in the clubhouse today—he shot a 67 on top of an opening 68—and I said, "I'm always helping you and you never give me a thing."

"Frank, you don't need any help," Miller said. "When the day comes you need it, I'll give it to you. Just ask me." Then he went off laughing.

Miller's a good old boy, and I'm glad to see him leading. I just want to catch up to him a little.

Dick Crawford and his wife stopped by for a visit tonight. Crawdaddy's a good fellow, very, very serious about religion, but usually laughing and cheerful. I think he's a good-looking guy. I think that mostly because people confuse us; they're always coming up to me and saying, "Hello, Dick." He started on the tour just a year after me, and everyone predicted he'd be one of the stars. He'd won the national collegiate championship twice, the only man ever to do that. But he's never lived up to his promise. He made the top sixty only once, in 1967, and was exempt from qualifying in 1968. But he missed the top sixty by about three thousand dollars last year and now he's got to qualify again. Dick missed the cut today, so he plans to leave for Pebble Beach tomorrow to start getting ready for the qualifying there. I'm sure the qualifying is weighing on his mind. It has to. It's a terrible thing. And it reminds me that this is something that could hapen to Frank Beard without warning. It's something I've got to guard against at all times.

January 18   It was rainy, cold, and nasty today, and we tried to play golf. I put on my rain suit and cranked up my hand-warmer and went to the tee knowing that, unless there was a miracle, we'd never finish eighteen holes. I hate to play in this weather.

For one thing, I wear glasses, and they always get wet and fogged up in the rain. I've tried various caps, and nothing makes any difference; the glasses still get wet. Besides, I just play badly in bad weather. I managed to get in six holes today, and I was two over par. The greens were flooding, the fairways were flooding, play was impossible. I waited in the locker room for the official cancellation, and Doug Sanders came in moaning that he was two-under, getting ready to go three-under, and I didn't know whether he was kidding or not. Some pros came in and said they were nine- and ten-over and praying for more rain.

I think most people, no matter how they're doing, are happy when a day like this is canceled. Golf's an art, and in miserable weather, you can't execute your art properly. People pay money to watch you, and you can't perform any better than they would in this kind of weather. You're all bundled up. You can't swing freely. Your footing's unsure and your grip's treacherous, and you feel like you're going to fall down or let a club go flying any moment. Half the time, you're trying to punch the ball into the wind, keep it low. You're improvising. You're not doing what you do best. Your swing gets all fouled up. It takes me about a week after I escape from bad weather to get my swing back into its groove.

Once play was stopped, we got up a bridge game in Bert Yancey's room—Yancey, Dave Hill, Deane Beman, Harold Henning, Tony Jacklin, Steve Reid, and me. We brought in sandwiches and some booze and sat around for about three hours playing bridge and watching golf matches on television. Yancey, a former West Point cadet, and I were playing together in the CBS matches—filmed last year—and we got beat, and then Yancey got beat again on the Shell Wonderful World of Golf. "Bert is the first man to lose twice in a day," said Harry the Horse.

"Hell," said Dave Hill, who always has something to say. "He lost three times—on Shell, on CBS, and here at Napa."

We were all kidding Bert about being a movie star, about hamming it up for the cameras. On one hole, a long par-four, he used a nine-iron for his second shot, and Dave said, "Boy, are you strong!"

It was a good afternoon, but I'd like to get back to golf.

January 19   I woke up this morning with intestinal flu, feeling like a dog, and I just didn't want to get out of bed. It looked like it was going to rain any minute, and I wanted the rain to come down quick and heavy so that I wouldn't have to go out at all.

The rain waited till I was on the sixth hole. By the ninth, it was coming down so hard I could hardly hold my clubs. I tend to hook normally, but my grip was so bad I hit a shot into a ditch way out on the right. I was two-over when they halted play.

One of my playing partners, Dave Stockton, was really upset that we couldn't finish. He's a young boy, reeking with confidence and ability, and he'd gotten hot and shot 32 and moved up among the leaders. With his score, I don't blame him for groaning when they called it off. Dave figured he'd shot an impossible round, and then Tommy Aaron came in even more unhappy, because he'd shot a 31. Dave's jaw dropped to the ground. He thought there wasn't anybody in the world who could've topped a 32 today.

Some players seem to thrive in bad weather. Doug Ford was always a great bad-weather player, and he's given me a few lessons on playing in rain and wind, little tips like not to overswing and to take a little more club on each shot. But nothing seems to help me enough in this kind of weather.

January 20 / Pebble Beach   They called off the tournament this morning. The rain was coming down so hard we couldn't have played in Napa next week, much less today or tomorrow.

Since we played only half the tournament, we get only half the prize money. I was tied for twenty-fifth, which normally would mean about $1,000 in a $135,000 tournament. But with the money cut in half, I'll just get a little more than four hundred dollars, not quite enough to cover expenses. I'm not happy, first because my game was starting to shape up and I figured I'd move up a few places and, second, because the rain-out makes the tournament unofficial. The top sixty money-winners are based strictly on official tournament earnings, and I haven't won an official penny yet this year. I've got to get moving.

I wonder what Miller Barber's thinking. He'll get half the first prize, $13,500 instead of $27,000, which is still more money than he'd have earned for finishing third in the whole tournament. I think Miller's got to be happy with that. It's hard to hold a lead through the last two rounds of any tournament; the halfway leader wasn't able to win the Masters, the Open, or the PGA last year, didn't even finish second, as a matter of fact.

But Charlie Coody, who tied for fourth at Napa and won close to three thousand dollars, wasn't at all satisfied. Charlie told me the way he was playing he'd have taken his chances on losing the three thousand to try to win twenty-seven thousand. Of course, he had better odds than Miller had.

After the rain-out was announced, I ran into Bob Goalby and Dow Finsterwald, and they were both a little irritated by the new rule that every person who makes the cut collects some prize money. In the past, only the first fifty finishers got money, but now each man who survives the cut gets something; everyone below the top fifty gets the same amount, sort of a token payment.

Bob and Dow joined the tour back in the middle fifties, when the total prize money was under one million dollars a year—now it's over five million dollars a year—and I could understand their feeling that guys were earning money too easily now. But I was one of the advocates of the new rule. I think any man who puts in a full week of his life at a tournament deserves some compensation; the guy who finishes dead last works just as hard as, or harder than, the winner of the tournament. Bob disagrees entirely. Dow's willing to go along with everybody getting something, but he feels the money should be scaled right down to last place. He thinks that would produce keener competition among the low-ranking players. He may have a point.

As soon as I could get back to the room, Patty and I began packing. Normally, we pack the night before a tournament ends, but we didn't know for sure we'd be moving today, so we had to jam things together as fast as we could. When we're packing and getting ready to travel is one of the few times that Patty and I ever argue. It's my fault. I don't like to travel, I don't like to pack, I get nervous, and I suppose I take it all out on Patty. I get very bossy, and then she gets upset. I guess by now she's getting used to my moods. I loaded the car, paid the room bill, which was about three hundred dollars, and went and paid my caddy, Pete. He worked four full days and two half days, and I gave him seventy-five dollars, probably a little more than he expected. He seemed happy with it. He's going to caddy for me at the Bing Crosby tournament, too.

We drove down the California coast in the rain and checked into the same motel we always use for the Crosby. It's a modest little place, comfortable and clean and close to the courses, and much more reasonable than the Silverado Country Club. If anything, the weather here's even worse than it was at Napa. They'd had seven inches of rain over the weekend.

I kind of enjoy Crosby week because there isn't much pressure on the individual. The tournament is a pro-am from start to finish, and my partner here is a real good amateur named Mickey van Gerbig. Mickey went to college about the same time I did, and he's a scratch player, but in this tournament, he gets about seven or eight strokes. That's not unreasonable. Billy Casper's playing with Michael Bonallack, the British amateur champion, and Bonallack gets four or five strokes here. Mickey and I won about eight hundred dollars in the pro-am division last year—even though I only tied for thirty-eighth on my own ball—so I figure I've got a good chance to collect some change here.

January 21   Naturally, it was still raining this morning, but Charlie Coody and I decided to go over to the Pebble Beach Country Club and register and see if we could work in a little practice. The registration setup here is more elaborate than usual. You pay your fifty-dollar fee and receive a bunch of gifts—a fifty-dollar shoe certificate, some shirts, some socks, a book about golf, and a lot of little trinkets for the wife.

Charlie and I heard the courses would be closed all day, so after we had some coffee with his pro-am partner, we figured we'd practice our putting. We picked up our balls and gloves from the local Titleist man, and Coody, of course, took forever to select his gloves.

We've both got the same size hand, and we got the box of gloves out and I tried on four gloves and three of them fit and I took them. But Charlie had to spend twenty or thirty minutes picking out just the right gloves for his delicate hands. I felt like screaming at him, he's so slow.

We got out on the putting green and decided we'd putt for a little money. There were nine holes on the putting green, so we said we'd play for fifty cents a round plus an extra fifty cents each time one of us made the long putt for an ace. It was low stakes, but we were planning to putt for two or three hours, so we knew it could add up. I firmly believe in gambling. I think every kid who starts out playing golf should play for money.

I'll probably get an argument from the mothers of America, but I think the best way any kid, ten years old and up, can sharpen his competitive desire, his will to win, his burning to be the best, is to gamble. Within reason, I mean. I don't want the kid to be a maniac, to gamble away his house or his clothes or his clubs. But the bet's got to be enough to hurt him if he loses. If he gets, say, a dollar allowance for a week, he should go out and play a twenty-five-cent Nassau. With a press, he could lose it all in one round. That way, he'll learn that the game's a struggle, that life's a struggle.

I know gambling helped my game when I was a kid. One day, when I was twelve or thirteen, I was chipping and putting, and a young Negro caddy walked up and said, "I can whip you at that."

"No, you can't," I said. I figured I was pretty good.

"Can," he said. "Play you for pennies."

I didn't want to bet. "This kid's so poor he's never held a club," I thought. I hadn't learned yet about the caddy yards, with their homemade courses, hand-dug holes, and beat-up old clubs. I'd never caddied myself. "Forget it," I said.

He kept bugging me and, finally, I said, "Okay, let's go."

I loaned him a club and a ball, and we began chipping and putting for pennies. I had fifteen cents, and he emptied me out.

I went home crying. I told myself I'd never let that happen to me again. I told myself I couldn't afford to let it happen again. I was getting an allowance of about fifty cents a week then. I know the whole thing sounds like a fairy tale, but that little incident gave me a determination I'd never had before.

I became a bit of a hustler. I played for cash every chance I had.

Two boys, five or six years older than me, used to play me a dollar Nassau every week, and I'd always take them for four or five dollars.

The kind of gambling I like is head-to-head gambling, whether it's on the golf course or at the bridge table, where you're backing your own ability and playing for reasonable stakes. I enjoy making five- and ten-dollar bets, too, backing my opinions on other sports. If, for instance, Kentucky is playing Houston in basketball, I'll go find me a golfer from Texas and set up a friendly wager. But I'm strictly opposed to big-time gambling, the kind that can corrupt sports, that involves bookmakers, the kind that got my brother into trouble.

Charlie and I were gambling today, just as an incentive to keep us concentrating, and as we got started, young Steve Spray came by. We decided we'd hustle Steve, get him into the game, and win us a little grocery money. Steve's an excellent putter, but Charlie and I are two of the best on the tour. We teased Steve and baited him and, finally, he said, "All right, I'll go get my putter." He came back, and we putted for about three hours, and Steve won five dollars from each of us. Our fish took our money and ran.

Before I left the course, I chatted with Mason Rudolph, who'd dropped out of the top sixty money-winners in 1968 for the first time in ten years. Mase had gotten off to a good start in 1969 with a tie for eleventh at Los Angeles, and I noticed that he'd gotten himself in much better shape. "What's your secret?" I said.

"Jogging," Mase said. "I jog a mile every morning."

My diet's kind of dragging, and I'm going to have to resort to something drastic. I don't know about jogging, though. That may be a little too drastic for me.

January 22   First thing this morning, I had to go through my weekly ritual of reporting all my expenditures and income to Johnny Owens, my accountant. Johnny's got me on a computerized accounting system, and each week I fill out a form for him. He's a solid tax man, and he takes good care of me. At least, the government hasn't tried to lock me up yet.

My partner, Mickey van Gerbig, and I played a practice round today with Charlie Coody and his partner, and before we got started,

Steve Spray spotted Charlie and me and asked us if we'd like to putt some more. "I enjoyed that game yesterday," Steve said. "If you'll putt with me every day, I think I'll quit the tour and just do that."

Charlie and I skipped the putting.

The Crosby's played on three courses—Pebble Beach, Cypress Point, and Spyglass Hill—but since two rounds are played at Pebble Beach, we decided to play that course today. The first tee was so crowded that we drove out to the middle of the course and teed off there. We got in our eighteen holes, not working too hard, just getting our distances. My partner wasn't too cheerful. He and his brother own the Oakland Seals of the National Hockey League, and he'd just heard that the league had turned down his application to move to Buffalo or Vancouver. He was pretty upset, and I hope it doesn't affect him too much during the tournament.

The golf courses here are fantastically beautiful, especially if you don't have to play them. The area itself is hilly, filled with large, wonderful pine trees and oaks. Deer run through the forest and practically come up and eat out of your hand on the course. You can see the ocean from many of the fairways, and the Pacific, at this time of year, is a cold, cold blue, a majestic blue. Some of the holes run along cliffs, offering incredible views, thrilling me every time I come out here.

The secondary view here is of all the celebrities who come each year to play in the Bing Crosby pro-am. Today I saw Clint Eastwood and James Garner, the movie stars, and Don Drysdale, the baseball player. I remember the first time I saw the celebrities here, from Bing Crosby and Bob Hope on down, I was awed. I still enjoy meeting them. One of my pet hobbies is wondering, any time I meet somebody special, what makes him tick—a champion in any field, an actor, a financier, it doesn't make any difference. Are they human? Are they down to earth? What makes Drysdale such a great pitcher? I don't know Don, but I'd like to sit down with him and try to find out what makes him a champion.

I have some theories about my own field, about what makes golf champions. I ran into Jack Nicklaus today, the first time he's been out this year, and we said hello and small-talked for a minute or two. That's about the extent of the relationship I ever have with a Nicklaus or a Palmer or a Casper. For a while, when Jack and I were both on the board of directors of the players' tournament committee, we spent more time together, but now I've drifted back in the crowd.

Jack Nicklaus is a golf champion, no question about that, one of the greatest players ever. If you judge by the past few years, the four greatest golfers in the world are Nicklaus, Palmer, Casper, and Julie Boros. I have nothing against any of them personally, but they're all off by themselves. They're isolated.

Cas tries harder to be friendly than the others do, but he's still in his own world. Palmer and Nicklaus don't have much contact with anybody except each other, and even that's mostly because they get thrown together, in business deals and social arrangements. I don't think either of them really enjoys the other's company. And Boros has nothing to do with anybody.

Remember, what I'm saying has nothing to do with these guys personally. I'm talking about them as champions, about the special life, the special style, of the champions. Leo Durocher once said, "Nice guys finish last." I don't go along with that exactly. I modify it a little. I say, "Nice guys don't finish first." You have to understand my definition of "nice guy." When I say a guy's not a nice guy, I don't mean he's a jerk or a cheat or a liar or a sinner or anything like that. I'm really talking about just one thing. My definition of a nice guy is somebody who puts other people first, who puts their feelings, needs, and desires ahead of his own. The opposite side is the guy who always puts himself number one, and everybody else second. My idea of the nice guy is somebody like Al Geiberger. He's as sweet a person as you could ever want to meet. He's friendly. He's considerate. He doesn't judge you. And he's a helluva golfer. He's made a helluva lot of money playing golf. But he's never been number one, and he'll never be number one because he just isn't egocentric enough. He isn't selfish enough.

The number-one guys have to be almost totally self-centered. They have to possess an incredible burning for success. They've got to be willing to do anything within morally, civically, and socially acceptable bounds to win. I don't mean they have to cheat, and I don't mean they have to go out of their way to stomp on people. Not at all. But they do have to stomp on people who get in their way. They have to ignore their friends and their enemies and sometimes their families, and they have to concentrate entirely upon winning, upon being number one. There's no other way to get to the top.

I'm sure I sound harsh, but I'm not really condemning them. They've got what we all want. They've got financial independence. They've got prestige. They've got power. I don't know anybody who wouldn't like to have his own airplane and his own secretaries and his own companies. There are many days I wish I had their drive, their singleness of purpose, their complete devotion to victory. I'm often tempted to try it, to push everything and everybody else out of the way and to pursue nothing but success. But I just can't do it. I don't mean I'm too nice a guy. I mean it's not my way. If I tried it, I'd fail. I couldn't survive that constant intensity, that constant burning. I admire—hell, I envy—their ability to burn and burn and burn.

My approach, the one that works for me, is less grueling. Basically, I'm content just to make a good living playing golf. If I make $100,000 a year, I'm very happy. If I slump to sixty or fifty or forty thousand dollars, I'll still be happy. I'll be able to pay my expenses, pay my taxes, and put a little bit away.

I can't get over the number of new faces out here. The rookies looked like a herd of ants on the practice tee today, maybe fifty or sixty of them who've gone through the school in the past year. You could line them all up in front of me, and for all the money in the world, I couldn't name one of them. I saw a few today who looked like they might be sixteen years old. I guess they're good golfers, though. I just keep hoping that they're not quite good enough to knock old Frank Beard off the tour.

January 23   The Crosby is an unofficial tournament, unofficial because, with amateur partners and team scores, our strategy's not the same as it'd be in a strictly pro event. Even though the money doesn't count toward official earnings and the scores we post don't count toward the Vardon Trophy—awarded for the lowest average score all year—I still want to do well. Unofficial money spends just like official money.

Mickey van Gerbig and I played Spyglass Hill today. We were

scheduled to play Pebble Beach tomorrow and Cypress Point Saturday. Everybody who survives the cut, which comes after the third round here, plays the final round at Pebble Beach. All the big names, Arnie and Jack and Cas, were at Cypress today, so that they could move to Spyglass tomorrow, then Pebble Beach Saturday. That's because the television cameras are set up at Pebble Beach, and when they go on national TV Saturday, they like to show the stars. We're just the little unknowns.

Mickey and I were paired with Don Massengale and his partner. Mas is another one of my friends who dropped out of the top sixty last year and is back qualifying after two years of exemptions. I seem to know a lot of guys in that category. It keeps me thinking.

I hadn't seen Spyglass since last year, since the players and the Crosby people had a war of words over this course. It's a pretty new course, designed by Robert Trent Jones, and we felt the course was miserable, totally unfair, punishing good shots and not properly rewarding great shots. Whenever we say we don't like a course, we get criticized in the newspapers. People call us crybabies and say we're afraid of tough courses. That's stupid. We play some of the toughest courses in the world every year—Akron and Flint and the Colonial in Fort Worth—and we get high scores, but we don't complain. Those are great courses. Going out and shooting a bad round on a great course is one thing; going out and making an ass of yourself on a bad course in such poor condition that the Lord himself couldn't shoot par is something else.

They've redone Spyglass a little and improved the greens. It's a better course now, but today it didn't make any difference. Mickey and I and Don and his partner almost laughed when we saw the course. It was underwater. The rain was still coming down when we teed off, and we felt sure there was no way we could play a full round today. It was crazy even to try.

But we tried. I played six holes in even par, then, on the seventh, a long par-five, gambled for the green on my second shot. I landed in the water guarding the front of the green and took a bogey. I bogeyed eight and nine, too, and I was three over par.

I wasn't upset. I could tell by the rain that we'd never finish. When we reached the sixteenth green, the PGA official in charge of the course suspended play. The greens were flooded, and we

figured we were through for the day. Then this official showed up and told us to resume play. He had a couple of workmen shovel the water off the green. "Now go ahead and putt," he said. I swear there was a river flowing through the green, and the official thought he could make it part like the Red Sea and have Don Massengale putt up the middle. Mas hit a good putt—and left it eight feet short. "Best I could do," Don said. Then Mickey left a nine-footer four feet short. That was it for the day. That was the end.

It's been so long since I've signed a scorecard and turned it in, I don't remember what it feels like.

January 24　I've heard we're going through the worst period of rain in the history of California, and I believe it. We played in the wet again today.

On the practice tee, I saw the official who'd made us putt through the river yesterday, and he sort of apologized. He said he was in a difficult position. He didn't want to see us get rained out of another tournament because it'd cost us all a lot of money. I can appreciate his position; he's got a thankless job. He said we'd certainly try to get in a round today. He'd ordered all the pins placed on high ground on the greens, so that the water would fall away from them.

Dan Sikes came over and joined the conversation. Dan was in law school at the University of Florida when I was an undergraduate, and even though he gave up law practice for the tour, he's still got a lawyer's gift for argument. Dan played in front of us yesterday, and he welcomed the rain-out because he was on his way to an 80. He told the official he wasn't going to putt through water today, that if the green's underwater, he just won't putt.

We teed off in a downpour, and I bogeyed the first hole when the club damn near flew out of my hand. I got another bogey with a three-putt on the fourth, and on the sixth hole, I ran into Bill Fleming from ABC-TV. Bill chased around Spyglass today because the rain-out yesterday means our section will be playing Pebble Beach tomorrow—Saturday. The little unknowns like Beard and Massengale are going to be on television instead of the big boys, so Bill had to gather some background material about our amateur partners. Just about then, Bing Crosby came along and joined us for a few holes. Bing's friendly with Mickey van Gerbig, and he knows Massengale pretty well because Don won the Crosby a few years back. I suppose Bing's not too fond of me because I was on the players' committee when we threatened to cancel this tournament on account of Spyglass and the various TV problems here. I'm sure it's hard for Bing Crosby to have a bad spot in his heart for anybody, but I can't blame him if he's not particularly fond of me.

Mickey had a beautiful round, getting pars on all the holes where he had strokes, and even though I had a fistful of bogeys, I picked up a few birdies. We came in ten under par, 62, as a team. I wasn't too happy with my own 74, but I figured we might have the lowest team score of the day, which would have been worth one thousand dollars to me. (The amateurs, of course, don't share in the money; they get trophies.) When we came in, we found out that Casper and Bonallack had a 61 at Cypress Point. Just to make the day complete, the rain started again.

January 25   I didn't see how on God's earth we could play today. It was pouring when I got up, and then I heard a Navy weather report that a blockbuster of a storm was going to hit here around one o'clock.

The committee should have called off play today, probably should have canceled the whole tournament. You have to draw the line somewhere; you can't just herd people through like cattle to finish a tournament. I spoke to some sportswriters and television people this morning, and everyone agreed the courses were absolutely unplayable. It was the worst day I've ever played in. The winds were at least fifty miles an hour, and it was miserably cold. The seventh hole at Pebble Beach is usually a wedge or an easy nine-iron, barely a hundred yards long, and today we had to hit four-irons.

The course was actually dangerous. On one hole, I hit my shot, then slipped, and it was just the grace of God that I didn't wrench my back or pull a muscle. Dan Sikes, playing in front of us, was so mad he could've spit nails. It was sheer insanity to play golf today.

But we played. My partner played well, and we came in with a team score of 68, which won't hurt us much. My own score was a 79, and I'm not ashamed of it. Don Massengale played fantastic golf and shot a 75. We got hit by the big storm; the players who teed off early finished before the storm, and many of them had excellent scores, 68s and 69s. I'm not complaining. I've had my share of the breaks, getting my round in before bad weather struck, but today the difference between teeing off early and teeing off late had to be six strokes.

Charlie Coody withdrew today. He just pulled out. He said he wasn't going to ruin his golf game in weather and on courses like this. If I didn't have a partner who was doing so well, I think I'd withdraw, too.

January 26　　The first thing I looked at this morning was the sun. I almost didn't recognize it. Then I looked at the papers and figured out I needed a 69 or, at worst, a 70 on my own ball in order to survive the individual cut here, the cut after the third round.

Mickey and I had the team cut made easily, but I wanted to make both cuts so I could have two chances at some money. We were at Cypress Point today, probably the easiest of the three courses, so I had a decent chance for a 69 or 70.

I saw one of the PGA officials and told him I thought they'd made a grave mistake letting us play yesterday. He hemmed and hawed about not wanting to lose all the money in the tournament, but I think he was embarrassed. He should have been.

I started off strong today, three-under after seven holes, shooting for a 69. I was pretty damn happy, considering that the course was so damn soggy my partner hit a shot on the second hole that actually buried itself in the fairway.

On the eighth hole, a squall moved in and, all of a sudden, our beautiful sunshine was gone. It was freezing, rainy, and windy, and then, to make things perfect, hail began flying around the course. The bottom fell right out of my game. My clubs were so wet I was throwing them down the middle of the fairway after each shot. I staggered in with a 75 on my own ball, not nearly good enough to make the cut, but, fortunately, Mickey was playing well, and we came in with a team score of 64, putting us in a tie for fifth place. We're only three strokes behind the leaders—young Tommy Shaw and his amateur partner—and since Tommy missed the individual cut, too, we're paired with them tomorrow.

Dale Douglass, a friend of mine who's never won a tournament, is in first place, a stroke ahead of Howie Johnson and two ahead of George Archer. I'm pulling for Dale to win; he's got a good game, and I think all he needs is one victory to get started on a great career.

I've got nothing against Howie or George, but I'm a little closer to Dale. Yet, to be honest, I expect George Archer to win. Dale's a bit too conservative. He doesn't seem to have the drive you need on the final day to win. You've got to be bold. You've got to go out and win it. They don't hand a tournament to you. I guess I'm no one to talk. Some people say I'm not too bold, either. Maybe that's why I haven't won a tournament in so long.

Dan Sikes, playing in front of me again, was so mad about the squall today he couldn't see straight. He went into the round needing only a 77 or 78 to make the cut, and on the famous sixteenth hole at Cypress Point, a long par-three along the ocean, he went for the green with a driver, instead of laying up with an iron. Dan missed the green and took so many strokes recovering that he missed the individual cut by six strokes. He finished the round with an 84.

At the end of the miserable day I bumped into Byron Nelson, one of the greatest players that ever lived. He's an announcer now for ABC and he said playing in a tournament like this does nothing but ruin a good golf game. You've got poor footing, you're not conditioned mentally or physically, and your whole approach to hitting a golf ball is altered. Maybe I'm just in a bad mood after missing the individual cut, but, I'll tell you, I wish I were somewhere else this week. It's not just that I'm hurting my golf game. I'm afraid I might drown to death.

Janaury 27 The sun popped out this morning, and everyone felt a little better. A bunch of the celebrities were on the putting green, joking and laughing with the pros, feeding us inside stories about show business. Most of these celebrities take their golf pretty seriously; they put on their little acts in the clubhouse and on the putting green, but once they get on the course, they're all business. I remember once I was playing with one of the funniest men in the world, Jim Backus, Mr. Magoo, and the funniest thing he said all round was "You're away."

I saw Howie Johnson before he teed off, and I asked him what he thought his chances of winning were, and he looked at me like I was crazy, like I was jinxing him, like it was somebody in the dugout mentioning a no-hitter in the eighth inning. I can understand Howie being a little touchy. He won two tournaments his first three years on the tour, and now he hasn't won one in ten years. He was jumping around, nervous as hell.

And, just like I figured, Howie and Dale Douglass both had trouble today. They finished in a tie for second, a stroke behind George Archer. Big George shot a 71, while Howie had 73 and Dale 74, and George collected first prize of twenty-five thousand dollars.

I didn't have much incentive today, except money, which is usually pretty good incentive for me. I played better than I'd been playing, and Mickey van Gerbig played very well, and on the front nine we could've had birdies every hole. But, between us, we missed five putts of less than five feet and we turned four under par. We finished with a 65, seven-under, in a tie for fifth or sixth place, I'm not sure.

I must've won about a thousand dollars, which isn't too bad, but I wonder if the money was worth the damage I did to my golf game. I kind of wish I hadn't played in the tournament, that I'd just gone down to San Diego and got myself in shape to win some official money in the Andy Williams–San Diego Open.

The one consolation was that we teed off on a beautiful day, and I got to see what it was like to play golf without three sweaters, six rain suits, and a hand-warmer. My irons are starting to improve, and even my four-wood's coming along.

For seventeen holes, we had sunshine, and then, as we teed off on eighteen, it began to pour. We played the last hole in the rain, a perfect ending to a perfect week.

January 28 / San Diego   Patty and I and the kids drove as far south as Santa Barbara last night, then went the rest of the way to San Diego today. I saw in the paper this morning that I won $1,100 in the team competition in the Crosby, and I guess I can't complain. That's not a bad week's work. There aren't too many jobs around for a boy my age with no really technical training to make over a thousand dollars a week.

Soon as we checked into our motel, I hustled right to the course. I was all fired up. My game needs work. When I got to Torrey Pines Golf Club, I found out that both courses there were being used for a pro-am. They've got two pro-ams here, one today for the guys who are pretty far down the money list, one tomorrow for the rest of us. There's just no way to practice on the course. I was damn upset. All I could do was chip and putt and, of course, I needed that, but I really wanted to work on my long game.

I saw Julius Boros and said hello. The old bear goes home each year around Thanksgiving and stays in hibernation until we get to some warm weather. Then he comes out of his cave and ambles around and hits a few balls and he's ready. He's forty-eight now, but he sure can play golf. I'm positive he'll be right up among the leaders again this year.

A couple of people from the Pensacola Open, which'll be held in March, were around, trying to line up entries for their tournament. They offer to help you get room reservations, anything they can do to get you to commit yourself. I don't promise anybody anything anymore. A few years ago, I committed myself to Minneapolis a month or so early, and they asked to use my name in their program. I said sure. Then Patty had trouble with her pregnancy, and I had to go home and miss the tournament, and they crucified me in Minnesota. The papers called me a temperamental spoiled brat, undependable, nice things like that. The Pensacola people asked me today if there was any way they could strengthen their field, and I said, "Sure, put up more prize money." That always seems to work.

One of the new young players was kind of strutting around at

Torrey Pines today. He'd finished in the top fifteen at the Crosby and made himself more than $1,500. I could tell he'd earned a pretty good check just by looking at him. He didn't have his bag and his practice balls the way the rabbits usually have. He had on his sport coat, and he was prancing around wanting to know where to register. Every week, there's somebody in that situation, some rabbit who's leaped out of the pack. He's dressed fit to kill and he's not going to practice. He's going to take a day off like the real tour veteran studs do. He's going to walk around and give a little advice to all the rabbits who are working. He's going to tell them all how he did it last week. He's out of their class now. And the odds are that he's probably had the only good tournament he's going to have all year and that within a week or two, he'll be back in the rabbit class, qualifying again.

January 29   I could tell today was pro-am day right from the beginning. I drove to the golf course and found that all the preferred parking spots had been given to the amateurs. I had to park about a mile up the road in some ditch, and I knew this was going to be a great day.

When I got to the locker room, the attendants couldn't find my golf shoes. We hunted around for a while till, finally, I found them in somebody else's locker. To top it off, rain had leaked through the roof last night, right down into my golf bag.

My three pro-am partners were good fellows, but we weren't going anywhere with any great team effort. I didn't play too well and, after a while, I picked up and stopped playing for score. I worked on my game instead. I found that I wasn't extending through the ball, that I was pulling up on it. I'm sure this came from the last two weeks in the rain. I'd been pulling up in an effort to pick the ball off the grass, to avoid going down in the slush. I concentrated on extending today and hit some real good shots.

I'm not too worried now about my game from tee to green. If I can only get my short game together and sink a few putts, I'll start winning some money. I've got to start making some putts on this California grass. If I don't, my confidence is going to be so low I'll have trouble getting it back up for the Florida and Texas tours. I can't help being concerned. I haven't won an official penny yet. I haven't finished four rounds of a tournament yet. I don't know whether it's California or old Frank Beard.

My amateur partners today were asking me about my plans for the future, and I told them that golf was just a business with me and that if the good Lord was willing and let me have two or three more years like I've had the past couple, then I'll get out of this rat race. I'm not going to stay out here forever. My family's going to be growing up and going to school, and my wife's going to be wanting to settle down, and I am, too. The touring life's no good for a family, any way you look at it. Of course, I keep coming back to one thing: I can't argue with the money.

I went to watch the San Diego Rockets play the Los Angeles Lakers tonight, and it was a good game. The Lakers won by a few points. It was a relaxing night, and it took my mind off golf completely. It was fun to see an athletic event that wasn't being played in the rain.

January 30   I got out to the golf course early this morning, two hours before I was to tee off. I don't usually show up until forty-five minutes or an hour before my tee time, but today I wanted to practice. I needed it. I concentrated on extending through the ball, hitting down and through and finishing as far out and as high as I could. I really got to hitting the ball well. It was one of the best practice sessions I've had in a long time, and I was really looking forward to going out and playing.

I felt even better after the first hole, a good-sized par-five. I hit two drivers in front of the green, then wedged up and made a ten-footer for a birdie. I should've quit right then. I parred the second hole, missed a simple six-footer and bogeyed the third, buried a four-wood shot in a bunker on four, and suddenly, I went from one-under to one-over, and I was on my way to a 74. It was nothing to be proud of, but I checked the scoreboard and saw that I was tied for about fortieth. I should be able to make the cut without much trouble, and if I have a good second round, I can move up and get in position to make some money.

Jack Nicklaus is leading with a 68, a stroke ahead of Dow Finsterwald, and Jack's going to be tough to beat. This course's long and wet, and with Jack's long, high ball, it's his kind of golf course.

I asked Patty tonight what our motel bill's going to be this week, and she said it'll be around $175. We've get a nice setup, two rooms and a kitchenette, but, I tell you, these rooms are getting out of hand. We spent $320 at Napa and $150 at the Crosby. In 1963, when I was a rookie, I was traveling with two buddies and we checked into a motel in Seattle, a small, clean place run by a little old lady. She told us we could have an apartment—a big room with two double beds and a pullaway couch, a front room with a TV, a bathroom, and a kitchenette. We asked how much it'd cost. "Twenty-one dollars," she said. "For the week."

We each stripped off two ten-dollar bills and a single and gave them to the lady, and she said, "No, no. It's twenty-one dollars total."

It cost us seven dollars apiece for the week. I spend that much now on one dinner for the family—unless I can find a good cafeteria.

January 31   With a 7:48 tee time, I had to get up at 5:30 this morning—more of the glamour of the pro golf tour. It was cold and wet again, so I slipped into my long underwear and my rain jacket and drove out to the course for breakfast. I'm a pretty demanding husband, but I don't expect Patty to get up at 5:30 and make me breakfast.

Miller Barber and I played a twosome today—our third man, Ken Venturi, dropped out with a bad hand—and we started at the tenth hole, a tough little dogleg to the right with a tiny green. I'd bogeyed it yesterday and the day before, but today I hit a drive and a three-iron and sank a ten-foot putt for a birdie, and I felt like I was going to get a good round started. Then, after two pars, on the thirteenth,

I let the ball slip to the right with a nine-iron and wound up in the fringe. It wasn't a hard chip shot, but the way I've been chipping lately, I figured I'd be happy if I could get it close. I hit the ball right into the hole. I was two under par after four holes.

I parred the next couple of holes, and we moved to the sixteenth, a long par-three. I hit a three-iron at the pin, but caught a bunker. Then Miller got up with a three-iron, and Mr. X whipped his shot right at the hole. The ball took one bounce and landed in the cup, a hole-in-one.

While Miller was accepting congratulations for his ace, I hit a bad bunker shot and took two putts for a bogey. On the par-five eighteenth, I caught another bunker and hit such a bad trap shot I didn't even get out of the sand. I took another bogey, bringing me back to even-par, and I was lower than a snake's belly. I wound up at 72 for the day, not too bad considering the wind. I made the cut easily and probably moved up into the top twenty-five or so, but still, after my strong start, I was disappointed.

I overheard two spectators talking when Miller and I were playing the front nine, and one said, "Hey, there's Miller Barber. He just made a hole-in-one. He's hot. Let's follow him. He's liable to get another."

I can't understand why people who don't know any more than that about golf spend good money to come out to a tournament.

Incidentally, when I passed the scoreboard, I noticed that the young boy who'd been strutting around Tuesday had missed the cut by thirteen strokes. He's got to qualify again next week. I guess he realizes the tour isn't quite as easy as it looked to him the other day.

February 1   Lee Trevino rushed up to me on the putting green today and said he had to tell me a story he'd just heard about the old days on the pro tour. According to the story, about fifteen years ago, when the tour was a lot smaller than it is now, one of the big pro stars went into the final round of some tournament trailing a young boy by about four strokes. The old pro bet the boy a thousand dollars he'd beat him out. Then he went to a friend of his, who was paired with the youngster, and said, "You got to help me out. I've got a thousand-dollar bet, and I don't have any money."

"Don't worry," his friend said. "I'll take care of him."

The kid birdied three of the first five holes, and when he came off the fifth green, the old pro's buddy took him to the side and said, "You know, when we get in, you got to show me that putting stroke of yours. I've never seen anybody hole putts the way you do—taking the blade back and opening it up to the outside and coming back so square. Never seen anything like it. You've got to teach it to me."

The kid started thinking about that, and by the fourteenth hole he'd gone from five shots in the lead to shooting 80. The old pro won the tournament, of course, and ran over to his friend and picked him up and hugged him and gave him a big kiss.

We're always hearing stories like that about the old days, about the hustling that went on before the tour went big-time, and I guess some of the stories are true.

Lee told me he's a little worried about his game. He's not getting the ball up in the air, he said; he's hitting it too low. I told him about my old friend Joe Campbell, who used to be on the tour. Joe always hit a real low ball, and once he told me that he was going to get on the tour committee and pass a rule that all tournaments have to be played in a gymnasium. "Any ball that hits the ceiling will be out of bounds," Joe said. "We play that rule, and I'll win every tournament."

"I'll go for that," Lee said.

Lee was paired with Nicklaus the past two days, and he said there was one incident yesterday that pointed up the difference between the two of them. "We're playing the ninth, the long par-five," Lee said, "and Jack hits a beautiful drive, takes a three-wood out and blanks the flag all the way in. But he's a little strong and hits the back edge, goes over, chips back, and two-putts for a five. I slice one almost out of bounds, duck-hook a three-wood so it hits some guy and drops down on the edge of the rough, flail a wedge up there, and hole a ten-footer for a birdie. I told Jack I'd give him a few tips."

The less said about my round today, the better. I shot 75, and it was a struggle. My mind was flighty as hell, wandering all over the place. And my putting didn't help. Actually, I rolled the ball up good, but nothing went in. Every putt lipped out or curled out or bounced out. I had to make a couple of birdies coming in to get my 75. It was one of those days that Chi Chi Rodríguez, the pro from Puerto Rico, is always talking about. "Man," Chi Chi says, "when you're snake bite, you're snake bite." I was snake bite today.

Outside of Gene Littler, who shot a 67 and moved into first place, two strokes ahead of Nicklaus, nobody was sensational today, so my 75 didn't hurt me too badly. Normally, a 75 in the third round'll drop you way down, but I just fell back from about twenty-fifth to thirty-fifth. I'm not too discouraged. I feel that with a good round tomorrow I can pass a lot of these cats and get up and make some real money. If I can get me a 67 tomorrow, I'll be at even par for the tournament—288—and I swear that'd put me in the top ten and be worth about three thousand dollars. Remember, tournaments are four days, not three, and I've shot more good closing rounds than just about anybody on the tour. That's a fact. My average score for the last round every year is lower than my average score for the other rounds.

I'm going to go out and win some official money tomorrow.

February 2   I got up this morning and set my sights on a 67. I went to the practice tee and, right away, a security cop started telling me where I could practice and where I couldn't. These security cops on the tour try to make everything more efficient, but sometimes they just get everything confused. Most of them, naturally, don't know much about golf tournaments or about golf, and they go strictly by the letter of the directions they've been given. Once, out in San Francisco, Ken Venturi came to the gate of the club where his father was the pro, and he was carrying his clubs, and the security cop wouldn't let him in the gate because he didn't have the required contestant's badge. The cop made Ken take his car out of the parking lot, park half a mile away, and then pay five dollars to get into the tournament.

I was paired today with Lionel Hebert and Harold Henning. Lionel is one of the sweetest people I've ever met. He's been on the tour almost twenty years. He won the PGA championship more than ten years ago, and even now he's a fine golfer. Lionel and his brother, Jay, and Gardner Dickinson are very close—they travel together and stay together—and they're three brilliant golfers who've won a bunch of tournaments. All the rest of us on the tour respect these fellows for both their records and their ability; but once in a while we like to tease them, in a friendly way, about how hard they work trying to find exactly the proper swing and proper shot for every situation.

Lionel, Jay, and Gardner are fanatics on mechanics, on working on the swing, on experimenting. When they play a golf course, they feel they have to hit a perfect shot for each stroke on each hole. They've got to fit a little three-iron in, or hook a little six-iron, or fade a little wedge. And all three of them, except maybe Lionel, are almost embarrassed when they have good putting rounds. They don't think putting's an art like hitting picture shots; they figure anybody can make a ten-footer, but only a real pro can deliberately hook one shot and then fade the next. They're artists all right, but over the years, if they'd just played their games and left all the mechanics alone, they might have run away from the rest of the tour.

I played like a bit of an artist myself today. I birdied the first hole, a par-five, then picked up six straight pars. On the eighth, I hit a five-iron in about a foot and a half from the hole and knocked that in for another birdie.

I came to the tenth two-under. I'd birdied the tenth hole Friday, but bogeyed it Thursday and double-bogeyed it yesterday, and I felt that if I could par ten, I'd shoot my 67. But I hit a bad chip shot and missed a six-footer and took a bogey and I was really down in the dumps. I felt like I'd blown the whole day. I could've collapsed right there, but I told myself to keep trying. I was still one-under. I parred the next three holes. Then, on the fourteenth, I pulled a six-iron onto the left fringe and I turned to my caddy and said, "Take that pin out. I got a feeling I just may chip this thing in." And I did. I chipped in for a birdie.

On fifteen, I lipped out a ten-footer, trying for a birdie. On sixteen, the hole Miller Barber aced, I hit a three-iron six feet from the cup and knocked it in for a birdie, and I was three-under with two holes to play, and the adrenaline was flowing. On seventeen, a real long par-four, I hit a good drive, but I was still a good three-iron from the green. But I was pumped up, and when the adrenaline's flowing, you're likely to hit each shot farther than you normally would. So I took a four-iron and busted it and came up five feet from the hole and sank the putt for a birdie, and then all I needed was to birdie the eighteenth, a par-five, and I'd have my 67.

I got greedy. I hit a big drive, and I knew I could hit a three-wood up short of the green. But I'd been hitting my driver out of the fairway lately, so I thought I'd give it a try for the green, maybe run it on and get an eagle. When things are going your way, you've got to capitalize on it. I overswung and half-topped the ball and wound up about 75 yards short of the green, out of cinch birdie range. I had to hit a full wedge in, came up about fifteen feet short, and two-putted for my par.

I'd have loved to have gotten my 67, but I was tickled to death with a 68. I checked my card carefully before I signed it. I've been fortunate. In all my time on the tour, I've never signed a wrong card. I've never signed for either a lower score (which would mean disqualification) or for a higher score (which would just mean I'd have to take the extra strokes).

Jack Nicklaus won the tournament—Gene Littler slipped to a 76 and lost by a stroke—and my 68 carried me up to a tie for ninth place. I won $3,325, official money, and, more than that, I won back my confidence. Now I know I'm capable of finishing in the top ten. Sometimes a check like this can give you more momentum than anything in the world. I'm out of the dumps and no longer wondering whether I'm ever going to play well. I feel like I can lick the world.

I paid my caddy $150, which is about ten dollars a day for five days plus three percent of my winnings. I didn't go into the tournament with ten-and-three in mind, but my caddy here was worth it. He knew the course. He kept me relaxed. He built my confidence.

On my way out of the clubhouse, I saw Rex Baxter, a Texan who's been out on the tour for about ten years. He was a great prospect when he came out—national collegiate champion and a former junior champion—but he never got his game going. He only won more than twenty thousand dollars in a year once and never got up among the top thirty money-winners. You just can't survive as a pro earning between ten and twenty thousand dollars a year; it's not enough to cover your bills. Rex recently got divorced and remarried, and now he's going to leave the tour and take a club job in Cleveland. He told me he's ready to settle down. He'll only play a few tournaments a year. It's kind of sad. I see Rex and I know he came out here with just as much physical ability as me, or more, and now, after putting in ten years of his life, he's giving it up for a new way of life. He's got a good personality. I'm sure he'll do well as a club pro and he may even do better in the few tournaments he plays. But it must hurt him, not to be doing anymore the thing he wanted to do most in the world.

I know it'd hurt me. I know it'd hurt my friends. I was glad to see that Steve Reid ended up in the top twenty-five here and won

Frank Beard's Record

TOURNAMENT	1ST ROUND	2ND ROUND	3RD ROUND	4TH ROUND
Southern Cal	69	70	—	—
Los Angeles	72	—	—	—
Kaiser	73	68	—	—
Crosby	74	79	75	—
Williams	74	72	75	68

* Unofficial. WD=Withdrew.
MC=Missed cut. T=Tie.

himself about $1,300. He hadn't finished in the top fifty at Los Angeles, Napa, or Pebble Beach, and he was starting to press.

Well, the first part of the tour is over—the West Coast swing— and I can't really complain. I didn't exactly burn up the bent-grass greens, but I made a helluva lot more money than I did last year and I played a helluva lot better. I'm ready to move inland, to the desert.

Patty and I got the kids to sleep early tonight, packed up all our clothes and all our groceries. Tomorrow morning, we'll load everything into the car and check out early. I'm really looking forward to Palm Springs, to the Bob Hope Desert Classic. I feel like I've got it in the bag.

TOTAL SCORE	FINISH	PRO-AM EARNINGS	INDIVIDUAL EARNINGS
139	T 6	—	$ 800.00*
—	WD	$ 187.50	—
141	T 25	—	414.97*
—	MC	1,100.00	—
289	T 9	—	3,325.00

2
The Desert Rat

TOURNAMENT	SITE	PURSE	DATES
Bob Hope Desert Classic*	Four different courses, Palm Springs	$100,000	Feb. 5– Feb. 9
Phoenix Open	Arizona Country Club, Phoenix	100,000	Feb. 13– Feb. 16
Tucson Open	Tucson National Golf Club, Tucson	100,000	Feb. 20– Feb. 23

* Unofficial tournament

February 3 / Palm Springs   The Bob Hope Desert Classic has a rather unusual format. It's a little like the Bing Crosby setup. During the first four rounds, we play on a different course each day —Indian Wells, La Quinta, Tamarisk, and Bermuda Dunes—with three different amateur partners each day. At the end of the four rounds, the pro whose four teams combined have the lowest score wins the pro-am part of the competition. It's sort of like playing in four separate pro-ams, and you know how much I like that.

Then—for the first and last time all year—the pros with the seventy lowest individual scores in the first four rounds play a fifth round. The amateurs sit out the fifth round, and all the pros play the host course—Indian Wells this year—to decide the individual championship.

I've always played pretty well in the desert here and in Arizona and Nevada. I won the Frank Sinatra Invitational here and the Tournament of Champions in Las Vegas, and a couple of years ago I won the pro-am section of the Hope Classic and collected $2,800 and a new automobile. I play so well here the sportswriters call me "The Desert Rat."

The Desert Rat's ready for this tournament. I'm really ready. That 68 yesterday has me all fired up. I've got a feeling I'm going to win this tournament and win it big, by five or six strokes. I wouldn't be surprised if I shot 68 every round here.

February 4   I started my diet in earnest again today. I had grapefruit and bacon and eggs for breakfast, nothing for lunch, grapefruit and steak and green beans for dinner. I'm looking pretty good. More than one person's come up to tell me it looks like I'm losing a little weight. I'm not down to Al Geiberger's size yet—he's got a thirty-one-inch waist—but I'm feeling better.

I played a practice round at Tamarisk today, and with a million members and guests swirling all around, Steve Reid and Jim Colbert and I were lucky to get on the course. I worked a lot on my bunker game. I think I've been playing the ball too far forward, keeping my hands behind the ball. I haven't been getting a crisp downward action through the sand. I've been sweeping the ball out instead of hitting down and through it. I moved the ball back today and I feel a lot more confident.

My good old four-wood seems to be coming along. I tell you, if I can get control of my fairway woods and my bunker shots, I'm going to be hell to beat.

In the locker room after my practice round, I saw Lee Trevino. They'd put out a little buffet for the players, and Lee was nibbling at some cheese. "You're gonna put on weight," I said.

"Listen, Beard," Lee said, "I've been playing like a rat lately. The only thing I can afford to eat is cheese."

February 5   Everybody's been kidding me about my fast finish at San Diego. Miller Barber came up to me on the putting green today with a big smile. He'd been three strokes ahead of me going into the final round at San Diego, and he'd shot 76, and he'd fallen back into a tie for thirty-fourth and I'd climbed up to ninth. "I went right by you last week, didn't I?" Miller said. "Just shot by you."

"Yeah," I said, "but in the wrong direction."

"I had it in reverse," said Miller.

I teed off today feeling like I could beat the world. I hit the ball well in practice and I was playing Indian Wells, probably the easiest of the four courses here, and I still can't believe what happened to me during the round.

I hit every single fairway with my drives. I hit seventeen out of eighteen greens in regulation. I hit every club well, except my four-wood. I used the four-wood three times on par-fives. The first time I hit it a little fat and came up short and settled for a par; the second time I hooked it into a bunker and settled for a par; the third time I hooked it real bad, over some bushes, took an unplayable lie, and wound up with a bogey, my only bogey of the day.

Would you believe this? With all that great golf, I picked up only three birdies all day.

On the greens, I've never been so snake bit in my life. I must've missed ten putts from less than fifteen feet; I must've missed five from less than seven feet. My putts hit inside the hole, hit the back of the hole, lipped out, and jumped out. I swear there was a gremlin inside the cup pushing my putts out.

The eighteenth hole sort of summed up my whole day. It's a good-sized par-five, and I hit a booming drive that left me a three-iron to the green. I busted that three-iron, just blanked the flag all the way in and came up six feet from the cup. I had a nice easy little putt for an eagle, a slight break right to left. I hit it firm, inside the hole, and the ball hit square in the back of the hole, jumped out, and just sat there like it was sticking its tongue out at me. Three perfect shots, absolutely perfect shots, and I wound up making a four, which probably some guy in front of me had made by duck-hooking a drive, blasting one up in front of the green, hitting a full wedge, and sinking a fifteen-footer.

I suppose it'll all even out eventually, and my putts'll start to fall. I've got to have patience and not get to feeling too sorry for myself. I believe that the person with the most even temperament is the one who's most successful on the tour. Gene Littler has the best temperament of anyone I know. I'm sure he could hit a shot up the side of a mountain and it wouldn't bother him at all. He'd just figure that's where that shot was supposed to have gone, and he'd go up and play down and never lose his temper or feel sorry for himself. Most people—like me—hit one bad shot and start thinking about it, and then they hit another. So much of this game is control, concentration and control.

I wound up with a 70 today, not a bad score, but I could have had a 65, 66 easily. Littler's among the leaders at 67, tied with Marty Fleckman, Tommy Shaw, and Lee Trevino. I guess Lee's eating better than cheese today.

My pro-am partners and I were thirteen-under, which isn't low for the day, but it's a good start. If I can get thirteen-under every day, I'll win the pro-am part of the tournament.

After I finished, I took my children into Palm Springs to buy them some new shoes. Two or three people—people I never saw—stopped me in the street and said, "Hi, Frank, how was the round today?" I'm not really used to being recognized off the course—or on the course, come to think of it—and it made me feel good, especially with all the big boys like Palmer, Nicklaus, and Casper walking around the same town.

I can't get too cocky, though. The last two rounds here are on national TV Saturday and Sunday, and the cameras are all set up at Indian Wells. Of course, the pairings are arranged so that Arnie and Jack and Cas and Trevino and those boys'll be at Indian Wells Saturday to smile at the cameras.

But not old Frank. Same story as the Crosby. Old Frank didn't quite make it with the big boys this year.

February 6   I've been coming here seven years, and I've never seen rain in Palm Springs—not until today. This is the year of the rain; it follows us to every tournament. The first person I saw at the club was Miller Barber, and Mr. X, who wears glasses just like I do, said, "Frank, we're gonna be in good shape today. We just love this weather, don't we?"

I put on my rain suit and decided I wasn't going to let this weather get me down. I was just going to bow my neck and forget about the weather and play my game.

On the practice tee, Gene Littler stopped to say hello. I congratulated him on his second-place finish last week. Gene's finished in the top ten now for three straight weeks. He told me in San Diego that he feels he's near the peak of his game and, I'll tell you, it couldn't happen to a nicer guy.

Gene's financially secure now, and he doesn't particularly enjoy the tour life. He'd rather be home with his family and with the old cars he collects. I think he's got a couple of Rollses and a Mercedes and a Jaguar and he fixes them up and polishes them, and he'd rather do that than play golf. Gene likes to earn his fifty or sixty thousand each year—he's been one of the top thirty money-winners fourteen of the last fifteen years—then go home and take it easy. He's the fifth-leading money-winner of all time—behind Arnie, Billy, Jack, and Julie—and he's probably had the least acclaim of any of the really great golfers. And he's great. Believe me, he's great.

We teed off in the rain, and after six holes I was two under par and feeling good, considering the weather. Then I got to talking to one of my amateur partners, a real nice fellow, and I just lost my concentration and hit a bad shot and bogeyed the seventh hole. When I walked off the green, angry with myself for losing my concentration, four ladies ran over to me to say hello. They'd met Patty and me last year, and they were so glad to see me they started hugging and kissing me, and that, coupled with the bogey, really made me lose my concentration. On the eighth, a long par-four, I hit a four-iron into a bunker. Suddenly, I faced the chance of falling back to even-par and ruining the whole day. I hit a fairly good bunker shot and stopped seven feet from the hole. And this putt was my critical shot for the whole round. If I'd missed it, I'd have been back to even, and my fast start would have been wasted. I was playing Bermuda Dunes, probably the second easiest course, and I thought, "If I go back to even-par, I'm sure as hell finished for this round and maybe for the whole tournament."

I made the putt. I saved my par. Then I parred eight and birdied the next four holes in a row to put me five-under for the round, seven-under for the tournament and sitting pretty. The wind blew up strong after that, and I parred five and bogeyed one of the last six holes, scrambling all the way, and finished at 68. I'm in third place, behind Trevino, who's at 136, and Red Funseth, a steady little golfer from Spokane who shot 66 today for 135.

One little incident today really broke me up. When I birdied one of the par-fives, a spectator ran up to me and said, "Boy, Mr. Beard, that was really a great four. Does that give you a net-three on this hole?"

I guess the way I was swinging, that fellow thought I should've been getting a few handicap strokes.

When I got home this afternoon, I had to take Patty to see a gynecologist. He says she's starting to dilate now and the baby should be here in another two or three weeks. I've got to send her home next week. I'm going to miss her, and I'll miss the kids, too. Danny's down with a little fever now, and he's crying a lot, but I'll even miss his crying when they go home. It's funny: I really don't want to bring my family on tour because it's no place to raise a family, but I sure as hell don't want to leave them at home. I need them with me. I feel better. I'm more relaxed. I'll be glad when I can settle down and stop this nomad life.

I still feel I'm going to win this tournament. I've felt it right from the start. With a good break in the weather, I could shoot 66 or 67 tomorrow at Tamarisk. If I don't win, I'm going to be very surprised.

February 7   Patty left the kids with a baby-sitter today and drove out to Tamarisk with me. When we got near the course, we found the only access road completely flooded from yesterday's rain. The one other way to get to the club was to turn around and drive back twenty miles and then approach the course from a different side. It was getting close to my tee time, so I told Patty to hold on, I was going to drive through the flooded road. I backed up, got a running start, slid and slushed through the mud and water, and made it. I was really proud of myself till I got to the clubhouse and found out, first, that my watch was running thirty minutes fast and, second, that because of the rain, the starting times had been pushed back half an hour. I would've had plenty of time to turn around and use the other entrance. At least I can tell the Buick people their car's a good mudder.

Patty and I ate breakfast with Art Wall, a veteran pro, a quiet, conservative individual who's been a friend of mine for a long time. Art and I got into a discussion of the importance of Arnie and Jack to the tour. Art, like a lot of older players, feels that the tour would have grown without Arnie and Jack and that their contributions to the game are exaggerated.

I can understand Art's point of view, but I can't accept it. All I know is that every time I collect any prize money, I mentally thank Arnie for twenty-five cents out of every dollar. I honestly think that's Arnie's contribution to the tour—twenty-five percent of every purse—and I'm grateful to him for it.

Lee Trevino stopped by Tamarisk to say hello to somebody, and he told me he'd never seen so much rain in his life. "Beard," Lee said, "I'm going to have to pump some sunshine up from El Paso for these California people. Hell, I haven't seen the sun in four weeks. If it doesn't come out soon, when I get back to El Paso, they're gonna let me sit in the front of the bus."

I birdied two of the first four holes, but my best shot set up a par on the third hole. After my second shot caught a trap, I decided to try out my new bunker theory. I took my stance with the ball farther back, and I hit through, and the ball popped out about five feet from the cup. I holed the putt. I parred the fifth hole through the twelfth, and then, on the thirteenth, I three-putted for a bogey, and my chin sank down on my chest. I was making a run at the leaders, my putting had come back and, suddenly, it had deserted me again.

On the fourteenth hole, a long par-three, I hooked my damn four-wood, made a bad pitch up, and left myself with a ten-footer. It was another one of those critical shots—like my seven-footer yesterday—the kind that can make or break a round. If I'd missed, I would've gone back to even-par.

It was a straight-in putt. I kept my head still, kept it firm, and stroked the ball right into the cup and saved my round. If I'd missed, I'm sure I would've gone up to 73 or 74. Instead, I parred in, finished with a 71, and remained in third place, still three strokes behind Funseth and two behind Trevino.

Lee's definitely the man to beat. He's playing Indian Wells tomorrow, the easiest course, and Rod and I are playing La Quinta, the toughest. But I still think I can win it.

My pro-am team went thirteen-under today, which puts me thirty-five-under for the tournament, very close to the top. First prize is three thousand dollars, so it's worth shooting for.

One thing that's very much on my mind this week is to take extra special care with my short putts, the tap-ins. I missed one last week at San Diego that couldn't have been more than fifteen or eighteen inches. Pure carelessness. That stroke cost me a thousand dollars.

I almost got in a hassle today with our lady scorer. At almost every tournament, the officials assign a woman to walk with each group and keep scores that are relayed to the scoreboards. These scores are purely unofficial; the only ones that count are the ones kept by the players themselves. But some of the women don't seem to realize their scores are unofficial; they think their tabulations and calculations are the most important thing in the world. This woman today kept pounding me with questions, like did so-and-so hit out of bounds and did he take an unplayable lie, and I did everything but just tell her to shut up and leave me alone. It's hard enough to concentrate out there with three amateur partners.

I've got a real good caddy here, a boy named Tony Mullins, who's on the golf team at the University of Wisconsin and caddies for me in Palm Springs each year on his semester break. When we left the course today, I wrote a check for Tony for twenty dollars because he needed some spending money.

We went to the bank together—I wanted to get some cash, too —and when Tony walked up to the lady teller, she looked at his check, made out to Tony Mullins and signed by Frank Beard. "You caddy for Frank Beard?" she said.

"Yes, ma'am," he said.

She cashed the check and gave him his money.

Then I stepped up and she saw my check, made out to cash. "Oh, you both work for Frank Beard," the lady said.

Before I could say anything, she said, "He must have a lot of caddies this week. What did he do—fire you?"

Tony and I both laughed and got out of there. It sure is great to be a famous professional golfer.

I played gin rummy with Patty tonight. We played for back rubs. I beat her out of three back rubs.

February 8   I knew I was going to play well today. I didn't care if I was facing the toughest course. I knew I could handle it. And I did.

The first nine holes were the greatest putting and chipping nine of my life. Just listen to this:

First hole. After a good drive, I put a seven-iron over the green, halfway down a slope, a tough little chip. I took out my old sand iron, blooped the ball up in the air, and it ran down and almost went in the hole. Tap-in for my par.

Second hole. On a long par-five, I hit two good drivers and came up just short of the green. I pitched up six feet behind the hole and sank the putt for a birdie.

Third hole. On a long par-three, I hit a three-iron into the left-hand fringe, then almost sank the chip. Tap-in for my par.

Fourth hole. On a very long par-five, I hit a booming drive, then a three-wood just short of the green, in the fringe, maybe ninety feet from the hole. I had to chip over a hill, then over a little hump, then downhill to the pin. I hit a firm eight-iron, and the ball popped over the hill, hit on the hump, ran down, made a little left-hand turn, and dropped in for an eagle. Three-under.

Fifth hole. After a big drive and a six-iron to the green, I sank a twenty-footer for a birdie. Four-under.

Sixth hole. On a par-three, I hit a three-iron into the left-hand fringe, chipped up, and lipped the hole. Tap-in for my par.

Seventh hole. A routine par.

Eighth hole. I missed the green with my second shot, but chipped up and knocked in a four-footer for my par.

Ninth hole. A routine par—for a 32 on the front nine of the toughest course in Palm Springs, even though I missed four of the nine greens.

By the time our foursome moved to the back nine, we had a

pretty good-sized gallery. I wasn't used to playing in front of so many people. I checked my amateur partners again, and there wasn't a movie star in the bunch. I guess the gallery was for old Frank Beard.

On the eleventh hole, a long par-four, I hit a bad drive into a fairway bunker. I got greedy and tried to hit a three-iron out, instead of playing safe with a four-iron, and I caught the lip of the bunker and just kind of squibbled out into the fairway. I hit a good-looking wedge from there, but it rolled about twelve feet past the hole. And from right there, putting for a par, I three-putted. I missed an eighteen-incher and wound up with a double-bogey six.

I could've quit right there. I could've given up. But, instead, on the next three holes, I sank a ten-footer for a birdie, sank a twenty-footer for a birdie, and just lipped out a fifteen-footer for an eagle. Three straight birds, and I was back to five under par for the round, twelve-under for the tournament. I parred the next three holes—helped by a good sand shot on the sixteenth—then, on the eighteenth, all pumped up, hit a nine-iron too big, over the green, missed a twelve-foot putt, and settled for a bogey and a round of 68.

As I came off the eighteenth green, Jack Tuthill, the PGA tournament director, grabbed me. "C'mon," he said. "We've got to get you over to the press tent at Indian Wells."

"Why?" I said.

"You're leading the tournament by two shots."

"What the hell happened to Funseth?"

"He took a triple-bogey on the first hole," Tuthill said, "and wound up with a 75."

"Trevino?"

"He shot 75 at Indian Wells. You're first at eleven-under, and Casper, Wall, and Montgomery are tied for second at nine-under."

I hustled over to Indian Wells and reviewed my round for the benefit of the sportswriters, fifty or sixty of them plus a flock of cameramen. I'd be lying if I didn't say it boosted my ego.

Outside the press tent, I saw Art Wall, and he was mad as hell. Art told me that some reporter had asked him how he felt being two strokes behind Frank Beard and did he think Beard was going to blow tomorrow. Art was hot. "They never give any of us credit for being good players," he said. "They write off everybody but

Casper and Nicklaus and Palmer. When anyone else wins, they say it's just a fluke or Nicklaus had the flu or something like that. Why don't they tell the truth and say that Beard is beating the hell out of Nicklaus and Palmer this week?"

I've got to agree with Art. It seems like if Arnie wins a tournament, the headline says, "Palmer Wins." And if I win a tournament, the headline says, "Palmer Loses." I don't blame Arnie—he doesn't write the headlines—but it can be awfully frustrating. It hurts the old ego.

Of course, my ego got built up pretty good today with the big gallery, the press interview, and the news that I tied for first place in the pro-am part of the Hope Classic. My team today shot eleven-under, which put me forty-six-under for the tournament and earned me $2,475.

I was all swelled up with myself as I was leaving Indian Wells, and I happened to bump into Phil Harris, the comedian. He'd been my partner in the Crosby a couple of years ago, and I've seen him a few other times, and he came up to me smiling today, and I thought he was going to say, "Frank, how ya doin', boy? You're really hittin' it good." Instead, he looked at me and said, "Hi, Mason. Been a long time since I've seen you. How's everything in Nashville?"

He thought I was Mason Rudolph.

When I got home tonight, I got a phone call from my father. Pro was ecstatic. Sometimes I think I play golf just for him. I feel that if I lose, it's going to break his heart more than mine, or if I win, it's going to mean more to him than to me. Mom tells me that when I play a good round, like today, Pro's out on the street, walking up and down, saying howdy to all the neighbors. But when I play badly, Pro just sits inside, in front of the television set, and doesn't say anything to anybody.

I'm nervous tonight, but I'm not scared. I feel the pressure of leading the tournament, but I'm past the fingernail-biting, no-sleep stage. I've won six tournaments. I've finished second or third eight times. I've been in contention and dropped out. I know what pressure is.

It's funny, but tonight I'm not thinking about the money I can win. Lord knows, that's why I'm out here on the tour—to make money—but tonight I'm thinking about victory. I want to win. I want to win a tournament on national television with the kind of field we've got here—all the big boys.

I want to win it for the money, sure, and for the prestige. I want to win it to make Bill Boone's job easier when he's selling me for exhibitions and endorsements. But, mostly, I want to win it just for the sake of winning.

It's been almost two years since I've won a tournament. Sometimes I wonder if I'm ever going to win one again. I am. I'm going to win this one. As long as I don't make any dumb mental errors, I'm going to win this thing.

I can't help thinking tonight about the first tournament I ever played in Palm Springs, the first tournament I ever had a good shot at winning, the Frank Sinatra Invitational in 1963.

It was my first year on the tour, and the week before, at San Jose, I'd missed the cut and since I didn't have an exemption, I had to qualify at Palm Springs on Monday. I just made it. I shot a 77 and, as I recall, the highest qualifying score was 78.

In the first round of the Sinatra Invitational, I shot a 68 and tied for first place with Bob Rosburg. I didn't feel much pressure. I didn't expect to stay up that high. The next day, I shot a 72 and fell back into a tie for fourth place with Rossy and several other guys. Dow Finsterwald and Ray Floyd, who was a rookie like me, were tied for the lead at 138, and Casper was only a stroke behind.

In the third round, Tommy Bolt shot a 67 and I shot a 69, and we were tied for first place at 209. The next morning, I went to Mass and, for the first time in my life—and the last—I asked God to let me win. Most times, I just ask Him to let me do the best I can, but that morning, I asked Him to let me win. I felt it could be a real turning point in my career. It could establish me as a professional. It would give me an exemption for the following year. I was more nervous than I've ever been since. I wanted to win so bad.

I played in the next-to-last threesome with Bob Rosburg and Jerry Steelsmith, who'd been playing the tour a few years. The final threesome consisted of Bolt, the former U.S. Open champion;

Mason Rudolph, one of the top ten money-winners that year; and Howie Johnson. Mason and Jerry Steelsmith were tied for second, just a stroke behind Bolt and me.

On the first four holes, I struggled for pars. Then I birdied five and eight, which put me six-under for the tournament and moved me into first place. But I bogeyed nine and then eleven, an easy par-five, and I felt like I'd blown my chance. All I could think about then was trying to hold on and get second or third or fourth money.

I scrambled for desperate pars the next four holes, and when we got to the sixteenth tee, with three holes to play, we saw an up-to-date scoreboard for the first time. Gardner Dickinson was in first place at five-under, and Steelie, Mason, and I were at four-under. "Wait a minute now," I said to myself. "I've faltered, and I'm still only a shot out. I can still win this."

The sixteenth hole was a dogleg to the left about 250 yards out, then another 220 yards to the green. I tried to cut the corner and hit some palm trees and just managed to trickle out into the rough, past the dogleg. I was still some two hundred yards from the green, and I had to hit out of the rough over a lake to reach the green.

Something possessed me, I don't know what. I had just a fair lie, and I should've played safe, out to the left and maybe bounce on the green for a two-putt, but I remember thinking, "You're never gonna have a better chance to win a tournament than right here."

I took out a four-iron and went right for the hole. My shot barely cleared the lake protecting the green, then rolled up within six feet of the pin. Steelie got on in two and two-putted, and I sank my birdie putt; suddenly I was tied for the lead. My head just about blew off from the heat and the excitement.

Gardner Dickinson was playing right in front of us, and we watched him on the seventeenth, a par-five bending to the right. He tried to reach the green on his second shot with a three-wood and hooked the ball out of bounds. He dropped a new ball and hooked another shot out of bounds. Gardner finally took a nine. About the same time, we heard that Bolt and Rudolph had played themselves out of contention behind us. There were only two holes left to play, and it was just me and Steelie, and I had a one-stroke lead.

I hit a big drive on seventeen, some 250, 260 yards, but in the rough. Steelie drove down the middle of the fairway. I must've been 220 yards from the green, but I knew from my lie that the ball was going to fly, going to take off. I had to get over some palm trees to reach the green.

I took an eight-iron—an *eight-iron*—one of the smartest moves I ever made. I really pumped it. I hit it almost two hundred yards, over the palms, right up in front of the green. Steelsmith hit his second shot to the edge of the green. I was away and I was shaking like crazy. I had visions of shanking the shot or topping it or just missing it completely. I hooded the club a little, to give me better control, and I chipped up to about eight feet from the pin. Steelie chipped up inside me, maybe five or six feet from the pin.

Again, I was away. I lined up my putt, sweating, shaking. If I missed and then he made his putt, we'd be all even. "Now, c'mon," I told myself. "If you make your putt, he won't be able to handle the pressure. He'll miss his, and you'll have a two-stroke lead."

I hit my putt a little too hard. If it'd been off-line, it would have gone way past the hole. But the ball went right into the center of the hole and stayed there. I just watched it and shook. I don't remember ever taking the ball out of the cup. I don't know how I could've, my hand was shaking so much.

Steelie missed.

Steelie and I have talked about that hole several times since, and he's convinced, and I am, too, that if he'd picked up a stroke on me then, he probably would have gone ahead to win the tournament and launch a great career. But that tournament, that hole, just broke his back. Steelie has never won a tournament, has never become the golfer he might've been.

We still had to play the eighteenth hole, even though I had a two-stroke lead. When I walked up to the eighteenth tee, I was still shaking. I looked down the fairway, and saw out of bounds on the left and bunkers on the right, and the fairway didn't look any wider than a pool table. Bob Rosburg walked over to me. "Frank," he said, "don't do anything stupid. You got this thing locked up. Take an iron and knock it down the middle and then knock it on the green and two-putt and win the tournament and forget it."

If Rossy hadn't said anything, I might've taken a driver and hit the ball out of bounds. But I just stroked a two-iron down the middle of the fairway, then watched Steelie drive his ball a mile, maybe fifty yards past me.

I was still about two hundred yards from the middle of the green, and something popped into my mind, that good rule I still follow: when you're pumped up, always take less iron than you think you need because you'll hit it farther than you normally would. For two hundred yards, I'd normally take about a three-iron. I took a five-iron. On a normal lie, under normal conditions, I couldn't hit a five-iron two hundred yards if my life depended on it. But I busted this ball right in the middle of the green, maybe twenty feet past the pin. If I'd hit a three-iron, I probably would've gone over the clubhouse.

Steelsmith hit a nine-iron and landed about three inches inside me. I had to putt first, and I was shaking, but I could still add. "If I can two-putt," I said to myself, "I win—even if he sinks his."

I lined up over the ball and I couldn't draw the putter back. My mind was telling my hands to bring the putter back, but my hands wouldn't listen. I must've tried three or four times until, finally, I brought the putter back and stroked the ball. It stopped a foot from the hole, twelve inches away. I walked up to putt out—I wasn't in anybody's line—and I couldn't even see my ball. My vision was all clouded up, sweat or tears or imagination or something. I still don't know how, but I tapped the ball in the hole, and I had my first tour championship.

I walked to the back of the green to wait for Steelie to putt out, and I was covered with goose bumps. I looked down at my shirt and, I swear to God, my shirt was palpitating, actually palpitating, because my heart was beating so hard.

After Steelie sank his putt for a birdie—cutting my margin of victory to a single stroke—they led me off the green for the presentation of the nine-thousand-dollar winner's check and the winner's jacket. Frank Sinatra was waiting for me, and Bing Crosby and Bob Hope and Phil Harris and Jill St. John, who was Sinatra's girl friend then. All I can remember about the presentation is that Jill St. John was wearing a white sweater and a big medallion around her neck, and the medallion was hanging down between her breasts, and all I could think, after winning my first tournament, was "Gosh, she's got big boobs."

I was just a country boy. I'd never seen anything like that.

I went right to the press tent and talked with the press, and then I called Mom and Dad, and Pro started crying, he was so happy. He couldn't say anything. He just cried.

I always figured when you won a tournament, you were a big hero, the center of attraction, but I guess I picked the wrong one for my first victory. There was a party in the clubhouse, and Dean Martin was there and Sammy Davis and a bunch of actresses, and I just stood in a corner and nobody paid any attention to me. After a while, I walked over to Sinatra, quietly thanked him, and left the clubhouse. Nobody noticed me leave.

I went back to my motel room and locked the door. I was so nervous I didn't want to go out, and I couldn't sleep. I ordered a cheeseburger and a Coke from room service, and I couldn't eat it. For three days, I couldn't handle a drop of food, I was so worked up.

I've won five tournaments since then, but I've never come close to the thrill that first victory gave me. The only thing in my life that even approached it was the birth of Danny, my first child.

Well, I've got to admit tonight that the pressure of being in the lead is a lot greater than the pressure of coming from behind. Still, I'd rather be in the lead. Any time I can have a two-stroke advantage over eighteen holes, I'll play any man alive.

I've got two strokes now, and they're going to have to come and get me.

February 9   What can I say? They got me.

I'm a pretty sad man tonight. I didn't win the Bob Hope Classic. Casper won. He shot 66. I shot 74 and wound up tied for fifth.

I don't think I'm going to jump off a bridge or anything. I've lost before and I'll lose again. But if only I'd shot a 69 and Casper had shot a 66 and beat me by a stroke, I wouldn't feel so bad.

I played miserably. I beat myself.

The day started badly. I woke up nervous. I can't remember the last time I woke up nervous, maybe because it's been six months since I went into the last round of a tournament in first place.

We got up and went to church and I snapped at Pat and I snapped at the kids and I stopped just short of snapping at the priest. We went to one place for breakfast, and it was closed. We went to another, and it was too crowded. We went to a third, and I told Patty I was uncomfortable because everyone was staring at me.

"Can I do anything to help you?" Patty said.

"Just leave me alone," I said. I was really in a beautiful mood.

I drove out to the course—Tony, my caddy, had gone out early to check a few distances and a few pin positions—and when I got there, I discovered I'd left my clubs back at the motel. I had to send Tony back to get them. That was the kind of blur I was in all day long.

Still, when I teed off, I felt confident. I'd hit my practice shots well, and the course wasn't playing hard. The conditions were perfect. Deane Beman shot a fantastic 62 today. Of the top twenty finishers, I was the only man who didn't break par; half of the top twenty shot in the 60s. I should have been in the 60s, too. I had just one person to beat today—Frank Beard—and he beat me.

I parred the first three holes, three-putted from about ten feet for a bogey on four, then birdied five. I parred six, then hit miserable drives on seven and eight, both easy birdie holes, and settled for two more pars. At the ninth tee, still even-par, I gave myself one of my little pep talks. "Now listen, Beard," I said. "If we're gonna win this tournament, by God, we're gonna have to buckle down and play golf like we know how. Don't be swinging like some old grandma. Tee that thing up and bust hell out of it."

I listened to myself; I hit a real good drive on nine. I left myself just an eight-iron to the green. I took the club and—this was the turning point—just cold quit on it. I made a terrible pass at the ball. Maybe I choked. I don't know. But I hit a bad iron and left myself thirty feet short of the pin. I left my first putt six feet short. And I missed that. I three-putted for a bogey and I turned one over par, and my momentum was gone, and so was my concentration, and so was my morale. I was in a total fog. I bogeyed ten and eleven, and you could stick a fork in me, I was done. I was finished. I picked up a stroke on par the last seven holes, but it was too late by then.

Just as I finished my round, Spiro Agnew, the Vice-President of the United States, came out to present the winner's trophy to Billy Casper. I just kind of slunk away. I walked out behind the stands, where nobody could see me, and I left without watching the award ceremony.

When you haven't played well, Sunday nights are the most miserable nights on the tour. Patty was sympathetic, sympathetic and quiet. She let me suffer in silence.

I've rented a car to drive to Phoenix tomorrow morning—Tony, the caddy, is going to return my borrowed Buick to Los Angeles— and tonight Patty and I put all our clean clothes in our suitcases and all our dirty clothes in a bag. We're ready to go.

Financially, I can't kick about the week. Between the $3,175 I won for finishing fifth and the pro-am money, I earned a little more than $5,600. If somebody had told me before I came over here that I'd win $5,600, I'd have kissed him right on Main Street. Yet now I feel so low.

And I've got nobody to blame but me.

February 10 / Phoenix   This felt like the longest, dullest day of my life. I had the blahs all day. I didn't know a poor finish could affect me so.

Patty and the kids and I got on the road this morning, and when we stopped for breakfast, I picked up a newspaper and read all about how Beard had choked and blown his lead in the Bob Hope Classic. The press never fails. If Cas or Arnie or Jack doesn't hold a lead, there's always some good excuse, like they were ill or they didn't get the breaks or something. But if Frank Beard doesn't hold a lead, you read about how he blew it, how he choked.

I don't think I choked. I just played terribly.

We moved into the Ramada Inn here—the place where that nymphomaniac failed to seduce me five years ago—and it was dead, nobody around except the wives of the fellows trying to qualify today.

I went out to the course, paid my registration fee for the Phoenix Open, and saw my caddy, Pete, the young boy who caddied for me at Napa and Pebble Beach. A few players were drifting around the clubhouse, and Al Balding, a Canadian pro, walked up to me and said, "Boy, I bet you got into the Scotch last night."

"I was feeling too bad to do that," I said.

Tonight, Dick Crawford and his wife came by to play a little bridge. A ball hit Dick on the elbow Saturday when he was practicing here, and today he shot a 75 and failed to qualify for the Pheonix Open. Dick's made the cut in only one tournament so far—and he finished next to last then—and he's really depressed. He's thinking about looking for a club job. This is the way qualifying can affect you. You're almost helpless.

I felt even sorrier for Dick tonight than I felt for myself.

February 11   Everyone was kidding Deane Beman today about the 62 he shot Sunday, and Deane was flexing his muscles—he's a little fellow, one of the shortest hitters on the tour—and saying he would've had a 58 or 59 if he'd been making his putts. Deane and I and Steve Reid and Jack Tuthill, the PGA tournament director, played a practice round, and I worked on trying to correct a hook I've developed off the tee.

I think I've moved my left hand a little too far over to the right. I slip into this grip every once in a while. It's a much stronger grip and, subconsciously, trying to get greater distance, I slip the hand over. Today I moved the left hand back on top of the club to weaken the grip and eliminate the hook. I drove a lot straighter than I had been.

Deane kept teasing me as we practiced. Last year, in one tournament he'd started with 64 and I'd started with 74 and we'd ended up tied, and I'd teased him like crazy, telling him I'd given him ten strokes in the first round and then caught up. Well, today, he wouldn't let me forget that going into the final round at Palm Springs, I'd had him by twelve strokes, and we'd finished in a tie. I finally got so hot I bet Steve and Deane ten dollars apiece that I'd finish ahead of both of them this week.

We walked off our distances very carefully. Flat golf courses like they have here in the desert are much more difficult to gauge by the eye than hilly courses. When you have hills, you get some depth perception. But in the desert, you can't trust your visual judgment; you've got to walk off every yard.

The course is pretty easy—par-71, less than seven thousand yards long—and I suspect it's going to take somewhere from sixteen to twenty under par to win, an average of 66 or 67 a round. That's bad for me. I do better on tough courses. Not that I'm a great player, but it just seems that the guys who shoot 65s on the easy courses shoot 75s on the tough courses, and I shoot 70 on both of them.

Patty went to see an obstetrician here today, and it looks like she's going to have the baby pretty soon. She's getting some pains, and I don't want her to have the baby out here on tour. She and the children are going to fly home this Saturday, and I'm really going to miss them.

I worry these days about working out a schedule so that I can see my family and be with them and still take advantage of the growing opportunities on the tour. It looks like we'll have about forty-five tournaments on the schedule this year, and the combined prize money will be close to six million dollars, and I know I'm right near the peak of my career. I'm as strong as I'll ever be and, if I can just push myself, I can make a pile of money and get out of this rat race.

I'd like to go home with Patty and the kids, but I can't afford it. Money's not going to grow on a tree out in the yard. Some of the fellows—Al Geiberger, for one—take off every third or fourth week, no matter what, but they're in better financial shape than I am. Jack Nicklaus says he's only going to play twenty tournaments a year, the minimum to satisfy his endorsement requirements. Well, if I had his money, I'd do the same thing.

Tonight I took the family to dinner at a cafeteria—that's the golfer's friend: good hot food, plenty of vegetables, at reasonable prices—then went home and played a little bridge with the Crawfords. I'm going to sleep early. Tomorrow's pro-am day, and I'll need all my strength.

February 12 With my usual early pro-am tee time, I got up at six this morning, stopped at the coffee shop, and just as I finished reading the papers, spilled a cup of coffee all over my britches. I had to go back to the room and change. I knew for sure it was pro-am day.

Naturally, when I got to the course, the security cop told me to go to one of the farthest parking places from the clubhouse. I ignored him. I parked near the clubhouse and gave him a look that said, "Pal, don't give me any problems, 'cause I'm all fired up for pro-am day."

I walked into the clubhouse and, right away, some guy ran up to me and said, "Hello, Frank, great to see you, haven't seen you since we played together in the pro-am two years ago, how you doing?" Like he was a long-lost buddy.

I couldn't remember him from Adam. I play forty pro-ams a year; that comes to about seven hundred pro-am partners over six years. And I'm supposed to remember this guy. I ought to do what Phil Rodgers does. If some guy comes up and says, "Hi, Phil, you remember me," he says, "Hell, no, I don't remember you." Phil says it with a big grin, and they laugh, and he gets away with it.

I can't do that. I just call them all "Pro," and say, "How ya doin', champ," and all that stuff and I couldn't drop their names if they paid me a hundred dollars to do it.

This guy this morning started telling me about every shot I hit two years ago, and I didn't know what he was talking about, but I tried to be nice to him.

"I'm really playing good these days," he said. "Just one problem. Remember how I was cutting the ball two years ago?"

"Oh, sure," I said.

"Well, that tip you gave me isn't working," he said. "Just isn't working." He shook his head, like he was sorry for me that my tip wasn't working. "Give me another tip today before I tee off."

I gave him the old standby about swinging smoothly, and off he went, happy as a lark, because Frank Beard had remembered him and given him a tip before he teed off.

After the round today—I shot a 69, which wasn't worth a cent, and the team score wasn't much better—I practiced my chipping and putting, and Gene Littler came over and told me not to feel too bad about my finish in the Hope. "Same thing happened to me the week before," Gene said.

Then he asked me a serious question. "What do you look at, Frank, when you're stroking a putt?" he said. "Do you look at the ball, a spot on the ball, the putter, a spot on the putter, the green, or the hole?"

"I don't know," I said. "I don't think I look at anything specific. I just try to keep my head steady and sort of watch the back of the ball, I guess. Why?"

"Just recently," Gene said, "I've found myself watching the putter go back instead of watching the ball."

"Has it hurt your putting?"

"No. I'm putting as well as I ever have in my life."

"Then what are you worried about?"

"I don't know," Gene said. "I just noticed I'm watching the putter, and I wondered if there was something wrong with that."

"Not if you're making the putts."

"Well, then," he said, "I'm not gonna worry anymore."

It started raining tonight—here in the desert, just to keep our record perfect for the year—and after we had dinner at the cafeteria, we came home early and Patty did all my ironing. She wants to have everything ready for me before I start bacheloring it this weekend. It sure is nice to have your wife with you to do the ironing and washing and picking up your clothes and keeping the room straight. There's no telling what this place is going to look like after she leaves. I'm going to miss her and all that nice treatment.

Well, maybe I can get started with a little 65 tomorrow.

February 13   I had breakfast this morning with Jacky Cupit, a Texan about a year older than me, and then I played with Chuck Courtney, a fellow from California who's a year younger than me, and seeing Jacky and Chuck, both old friends, made me kind of think. Like me, they both won tournaments their rookie years. Like me, they both made the top fifty money-winners their rookie years. And now both of them have problems. Jacky pulled a back muscle a couple of years ago, and his earnings dropped from fifty thousand dollars in 1966 to under twenty thousand dollars in 1967 and 1968. Chuck's earnings dropped from twenty-five thousand dollars in 1967 to about sixteen thousand dollars in 1968. Both of them lost their exempt status.

All the time, I live in fear of a slump like Jacky and Chuck have suffered. It can happen so quickly, without warning, to anybody. At least Jacky knows the cause of his slump—the muscle pull. Imagine how Doug Sanders feels. His tournament earnings fell from more than $110,000 in 1967 to less than $40,000 in 1968. He dropped from sixth place in money-winning to clear out of the top forty. It scares me. It could happen to me.

I cheered myself up a little with my round today. I shot 66, hit every fairway and every green in regulation, scored three birdies, and chipped in once for an eagle. My putting left a bit to be desired. I missed eight putts of twelve feet or less for birdies. If I'd made half of them—which I ought to do, with my stroke—I'd have had a 62. I've never shot lower than 64 in tournament competition.

Even with a 66, I was only in eighth place, behind seven— seven!—65s. Still, I'm happy, with my score and with my game. The only time I got into a bunker, on the par-five eighth hole, I hit a great wedge three feet from the cup and got a birdie. And, by moving my left hand on top of the club and weakening my grip, I've cut down my hook off the tee. Most important, my concentration's improving week after week. I'm starting to get into my good old rut—eight-to-five going to the office—and that's when I play best.

The guys are starting to talk about my waistline again. My diet's kind of gone to pot for the past week or so. Well, Lent starts next Wednesday, and I'm going to give up bread and potatoes for Lent, and maybe by the time summer comes around, I'll have this thing under control. It upsets me that I don't have the willpower to start a diet and stick to it. Of course, it's not the first time for me.

February 14   A long time ago, my father gave me some good advice. "Most people don't have the patience to remember this," Pro said, "but don't you ever forget it: three is always better than four, and four is always better than five, and five is always better than six, and six is certainly better than seven. Don't ever be dissatisfied with a bogey, 'cause if you are, sure as the world you'll wind up with a double-bogey."

Pro's advice paid off for me today. After I'd birdied two of the first four holes, I hit my drive on number five close to some trees on the right. Trying to cut the ball around the trees, I didn't slice enough and I landed behind some more trees just to the left of the green. Then I tried to chip through the trees and hit one of them and dropped down. I was lying three, under a tree, and my chances for making a double-bogey-six looked excellent. But I remembered what Pro said and, instead of quitting, I buckled down, chipped up to three feet from the cup, and sank the putt for a bogey. The next hole, I hit a fantastic wedge after missing the green with my second shot and salvaged a par there. That was really the turning point for me today—a bogey and a par where I could just as easily have had a double-bogey and a bogey. I felt like I'd robbed a bank. And I really began to move.

I birdied the seventh and eighth holes, parred the ninth, then birdied ten and eleven, four birdies in five holes to put me five-under for the round and ten-under for the tournament. I came in with a 65.

I'm tied for first place with Billy Maxwell, a peppery little Texan, at 131, eleven-under, and the scores here are just amazing. The cut came at 140—two under par—and there were a couple of 64s and an incredible 62 by a part-time tour player named Johnny Stevens. His 62, after an opening 71, didn't even put him in the top five.

After the round, I went into the press tent to talk with the reporters. It's a nice habit to be getting into—my second visit to the press tent in two weeks—but I'd kind of prefer to be there Sunday afternoon, when the tournament's over.

I saw Lee Trevino afterward. Lee'd just made the cut at 140, and he wasn't happy.

"Those greens sure are bumpy, aren't they?" I said.

"I wouldn't know," said Lee. "I haven't been on many of them."

February 15   I got up early this morning and took Patty and the kids to the airport and put them on the plane, and I felt very sad. It's not natural for families to be apart for any length of time. I had nothing to do back at the motel, so I got out to the course around 10:30, two and a half hours before I was going to tee off, and just kind of wandered around the clubhouse. I kidded with Billy Maxwell awhile. He's a beautiful fellow. He's got the most colorful vocabulary of any man on the tour, and every now and then, when he uses some of that vocabulary out loud, he gets in trouble with the PGA officials.

I walked down to the practice tee with Steve Reid, and Steve had lost his practice bag. Some airline had misplaced it, so Steve was carrying his practice balls in a brown paper sack. Lee Trevino came running up, took one look at Steve's brown paper sack, and said, "Hey, Steve, I'll trade you a ham-and-cheese for a tuna fish."

On the practice tee, Gene Littler shook his head and said to me, "This is the only tournament I've ever seen where a guy could shoot 70 and go from first to last." He was exaggerating, of course, but not by much. Gene went out and shot 62, which moved him from a tie for about twentieth right up into first place. And I did just the opposite. I shot 71—even par—and slipped from first place back to a tie for ninth. I went into my blur, my coma, my fog. I don't know what happened. The whole round seemed to flash by in a second.

I three-putted from ten feet on the first hole and took a double-bogey. Of the next sixteen holes, I parred thirteen and birdied three. I came to the par-five eighteen, an easy birdie hole, figuring I'd get a birdie and a 69 and be thirteen-under for the tournament, only three strokes behind Gene.

For fifty-three straight holes, I'd placed my drive in the fairway.

For fifty-three straight holes, I hadn't caught the rough. Right there, on the fifty-fourth hole of the tournament, I hit my tee shot out of bounds. On my second ball, I made a four, but that gave me a bogey-six for the hole and a 71 for the round.

Tonight, with my family gone—I called and found out they made it home all right—and my chances for winning the tournament almost gone, I'm really depressed. I'm really low.

I'm starting to worry about my fogs. It's got to be some kind of mental problem, some kind of psychological block. Am I afraid to win? Have I lost the drive you need to finish first? Do I want, subconsciously, to be a loser? I don't know. I just don't know.

February 16   If anybody ever has a day like I had today, they should go jump off the highest bridge they can find. This was the worst day I ever spent on a golf course. It's a good thing I'm too old to cry.

I can't understand what's happened to me. I'm not playing badly. Hell, I'm playing better than I ever have in my life. On the first hole today, for instance, I hit a good drive and left myself an easy nine-iron to the green. I hit a beautiful nine-iron, just blanked the flag all the way to the green. I almost thought I was going to make a two. The ball carried behind the hole, didn't bite, took one hop, and went over the green. I pitched back up, missed a four-foot putt, and took a bogey. The second hole, my drive took a weird bounce to the left and the ball ended up under a tree which was practically on the fairway. I stood behind the tree, reached around it to chip at the ball, caught my club on a limb, and whiffed, missed the ball completely. I wound up with a double-bogey-six. The third hole, I missed a three-foot putt for a birdie, and it was all over. I knew it. On the back nine, I missed two four-footers and wound up with an unbelievable 76.

I dropped from a tie for ninth place clear out of the top fifty. A tie for ninth was worth about $2,500. I won $143. And I lost twenty dollars to Deane Beman and Steve Reid. I was five strokes in front of Deane after two rounds, and he ended up eight strokes in front of me. There was only one score all day worse than mine— one 77. Lee Trevino shot it. He finished last.

Gene Littler won the Phoenix Open. He finished with a 66 for 263, twenty-one strokes under par. The scores were fantastic. Howie Johnson shot four straight 68s—some guys go a whole lifetime without ever shooting four straight 68s—and didn't even finish in the top fifteen. A fellow named Horace Moore shot four straight sub-par rounds—four 70s—and finished in a tie for sixty-second.

I'm lower than a snake's belly, missing my wife and missing my kids, and yet I can always find something that makes me realize how fortunate I've been. I saw Jerry Steelsmith today, the guy I beat out for my first tournament victory six years ago. Jerry failed to qualify for the Los Angeles Open, the Kaiser, or the Crosby, then skipped San Diego, then failed to qualify for the Hope. He qualified here, and at the end of three rounds, he was tied with me for ninth place. He shot 72 today and fell back to around thirtieth. He won $725. That's all he's got to show for six full weeks on the tour. "I just can't take it anymore," Steelie told me. "I'm going to play one more week, then go home and try to find a job at a club."

Steelie's got natural ability. He's got desire. He wants to play the tour. But now he's got to go home and, to support his wife and his children, do something he doesn't really want to do. A few more days like today, and I'll be looking for a club job, too.

February 17 / Tucson   It's only the first day of the week, and already the boys are having fun with my performances of the past two weeks. "Frank," said Al Balding, "you look like a sprint horse trying to run a mile race."

Deane and Steve are calling me "Fast-Start Beard," and Deane, who's been very successful in the insurance business, has offered to sell me insurance on my Sunday rounds. It's a million laughs.

Well, maybe things are changing. Maybe this is going to be my week. I won money today playing bridge and golf. A fellow named Dave Eichelberger and I played a scramble against Deane and Steve. A scramble works this way: both of us drive, and then we pick the better drive and both of us hit a second shot from there. Then we pick the better second shot, and both of us hit—or putt—from there. It was fun, and profitable. Dave and I won twenty dollars apiece.

I'm rooming with Deane and Steve this week—we're all temporary bachelors—and, for excitement, we went to Shakey's tonight for a pizza and some black beer. Then I went back to the room and called Patty. I call her every night. It's not that I'm a big spender. I just like to hear her voice. Besides, I always call after eight o'clock, when the rates change, and I only talk for three minutes, so it's not too expensive.

February 18 Harry the Horse has a new theory. Henning says he's not going to play golf anymore on Mondays or Tuesdays. He says he'll be more relaxed that way.

We all love Harold on the tour. He's fun to watch. He's a wild scrambler. He's got a less than classic golf swing, and he's not exactly perfect from tee to green. The other day, he was paired with Deane Beman and George Knudson. George is really an artist, a picture player who hits every ball down the middle and blanks the flag with every approach. While George was playing his usual classic game the other day, Deane told me, Harold was hitting little old toe hooks off the tee and yelling, "Run, you beauty, run, stay away from that rough, you beauty." Harold beat George by a couple of strokes.

In our bridge game yesterday, Harold's partner, Steve Reid, lay down a dummy with the ace, king, queen, and jack of clubs, and Harold grinned and said, "Ah, a full set of McGregors." McGregors, of course, are a brand name for clubs, golf clubs.

I can understand Harold's theory about not playing Mondays and Tuesdays—it does give your mind a chance to rest—but I can't do it myself. My conscience hurts me if I'm not playing.

I had a practice match set up today with Dave Hill as my partner, and just before we teed off, Dave said he had to go back to the clubhouse for a minute. When he came back, he was holding his wrist.

"What happened?" I said.

"I was coming down the clubhouse steps," Dave said, "and I slipped. I tried to brace myself and twisted my wrist."

Dave tried to play, anyway, but on the third tee, he just dropped his ball and said, "That's it, my wrist hurts too bad." He walked off the course and withdrew from the tournament. It's frightening. Dave's finished in the top ten in three tournaments this year—he's one of the ten leading money-winners so far—and now, just when he's hot, he's got to give up one tournament, maybe more. He could drop clear off the money list by the time his wrist heals. I feel sorry for him, partly because I know the same thing could happen to me.

On the way in from my round, I spotted Trevino, and he said, "I'm pooped. I've had about nine hours of sleep in three days." Lee'd flown from Phoenix to New York to Los Angeles to Tucson, all so that he could speak at a banquet in New York. "I went there for six inches of snow, six inches of garbage, and some bad food," he said. "No more banquets for me."

I got a new contract in the mail today from Hillerich & Bradsby. They gave me a nice raise. I guess they must've sent out the contract before the last two rounds at Phoenix.

February 19   Tommy Shaw, one of the young fellows on the tour, and I were on the practice tee this morning before the pro-am, and we decided to play a little joke on Kermit Zarley.

Kermit's very religious. He participates regularly in the Tuesday-night prayer meetings some of the fellows attend on tour. Tommy and I walked up to Kermit and I said, "Kermit, Tommy and I have a bet, and we figured you could settle it 'cause you know a lot about the Bible."

"I'll try," Kermit said.

"I've bet Tommy that skin will stretch farther than rubber."

"How can I help you?" said Kermit.

"Well," I said, "doesn't it say in the Bible that Abraham tied his ass to a tree and walked a mile?"

Tommy and I broke up laughing—it wasn't very nice of us; Kermit's really a good fellow—and Kermit said, very seriously, "Well, Frank, it just depends on how you interpret that."

He was still dead serious.

I had the most fun I've had in a long time in the pro-am today. I had three of the nicest partners I ever had, three old country boys from Dodge City, Kansas. They chewed tobacco, had no pretenses about acting fancy—they'd hit oil in Kansas—and, best of all, they didn't care whether they won or lost. They just wanted to have a good time, shoot the breeze a little, and relax. I relaxed, too, and shot a 70, two under par, which earned me about two hundred dollars in the individual event. If I could get three fellows like that every week, I'd love pro-am day.

We finished early, before a rainstorm hit, and when I got back to the motel, I found a letter from my mother. She's probably the smartest person I've met in my whole life, at least as far as knowing me is concerned.

In her letter, Mom told me that I had nothing to worry about, that I had a lovely family, that Pat and the baby were going to be fine, that I had money in the bank, that I'd lost no face the past two weeks with the people that counted, that regardless of how I played, they all loved me. I really needed that letter. I almost cried when I read it.

I thought about all the things that I have to be thankful for. Steve Reid has three deaf children. Deane Beman has a retarded child. I don't have any problems. I've got everything any man could want.

February 20   Don't laugh, but I'm on my diet again. Lent started yesterday, and I'm off bread and potatoes. And I'm doing sit-ups to get in shape. I did four or five of them this morning.

At breakfast, a few of us were talking about an article Gary Player's just written. It's called "Jog Now and Win Later" or something like that. Gary's a real physical-fitness bug, and I asked Harold Henning if all that exercising really helped his fellow South African's game.

"When I'm playing Gary head-to-head in a tournament," said Harold, "I'll walk up to him on the tee and say, 'Gary, you don't look well. Do you feel all right? Have you lost some weight? Have you been ill?'

"Immediately, Gary starts worrying. 'Do you really think so?' he says. 'Do I look ill?'

"From then on, he's mine. Just make a reference to his health, and that'll take care of him every time."

I had a real Frank Beard round today—fourteen pars, two birdies, and two bogeys—a par-72 that should've been a 70. Twice I three-putted, once missing an eighteen-incher. I'm in the top thirty-five or so. Miller Barber's leading with a 65—old Mr. X is really hot; he finished 66-64 at Phoenix—and Lee Trevino and Dale Douglass came in with 67s. I guess the snow and garbage in New York didn't do any permanent damage to Lee.

When I walked in the locker room after my round, Don Cherry, the nightclub singer who's also a professional golfer, greeted me and started laughing. "Hey, Beard," he yelled. "They got a little two-round tournament in Oklahoma City for you next week if you want to go down there."

Everybody had a good laugh, and then Charlie Sifford came up to me and said, "Frank, I used to caddy. You don't start finishing better, I'm gonna have to go back to my old trade, give up the tour, and put your bag on my shoulder. I'll have to lead you around. You're too good a player to be finishing up like that."

Charlie was teasing, of course, but if things don't go better soon, I may have to hire him—as long as he doesn't expect ten-and-three from me.

February 21   I had a strange round today. In the first place, I three-putted five holes, including three of the first four, all of them from thirty feet or less. I had only eight pars, five bogeys, four birdies, and one eagle for a one-under-par 71. I'm worried about my putting—seven three-putt greens in two days. That's just not like me. I'm one of the best putters around, but I haven't looked it lately. I don't know whether I'm flinching on my putts, moving on them, reading the greens wrong, or what. It's got me scared. I'm hitting the ball as well as I ever have, or better, from tee to green, but I'm not getting the ball in the hole. I've got to get straightened out, or I'll be deep into one of those slumps I'm always thinking about.

My 143 puts me in the middle of the pack. Johnny Pott's leading at 135, Douglass is at 136, Trevino and Barber are at 137, and 146 made the cut. I noticed that Jerry Steelsmith missed the cut by five strokes, but I was glad to see that Dick Crawford made it at 145. Steve Reid made it, too, but Deane Beman woke up this morning with a painfully stiff neck and had to withdraw after an opening 71.

I played bridge this afternoon, and I've never had a run of cards like I've had here. Just unbelievable. We don't play very high stakes, but I've won close to $150 this week. I hate to mention it, but that's more than I made for the whole golf tournament last week.

February 22   It was so cold and windy this morning in sunny Arizona that, after breakfast, I had to go back to my room and put on my long underwear and my long turtleneck shirt and start up my hand-warmer.

On the putting green, before I teed off, I got to talking with Orville Moody, the old Army sergeant who started on the pro tour last year at the age of thirty-four. "I hope it blows up to forty miles an hour," Orville was saying, " 'cause if it does, I'll pass me a few cats today." Orville told me he learned to play golf in El Paso, and he got used to playing in forty-mile-an-hour winds. "I sure hope it blows and blows and blows," he said.

I was playing with Dave Stockton and Jacky Cupit, and I told Dave what Orville had said. Once we started playing, the wind did whip up to about forty miles an hour, and every time I hit what looked like a perfect shot, the wind blew it off line. "I hope it's blowing hard enough for Orville," I kept yelling to Dave.

Then Dave'd hit a shot, and the wind'd sweep it away, and he'd shout back to me, "I hope Orville's happy."

We couldn't wait to get into the clubhouse to see what Orville shot. The scores were really running high; only four guys broke 70 all day (compared to thirteen a day Thursday and Friday). "Orville probably got himself an 80," I said.

We looked at the board—I'd shot a steady 72, and Dave'd shot 74—and old Orville, who'd only made the cut by one stroke, had come in from the wind with a 69. Dave and I stopped laughing.

Right after we finished, play got delayed for half an hour, first by a sandstorm, then by a hailstorm, then by rain. Imagine how good a score Orville would've had if he could've played in the storms.

I moved up about ten spots today, into the top twenty-five. Super Mex Trevino shot a 68 in the wind—Lee's from El Paso, too—and he's leading everyone now by five strokes. I'll tell you, that traveling from Phoenix to New York to Los Angeles to Tucson in two days really helps your game.

Some fellow I'd never seen in my life walked over to me in the clubhouse and said, "Frank, how'd you play today?"

"Oh, not too bad," I said.

"What'd you shoot?"

"Seventy-two."

The guy looked at me very seriously. "Hmmm," he said. "That's not too bad—for you."

He walked away, and the whole locker room cracked up.

I think these people who come to golf tournaments are half nuts anyway.

Hey, my diet's coming along great. I was down to 187 today— before I had a few beers.

February 23   I was paired today with Charlie Coody and Mason Rudolph, and I knew old Charlie was planning on a strong round. He was wearing his red socks.

Whenever Charlie needs a good round—to make the cut or win some money—he wears red socks. It's the only way we can tell he's determined, because his expression never changes.

Coody's a superstitious old boy. He plays a Titleist ball, and on Thursdays, Fridays, and Saturdays, he'll play any number Titleist. But on Sundays, Charlie'll only play a number one or a number four. Don't ask me why. We've got a bunch of superstitions out here on the tour. Some guys will wear the same shirt the same day of each week as long as they're going good. We've got one guy who, if he goes into the john one morning and uses a particular urinal and has a good round, he'll use the same urinal the next morning even if there's a line a mile long. Even if he doesn't have to go.

Charlie's superstitions didn't help him too much today. He shot
74 and fell back to around thirtieth, tied with, among others, Dick
Crawford and Steve Reid. Trevino won by seven strokes, only a
week after finishing last, and Gene Littler came in fourth. Gene's
been in the top ten now six straight weeks and he's won more than
fifty thousand dollars. He's way ahead of schedule. He's on his
way home to his old cars now. I hear he's planning on skipping the
whole next month of tournaments in Florida. I wish I could afford
to do that.

Mason Rudolph shot a pretty good round, a 70, and while we
were playing, we talked about Orville Moody. I told him about
Orville and the wind. I told him I thought Orville was going to
become one of the best players on the tour. "Orville's a good fellow,"
Mason said, "and a good golfer, but he's got to learn one thing. He's
got to learn that if he shoots a bad round, nobody else wants to
hear about his problems."

Mason smiled. "Out here," he said, "you've got to realize that
if you take an eight on a hole, ninety percent of the other pros don't
care and the other ten percent wish it had been a nine."

I had no complaints myself today. The key for me was the second
hole, a par-five. I hit a big drive and took out my two-iron and
studied my shot to the green. "The hell with it," I told myself. "It's
not a two-iron shot. It's a four-wood shot, and you've got to hit
the four-wood." I cut a little four-wood right in to the pin, wound
up ten feet from the hole, and sank the putt for an eagle.

Frank Beard's Record

TOURNAMENT	1ST ROUND	2ND ROUND	3RD ROUND	4TH ROUND
Bob Hope	70	68	71	68
Phoenix	66	65	71	76
Tucson	72	71	72	68

* Unofficial

I birdied the seventh and eighth holes to go four-under for the day, then cooled off and finished with eight pars, a birdie, and a bogey for a total of 68, which really bolstered my confidence. After my 76 last week and my 74 the week before in the final rounds, a 68 felt good. I should be somewhere up in the top ten or fifteen; I rushed away from the course to catch a plane, so I won't know till I see the paper tomorrow.

Right now, I'm sitting in the Los Angeles airport, waiting for the red-eye overnight flight to Atlanta. I'll switch planes in the morning and get into Louisville around eight o'clock. I can't wait to see Patty and the kids and just lie around the house for a day. I could use a month at home.

But, early Tuesday morning, I'll kiss my wife and children goodbye again and leave for Miami to start the Florida part of the tour.

I wonder about this kind of life. I really do.

February 24 / Louisville   I saw in the paper that my 68 got me a tie for eleventh place and won $2,200—official money. I've now won almost $5,700 official money in four official tournaments. That's a good enough pace to put me in the top sixty easily. You only have to average about nine hundred dollars each official tournament to make the top sixty.

5TH ROUND	TOTAL SCORE	FINISH	PRO-AM EARNINGS	INDIVIDUAL EARNINGS
74	351	T 5	$2,475.00	$3,175.00*
—	278	T 52	—	142.86
—	283	T 11	200.00	2,200.00

I relaxed today. I felt as if I hadn't seen the family in a hundred years. I guess they felt the same way. They were all out at the airport at eight o'clock this morning waiting for me. It's worth a whole night of flying for the chance to see them even for a day.

My folks came over this evening, and Pro and I discussed my game at some length. Pro said that from what he'd read and from what I'd told him, he figured that I was playing well, but that my concentration had slipped. "You get overorganized," he said. "You get concentrating so much on leading that you forget it's just another day. Sunday is Sunday, whether you're leading or last. A 67 counts the same on Thursday as Sunday."

Pro really calmed me down, made me see what I was doing, made me feel like I could lick the world. Well, I'm ready to go to Florida. I went to school there and I always play well there. Let's go. Old Frank Beard is ready to win a tournament for a change.

3
Vichyssoise
and Soup, Too

TOURNAMENT	SITE	PURSE	DATES
Doral Open	Doral Country Club, Miami	$150,000	Feb. 27– March 2
Citrus Open	Rio Pinar Country Club, Orlando	115,000	March 6– March 9
Monsanto Open	Pensacola Country Club, Pensacola	100,000	March 13– March 16
Jacksonville Open	Deerwood Country Club, Jacksonville	100,000	March 20– March 23
National Airlines Open	Country Club of Miami, Miami	200,000	March 27– March 30

February 25 / Miami   I flew into Miami this morning, half expecting to land in Havana, checked into my room at the Doral Country Club, the site of the Doral Open this week, and went out to hit a few balls. As soon as I reached the practice tee, Homero Blancas, a good friend of mine—he played for the University of Houston when I played for the University of Florida—came over to me and said, "I want you to see my new driver."

"I don't want to see your driver," I said. Homero's got the worst collection of drivers in the world.

"You got to see this one," he said, and he whipped out a driver with a psychedelic head, painted red, orange, and yellow. I just burst out laughing.

Homero's a puzzle to me. He's been on the tour for four full years, always in the top sixty, always earning more than twenty-five thousand dollars a year. But he's won only one tournament, and he's never gotten up into the top thirty, and, I'm telling you, he's got the kind of game he ought to be earning $100,000 a year.

He's a Mexican-American, born in Houston, and he used to have a standard line whenever anyone asked him how he did in a round or in a tournament. "I was low Mex," he'd always say. Then Trevino came along, and Homero started giving a different answer. "I was second-low Mex," he'd say.

Now, Homero told me today, he's back to being low Mex. "Since Lee won all that money last year," Blancas said, "he's turned Spanish. He's not Mexican anymore."

As Homero and I were talking, Doug Sanders came up next to us. Homero waved his psychedelic driver at Sanders and said, "I'm going to whip you this week with this driver."

Sanders laughed. "That's too much for me," he said. "It just doesn't match a thing I'm wearing."

Doug was in his lavender outfit—lavender shirt, lavender slacks, lavender shoes, and lavender golf bag.

I hadn't seen Doug in a few weeks, and he explained he'd been down in Houston, fishing and playing tennis with his son. I'm worried about Doug and about his game. After his slump last year, he hasn't done a thing this year, and I'd hate to see him just drop out of the tournament picture. With all his color and glamour, he's an asset to my business. He brings something special to the tour— something I could never supply—and I'd hate to lose someone like that.

Doug isn't going to starve or anything—he probably earns more on his clothes contracts than I earn on the tour—but I'm afraid his game is going. I may know why. When I first came on the tour, Gardner Dickinson took me aside one day. "I like the way you hit the ball," he said. "You've got a good future in this game, but you've got to do one thing."

"What's that?" I said.

"You're gonna have to lengthen your swing," Gardner said. "As you get older, your muscles tend to contract and shorten your swing. If you start with a big swing now, it won't bother you so much later."

I don't know how sound Gardner's theory is medically, but way back then he predicted that Sanders would have trouble in five or six years. Doug's swing is so compact it's become famous; the standard line is that Doug could swing in a telephone booth. If you accept Gardner's theory—and it may explain why Sam Snead and Julie Boros, with their big swings, have lasted so long—then Doug couldn't afford to lose any of his swing. Now he has. His swing used to be short and smooth, but now it's short and choppy. I know Doug won't give up without a fight. He's a battler.

I played a practice round with Dick Crawford and Charlie Coody and lost a few dollars, nothing serious, but I was kind of laughing at old Charlie. His frugality was put to the supreme test today. He was supposed to room with Art Wall here at Doral, but Art had some kind of trouble with his back and had to cancel. That left Charlie all alone in a room that was going to cost twenty-three dollars a day. Naturally, he started looking around for a new roommate.

One of the PGA officials came up to Charlie and told him about another guy who'd lost his roommate and was in the same position as Charlie. This other guy happens to be one of the very few really obnoxious people on the tour. Nobody likes him. "Charlie," I said, "this is the day I've been waiting for. Tell me, are you gonna save $11.50 a day and room with *him?*"

I've got to admit Charlie didn't hesitate. "I wouldn't room with him," he said, "if the rooms were forty-six dollars a day."

Charlie finally did find a new roommate, and I'm glad. If he hadn't, he would've moaned from now to Sunday.

I'm rooming with Steve Reid, and before we went out to dinner tonight, after we'd had a few Scotches, he got to talking again about how badly he wants to play on the tour, how badly he wants to be a good tournament player, how badly he wants to become one of the stars. This game just eats him up, he's so intense. Steve's off to a fairly slow start this year—he hasn't finished in the top twenty in a tournament yet—and he told me that the other day he was complaining on the phone to his wife about his game, and she said, "Well, you can always come home and run a filling station."

Steve said he got so angry he slammed the phone down and didn't call his wife for three days. He once had to quit the tour and take a club job for a while because he ran out of money, and he doesn't ever want to do that again. I've never seen anyone who burns more with the desire for success. I don't mean just financial. I think it's a lot more than that with Steve.

He and I went to dinner tonight with some friends, and as we were sitting in a nice Italian restaurant, some fellow from a nearby table got up and walked over to us. "Aren't you Frank Beard?" he asked me.

I said I was, and he introduced himself—Lou somebody from Philadelphia—and I felt kind of good being recognized and kind of bad that he hadn't recognized Steve. I guess that's what Steve's really striving for—recognition.

Philadelphia Lou wouldn't just say hello and leave us alone. He had to carry on a whole conversation. Finally, he said to me, "I want to trade ties with you. I'll give you mine—it cost me six dollars at Lord and Taylor's—for yours."

Well, I thought his tie was about the ugliest thing I'd ever seen, but I think I'd have traded pants to get him to leave us alone. Besides, my tie only cost a buck and a half. I agreed to trade with him.

Lou took his tie off, and I took mine off, and we swapped, and as Lou started back toward his table, Steve couldn't resist needling me about my recent finishes. "Just be careful of one thing, Lou," Steve yelled. "If you wear Frank Beard's tie on Sundays, wear it loose."

February 26   One of my partners in the pro-am today had the fastest backswing I've ever seen. Someone said to me the only thing faster was if you took a snake's tongue, greased it, and hung it on a lightning bolt. It was a miracle he ever hit the ball.

We struggled around the course and didn't do anything as a team, and I shot an unexciting 72 on my own ball. I had my own personal gallery of one, a brilliant golf fan who kept asking me the same question all day, "What did you lay on to it with there?"

I guess he meant what club did I use.

On the second hole, I hit a low seven-iron to the green, and this fellow said, "What did you lay on to it with there—a five-iron?"

I wasn't paying much attention, and my caddy turned to the guy and said, "He hit a three-iron."

A little later, I hit another seven-iron, and the man turned to a young boy who was with him and said, "See, he laid on to it with that three-iron again!"

At one point, the same man walked over to me and grabbed my

driver out of my hands to look at it. "This the way you put your grip on it?" he said, and he demonstrated some weird grip.

"Yeah," I said, and grabbed my club back.

If he'd ever done something like that to Lionel Hebert, Lionel would've popped him. Liney's not the type to get upset easily, but he once told me doesn't want anyone ever touching his grips. He said that the oil from somebody else's hands might mess up the feel of his grip.

I was pretty upset myself. It was like walking onto a football field in the middle of a game and asking Joe Namath how to grip the ball for a pass.

February 27   I was paired with Jack Nicklaus today for the first time this year, and on the first tee, he walked up to me, put his arm around me, and said, "How's the family, pro?" Jack tries to be friendly, but I just don't feel comfortable with him. I feel like we're on different levels, which, of course, we are. Unlike Arnie and Cas, Jack's never been just another pro. From his first day on the tour, he's been in the superstar class.

Bruce Devlin, who was playing with us, is an Australian, one of the most likable people on the tour. I hate to go out of the United States, to England or the Far East or even to Canada—I just don't enjoy being in any other country—yet I find the foreign players, golfers like Devlin and Tony Jacklin and Harold Henning, to be much more interesting and more pleasant than the Americans. They seem more intelligent, more polite, and more aware of things that are going on.

Bruce is one of the very few golfers I've ever seen or heard of who took the time and heartbreak and energy to actually change his whole golf game in the middle of his career. From 1964 through 1966, he was always among the top twenty money-winners. He won a few tournaments and he had a fine golf game, but he had one flaw that prevented him from moving up among the top stars: he had a very strong grip which made him a definite hooker.

At the end of 1966, when he'd won about fifty thousand dollars for the year, he decided he was going to get rid of the one flaw in his game. He moved his left hand over on top of the club, weakening his grip to eliminate the hook. For a full year, while he tried to master a new style of play, Bruce gave up any chance of winning a tournament. It took an awful lot of intestinal fortitude. His earnings fell to around twelve thousand dollars in 1967, and he slipped right out of the top sixty. But last year, using his new game, he bounced back, finished second in the Crosby and fourth in the Masters, and won about forty thousand dollars. This year, I expect great things from Bruce. So far, he's among the top ten money-winners, and I'll bet right now that he wins a tournament before the year's over.

We teed off early, so Jack's gallery wasn't too big at the beginning, and fortunately, we had a whole crew of marshals to keep the crowd under control. A couple of times, Bruce got a little upset when the gallery made too much noise, but it wasn't bad. Often, when Jack was away from the hole, he let Bruce and me putt out first, so that our putting wouldn't be disturbed by the gallery moving after he'd putted. Jack's good about doing that. Arnie'll do it, too, but not as often as Jack.

Our gallery built up after Bruce shot a six-under-par 30 on the front nine. He cooled off slightly on the back nine and came in with a 66, one stroke off the lead. Tommy Shaw and Dan Sikes set a Doral course record with 65s.

I was really surprised by the way Jack played today. He used a new driver, one with a weak, ladylike shaft, and he lost a lot of distance with it, maybe twenty or twenty-five yards a drive. On the first tee, he hit a shot that looked like it was going into orbit, and still I outdrove him. I outdrove Jack most of the day, and it had to be the equipment. Bruce knows Jack pretty well—Bruce has a home in Florida, too—and he told me afterward that Jack picked up this new driver somewhere and just likes it. I don't understand it. Every time he got to the top of his backswing, that club bent like a bow. A guy like Jack ought to use a stiff shaft. Hell, with his strength, he ought to use an ax handle.

Jack had to struggle to shoot a 72, and I had a very unspectacular 71—fifteen pars, two birdies, and a bogey.

After my round, I bumped into an old college friend, Roy Smith, who now lives in Hattiesburg, Mississippi. He's on the committee for the Magnolia State Classic, a little tournament that's being held in Hattiesburg the same week as the Masters this year. Roy told me he's trying to get official status for his tournament and he asked me to try to influence some of the players who wouldn't be going to the Masters to enter at Hattiesburg. Then he mentioned that they were raising money for the tournament by selling sponsorships, and old Frank opened up his big mouth and got himself in trouble.

Each guy who buys a sponsorship, Roy said, gets to play in their pro-am. I thought he said they'd already sold 250 sponsorships for fifty dollars apiece. I don't know what got into me, but I said, "Look, I'll buy a sponsorship. You can give my place in the pro-am to a junior golfer who otherwise wouldn't be able to play."

Roy thought my idea was terrific, and he got all worked up about holding a Frank Beard Junior Tournament, with the champion getting into the pro-am. I couldn't figure out why he was getting so excited about a little old fifty-dollar offer and then, in the course of our conversation, I found out that he hadn't said anything about 250 sponsorships for fifty dollars apiece. He'd said *fifty* sponsorships at $250 apiece.

What could I do?

I couldn't say, "Oh, I thought it was fifty dollars."

It was too late for good old Frank, the big spender from Louisville. I'll never learn to keep my mouth shut. I'm always promising people back home I'll play golf with them and telling them I'll get them tickets for tournaments, and half the time, I guess, I've had a couple of Scotches and I don't remember my promises. But they always remember.

Roy's not going to forget about my $250.

February 28   I'm no meteorologist, but when I got up this morning, the day had an ominous look to it. It was too warm, too calm, and I've been coming down here long enough to know that when it's like that in the morning, the wind starts kicking up in the afternoon. I was right. I had a late tee time, and the wind blew up, and there must've been two or three strokes difference between playing in the morning and playing in the afternoon.

Nicklaus, Devlin, and I were playing the back nine first, and the wind wasn't our only handicap. We had a much bigger gallery than yesterday, and no marshals, and the crowd was just terrible. I guess all the marshals had gone off with the morning players, and I had to walk off the green a few times and tell the gallery to quiet down so that Bruce could putt.

I hit sand traps just about every other hole, and—I'll admit it— my bunker game was astounding. I kept popping the ball into one-putt range, and after eleven holes, I was one-under for the day and feeling good, feeling that I'd been battling the wind well, that I'd been scrambling, but saving myself. As I came off the second green—my eleventh hole today—one of my pro-am partners from the other day jogged up to me.

"Frank," he said, "remember what you told me about relaxing? Remember? Well, you relax now. Take it easy."

And, as I walked to the third tee, he gave me a back rub and kept saying, "Relax, Frank, take it easy, relax."

I didn't know whether to laugh or cry. I really don't think the back rub had anything to do with it, but, suddenly, my game just fell apart.

On the third hole, I missed a six-footer and took a bogey. On the fourth, a par-three, I hit the worst iron I have hit since I was twelve years old. My wife could've hit a better iron; my son, Danny, could've, and he's two years old. I landed in the water, nowhere near the green, and took a double-bogey. Then I bogeyed the next hole. In three holes, I'd gone from two-under for the tournament to two-over.

I was in real danger of missing the cut. I figured 145, one-over, would probably be safe to make the cut and 146 would be the absolute top, and the strangest thoughts started going through my mind.

I began thinking that if I missed the cut, I'd have to call Patty and tell her, and she'd want me to fly home tonight, and I'd tell her, "But, honey, it's a hundred dollars to get home and a hundred to get back, and I've got to play in a special pro-am Monday, and I'd only be home for two days," and she'd say, "You don't want to see us anymore," and, being pregnant and taking care of two kids by herself, she'd get all upset, and I'd get all upset. I should've been thinking about shooting a few birdies and catching up and making some money, and, instead, all I could think was that I wanted to make the cut so that I wouldn't have a fight with my wife.

I don't like missing the cut, anyway. I know it's going to happen sometime this year, probably a few times—Billy Casper was the only man on the whole tour last year who never missed a cut, and I've never gone a full year without missing a cut—but it's the worst feeling in the world. It's Friday afternoon, and everybody else is going to play golf Saturday and Sunday, and you don't know what you're going to do, and you just feel totally useless.

For my wife, for my friends, and for my ego, I felt I just had to make the cut. So I went out and parred the next two holes, then birdied the last two, and came in with a 73 and made the cut comfortably. As it turned out, if I'd just parred the last four holes and come in at 146, I'd have made the cut.

Nicklaus shot a 71 to move past me, and Devlin shot a 75 to move back toward me. I'm a realist. I know I'm not going to win this tournament. I'm even-par now, and the leaders—Shaw and Sikes and Tommy Aaron—are at nine-under, and I'm not going to catch all of them. But at least I've made the cut and, with a couple of decent rounds, I'll be able to earn some money to add to the big thirty dollars I got for my 72 in the pro-am.

I went out to dinner tonight with Paul Grossinger, the man who owns Grossinger's resort, and some other people, and we went to a nice French restaurant. I was pretty hungry, so first I ordered vichyssoise and then I said to the waiter, "And what kind of soup do you have?"

The waiter and everybody at the table looked at me like I was crazy. After a while, somebody broke the news to me, gently, that vichyssoise was soup. I'd gotten mixed up. I'd been thinking of a cheese thing I'd once had. I'd been thinking of quiche Lorraine.

After dinner, I called home to see how the family was doing, and Patty told me she'd driven my brother, Ralph, and his wife to the airport this morning to catch a plane to New York. Little Danny went along for the ride, and he thought he was going to pick up Daddy. He'd never been to the airport for any other reason. When he saw that I wasn't at the airport, he started to cry. He cried all afternoon.

I spoke to him tonight and calmed him down, and he signed off by saying, "I'll see you after my nap, Daddy." Patty told me that every day, when he wakes up after his nap, his first question is "Where's Daddy?" If that won't break your heart—what a weasel!

March 1   Don Massengale walked up to me on the putting green this morning and said, "Did you hear about Jack Montgomery?"

"What happened?" I said.

"He's got to have an operation Monday," Don said.

Jack had withdrawn the other day after playing a few holes, complaining about pains in his side. Evidently, he's had a cracked rib all year, and now his doctors have found a cyst growing on it. They're going to operate, and he won't be able to touch a club for at least three months, which is really a terrible thing. Just when Jack's finally made the top sixty, for the first time in his four years on the tour, something like this comes along and knocks him out of action. By the time he returns, it'll be almost impossible for him to make the top sixty this year, and he just might be eliminated from the golf scene. I mean, for the rest of his life. Once you lose that exemption, it's so damn hard to come back.

Almost exactly five years ago, I got knocked off the tour by illness myself. In New Orleans, in 1964, I thought I was coming down with the flu. My head was stuffed up, and I was running a slight fever. I tried to shrug it off, but the next week, at Pensacola, I didn't feel any better. A week later, in St. Petersburg, I began running a good fever and went to see a doctor; he gave me a few pills. That whole week, I couldn't sleep, I couldn't eat, and I lived on Cokes.

From St. Petersburg, the tour moved to Miami for the Doral Open, and I still felt miserable. I went to another doctor, and he told me that I probably had German measles, a strep throat, or mononucleosis; he gave me some more medicine. Throughout the Doral Open, I lived on Cokes again and slept about eighteen hours a day; I still managed to finish in a tie for ninth place.

At the end of the Doral, I decided to go home and rest for a week. It's about 1,200 miles from Miami to Louisville, a solid day of driving normally. It took me three days to get home. Every thirty minutes, I pulled off the road, set an alarm clock, and slept for five or ten minutes. I got home Wednesday. Thursday morning, I fell out of a chair and went into a coma. I had encephalitis—

sleeping sickness. A priest gave me the last rites. Seventy-two hours later, on Easter Sunday, I woke up. I spent five weeks at home re-cuperating—it just felt like I was getting over a case of the flu—then returned to the tour.

The golf writers later wanted to give me the Ben Hogan Award for the comeback of the year, but I couldn't accept it. I didn't deserve it. I hadn't done anything courageous. All I'd done was get better.

I played with Dave Hill and Bert Greene today, and Davy impressed me. He seems like a new man on the golf course. The one word I always think of when I think of Dave Hill is "volatile." As long as I've known him, he's had an explosive temper. I remember once, in a bridge game, when I started telling him after a hand how he could've made his bid, he got so mad so quick he was ready to hit me. His temper's hurt his game in the past. He's broken clubs and walked off courses.

A couple of years ago, playing with Chuck Courtney at Tucson, Dave had a putt of ten feet or less for a birdie on each of the first four holes. And after four holes, he was one over par. He'd missed all four birdie putts and three-putted once.

On the same holes, Chuck missed all four greens—and was two under par. He one-putted twice and chipped in twice. The second time Chuck chipped in, on the fourth hole, Davy walked off the course. He just cold quit. "If I'd gone any further with that man," Davy said afterward, "I'd have killed him."

(I've walked off courses myself. Once, in Canada, in the middle of my second round, when I knew there was no way in the world I could make the cut, I quit. Under our rules, you're not allowed to withdraw unless you've got some physical ailment. I came in and said I had a bad hand. I hated to do something like that, but I wasn't completely lying. My hand hurt from taking too many shots.)

Davy was very calm today, by his standards. One time, early in his round, he hit a shot into a soft spot in a bunker, and the ball buried itself under the lip. The old Davy would've kept swinging at the ball all day or at least till he'd broken a club, but today he quietly took an unplayable lie, dropped the ball, took a double-bogey, and didn't lose his temper at all. He kept going, made up for the double-bogey, and came in with a 71.

I don't mean Dave's reached the stage where he's entirely placid on the course. He was talking out loud to himself a lot today, asking himself questions, discussing his game with himself, often gabbing with the gallery. He was puffing on cigarettes all the time, practically running from shot to shot, barely lining them up. He's such a nervous, intense fellow that he's got a regular traveling caddy who lines up all his putts for him. I can see it in Davy's case; he's just too impatient to do it himself. And he was using two different putting strokes today—an orthodox grip on putts of about four feet or more and a cross-handed grip on the short putts. That's typical of Davy; nobody else'd try that.

Bert Greene had a rough day. He shot a 79. He's gifted with a fantastically strong, prodigious type of golf swing, but he has no finesse at all. He thinks he has to kill every shot, whether it's a driver or a nine-iron. In every other respect, Bert's a smart young player. With his swing, if he stops trying to hit every shot five hundred yards, he could be a successful player. But right now he's absolutely atrocious. This is his seventh tournament this year, and he hasn't earned a total of five hundred dollars yet.

I started off very well today, especially considering that I was playing in a strong wind, and with some more fantastic bunker play, I was two-under after eight holes. The ninth hole is a par-three, with water surrounding the green. As I got up to hit, a little wind was blowing from right to left. I couldn't have asked for better conditions. I decided to just cut a little shot into the wind, and with the canceling vectors—the wind blowing one way, the ball fading the other—I figured I'd hit the green softly and maybe get myself in birdie position.

I don't know what happened. I was feeling good. I was concentrating. I knew exactly what I wanted to do. And I fanned a seven-iron off to the right and into the water. I walked up, took my penalty stroke, dropped a new ball, and hit a wedge that landed just short of the green and rolled back into the water. The ball was on the edge, half in and half out, so I elected to play it. Actually, it's no worse than a buried lie in a bunker, probably even a little easier to hit. I popped it out and two-putted for a triple-bogey, and that was it for me.

There's only one way to describe my feelings after the round. I was numb. I'd really missed just one shot all day—that tee shot on the ninth—and, still, I ended up with a 74. I almost couldn't believe it.

When we came in off the eighteenth green, my caddy said to me, "Do you want to practice?"

"What the hell can I practice?" I said. "Seven-irons over the water?"

March 2   I didn't quit today. I went out to play the best I could, and I did manage to hit the ball pretty well. But I couldn't sink a putt. I don't know what's wrong with my putting. I'm putting the ball just where I'm looking every time, but the ball won't go in the hole. I've got to be patient, I guess, and they'll start dropping. I hope it's soon.

Cliff Brown, a young Negro player—I've heard he's sponsored on the tour by the Supremes—and Bruce Devlin were paired with me today, and Bruce shot a 69 to go with his opening 66. But in between he'd shot a 75 and a 77 and he didn't even make the top thirty. Cliff shot a 77 today, and I shot a 71 and finished in a tie for forty-third place, one over par for the tournament. My friends didn't do too well here, either. Steve Reid came in a stroke ahead of me, Charlie Coody was four strokes behind me, and Jimmy Colbert, who hasn't finished in the top fifty in a tournament since Napa, didn't even qualify here. I was glad to see Dick Crawford come in with a closing 68 and climb up into tenth place and win about $3,500, Crawdaddy's biggest check in a year.

I earned less than five hundred dollars, and I just feel like it was a wasted week, a week I should've spent at home with my wife and children. I'm playing too damn much, nine straight weeks now, counting the Southern Cal Open. That's too much golf. You'd think I'd have learned by now to pace myself, to get myself refreshed once in a while, but I just hate to pass up a tournament. I told Patty tonight I'm definitely taking off the week after next, the week of the Monsanto Open in Pensacola, no matter whether she's had the baby or not. I hope she has it when I'm home.

Tommy Shaw won the Doral Open, his first tour victory ever, and he beat Tommy Aaron by one stroke. Poor Aaron's never won a tournament. He's finished among the top sixty money-winners for nine straight years, he's earned a quarter of a million dollars, he's come in second eight times and third seven times, but he's never come in first.

It's become sort of a psychological thing with Aaron. We went to school together at the University of Florida, so, naturally, I know him pretty well. He's a nondrinking, early-to-bed type who never shows much emotion. But I know that inside Tommy's got to be dying for a victory. He's just too good a golfer not to get one.

All around the course today, people were walking up to me and congratulating me. The final round of Shell's Wonderful World of Golf was shown on television this week, and I won the championship. I won three straight matches, beating Palmer, Boros, everybody.

Everybody was slapping me on the back today like I was a real hot golfer. Those matches were filmed last year.

March 3 / Orlando   I stopped at Lost Tree Golf Club today, near Palm Beach, to play in a pro-am in pouring rain. A bunch of us played as a favor to Dow Finsterwald, who organized the event. The rain was miserable. My clubs got soaked, I ruined all four of my golf gloves in the first six holes, and the bottom of my new golf bag got ripped right out. Still, my team came in with a 60, twelve-under, and finished first, which meant about a $1,200 prize for me. That's more money than I've won in two out of my last three tour events, so I won't complain too much about the wet clubs, the ruined gloves, and the torn bag.

Charlie Coody, Don Massengale, and I drove up to Orlando tonight—we split the cost of a rented car—and I am just pooped. I can't wait to get this week over with and go home and rest.

March 4   I got a big break this morning. One of the PGA officials came up to me and told me I shouldn't buy a sponsorship in that Hattiesburg tournament, that it just wouldn't look good for a player to be involved in a sponsorship where he might influence pairings and tee times and things like that. So I wrote a letter to my buddy in Hattiesburg, explaining what the PGA had said and saying that I was sure the tournament could get along fine without my $250. I didn't tell him that I'd thought originally I was only committing fifty dollars.

Then I got another break this afternoon. I withdrew from the pro-am tomorrow, the first pro-am I've skipped all year. I told the tournament people I've got a sore hand. The truth is I'm beat, I'm dead, I've got to rest.

I weighed myself tonight and I'm down to about 187 pounds. My diet's going good right now. I started on it again yesterday.

March 5   I had a nice relaxing day, without any physical exertion at all. Steve Reid's thinking of moving to the Orlando area, so he and I went to visit a school for the deaf this morning. Steve's very proud of his children, of how much they've accomplished to overcome their deafness, and before he moves down here, he wants to make sure they'll have the proper educational facilities. He was impressed by the school we saw today.

Afterward, we went over to the Rio Pinar Country Club, and while Steve hit a few balls, I just took it easy around the putting green. I saw one of the funniest sights I'll ever see—Art Wall and Charlie Coody over on a corner of the green, giving each other putting lessons. They're two of the greatest putters in the world, and they're both looking for help.

"Watch me, Art," Charlie said, "and tell me what I'm doing wrong."

Then Charlie put down three balls, about ten feet from the cup, and knocked all three in the hole. "Art," he said. "How's that look?"

I just laughed and laughed.

Bob Goalby came over and proposed a deal to me. He's working with the Amana people, the ones who make deep freezers and refrigerators and things like that, and he wanted to know if I'd be willing to wear an Amana hat, just a regular golf hat with Amana written on it. Bob told me I'd get fifty dollars a week for wearing the hat; he said I was one of twenty pros he was asking. I told him to put me down and I'll start tomorrow if he wants me to. I don't like to wear hats—I think I look like Donald Duck in them—but for fifty dollars a week, I'd wear feathers in my hair.

I spoke to Bill Boone this evening, and he told me that he's getting a lot of calls about exhibitions because of my victory on the Shell show. It's kind of nice to hear that a few people actually have gotten to know my name.

March 6   All the guys were ribbing me this morning about the big rip in my golf bag. Somebody said I ought to get a bonus from Golf Pride, the grip company I represent, because I'm the only golfer on the tour with all his grips showing through the bottom of his bag. Somebody else said my bag was starting to look like my game—ragged. I finally had to go and borrow an old practice bag from the pro shop or my caddy would've been spilling my clubs all over the course.

I played with Bob Rosburg and Tommy Aaron in the first round of the Citrus Open, and I told Tommy I was pulling for him to win the other day. The wind blew up strong again, and I had to use my old first-aid kit, my emergency repair kit, to save some of the wild shots I hit. I'll tell you, your mother could hit better shots than I hit sometimes in the wind. I'm really getting psyched up about it.

Rossy had his troubles, too, with the wind and with some miserable pin placements, and whenever he hit a bad shot, he went through his regular routine. It's almost like Rossy's trademark. If a shot doesn't turn out the way he'd like it, he turns his back on the hole, jams his hands in his back pockets, and walks away with his nose up in the air.

Even with our troubles, Rossy and I managed one-under-par 71s. Tommy shot a 69, which left him one stroke behind the leaders, Tom Weiskopf and Rod Funseth. Weiskopf, who just finished serving five or six months in the Army, returned to action last week and won himself $1,300 loosening up at Doral. Now that he's back, with his power and his touch, there's a big chunk gone out of the pot each week.

Late in the afternoon, Ken Still came into the clubhouse with Bob Allison, the Minnesota baseball player, and I really enjoyed meeting a big baseball star. Kenny plays the golf tour, but he's a sports nut and he knows guys on all the baseball and football and basketball teams. He's a Dodger fan in baseball and a Lakers fan in basketball and a Kings fan in hockey, any team from Los Angeles, and he and I are always betting on games. If Kenny spent as much time on his golf as he does following other sports, he could be a big winner on the tour.

March 7   Bob Goalby gave me my Amana hat today, and I looked like hell in it. But the price is right, and now it's part of my standard equipment.

I had a late tee time, and the wind, which had been blowing all morning, stopped just about when I teed off. So I got even quick for that day last week when I caught the afternoon wind at Doral.

My round was pretty uneventful, one bogey and four birdies, and I came in with a 69, which put me four-under for the tournament. Rosburg struggled around the first nine in one over par, storming and groaning and tossing his putter around and, finally, telling his caddy to pack up his clubs. He said good-bye to Aaron and me and went over to the officials' tent to withdraw. Tommy and I moved to the tenth tee, and, suddenly, Rossy came running up to tell us he'd changed his mind. Then he shot a 34 the back nine for a 71.

Aaron shot a 31 the back nine and came in with a 67 to tie for the lead at 136, eight under par. I'm not in bad shape myself, only four strokes off the pace, the closest I've been after the second round since Phoenix.

Dave Hill came up to me in the clubhouse afterward and thanked me for my advice. He'd shot a 75 yesterday, and he was ready to withdraw. In fact, he'd made a plane reservation to leave town last night, and I talked him out of it. I told him the cut'd be up around 147 or 148 and that he shouldn't pull out. As it turned out, it took 145 to make the cut, and Davy shot a 69 today to make the cut with a stroke to spare. He'll probably end up beating me in the tournament. I should've let him go.

March 8   Sam Snead walked over to me on the putting green today. I don't know Sam real well—sometimes he's perfectly congenial to me, and sometimes I don't think he knows my name—but I respect him for his great record over the years. He wanted a putting lesson. He's always moaning about his putting and looking for a lesson, but he's not going to get much sympathy from anybody. Sam's won more than a hundred tournaments, and you don't win all those tournaments without getting the ball in the hole.

He dropped three balls on the green about twenty feet from the cup and said he just wanted to get a look at my stroke. I stepped up and putted the first ball and missed it. "That's just to get the line," I said to Sam. "I'll buy you a steak dinner if I don't make these next two."

Of course, I was only kidding about buying him a dinner, but I'll be a sonuvagun if I didn't step up and knock the next two right into the hole, a pair of twenty-footers. Old Sam's eyes opened wide, like he was thinking, "If I could putt like that, I really would've won me a mess of tournaments."

I laughed like I could do it all the time. I wish.

We started a new system today, playing twosomes instead of threesomes every Saturday and Sunday. I was paired with Larry Hinson, a young boy from Georgia who's got a withered left arm, something like Ed Furgol, the man who won the U.S. Open back in 1954. Larry didn't have a very good day—he shot a 74—but he impressed me both with his game and his personality. Obviously, he's got a lot of guts and determination to overcome his handicap, and I'd love to see him have a good career out here on the tour.

We played in a light rain all day, and I had one interesting hole, the seventeenth. I was on the tee, getting ready to drive, and just as I started my downswing, some television people up on a tower let out the shrillest whistle I ever heard. I almost jumped out of my skin. I duck-hooked the ball over to the left of some trees bordering the fairway. It looked like I didn't have any shot from there, except a chip out to the fairway. I was afraid I was heading for a five or a six on what's normally a fairly easy birdie hole.

I studied my position and studied it and studied it, and, finally, I figured out a little opening through the trees. I could just fit a nine-iron through there and maybe come up close to the green. I threaded a needle with that nine-iron, came up about two feet from the green, chipped up stiff, and saved my par.

I came in with a 70 and now I'm six-under for the tournament, still four strokes behind the leaders, Bert Yancey and Johnny Pott, but up in the top fifteen or so. I need a hot round tomorrow, a 68 or a 69, and I'll be right up near the top. I don't think I can win—there're too many guys to pass—but a high finish and a big check would help me get back the confidence I've lost over the past few weeks. I'm going home tomorrow night, and the trip'll be a lot more pleasant if I've got a few thousand dollars recorded on the money list.

When I got back to my motel room tonight, I noticed my pants were so baggy I couldn't believe it. They were really hanging loose. I guess my diet's going good, finally. Either that, or my pants have stretched.

March 9   Everybody was talking this morning about a story in one of the local papers, an interview with one of those wonderful touring caddies, a fellow called The Baron. I guess somebody didn't give him as much money as he thinks he's worth, so he sounded off about how stingy all the pros are, how everybody except Palmer and Nicklaus is just too tight.

The Baron said that the caddies were worth about five strokes a round to the golfers and that he'd like to see anyone shoot a 66 without a good caddy. I don't know who was dumber, the caddy or the reporter who wrote up the story.

I wasn't in a good mood anyway this morning, and that story didn't help. When I got up, I saw how hard the wind was blowing—it must've been forty or fifty miles an hour—and I knew old Frank was in for a bad day. I've tried everything I know to play better in the wind. I've talked to every man on the tour who plays well in the wind. But nothing helps. You can call it giving up or pessimism or alibiing or whatever you want, but all I know is that I absolutely dread the wind these days.

For me, the hardest thing about playing in the wind, strangely, is the putting. I simply cannot maintain my equilibrium in the wind. I have sort of a delicate type of putting stance. I don't dig in and jam the ball in the hole. I approach it more with a feel, kind of a velvet touch, and when I can't maintain perfect equilibrium, it throws my whole stroke off. That's all there is to it. I'm going to have to overcome this problem because we don't play in perfect weather all the time and, if I'm going to make my living out here, I've got to learn to play in the wind.

I played with Bob Charles today, the only lefty who's ever done well on the tour. He's one of the most underrated pros in the world. Bob's a great putter and much better from tee to green than most people give him credit for. He shot a 74 today, which brought him home in the top fifteen.

My round was a struggle from start to finish. The wind kept kicking up at the worst moments, pushing my shots around, and my putting was atrocious. I must've missed half-a-dozen putts of six feet or less. It was so discouraging; just when I felt I was getting my touch back on the greens, I lost it completely. I finished the round, appropriately, by missing a three-footer on the eighteenth, and came in with a 75. I still finished in the top twenty and earned about $1,200, but the way things turned out, if I'd shot a 70, I'd have finished in the top five, and if I'd shot a 68, what I was aiming for, I'd have tied for first place.

Kenny Still won the tournament, his first victory in nine years on the tour, and he was even more excited than if the Dodgers had won the World Series. Miller Barber finished second and climbed up to second place on the money list, over fifty thousand dollars, only a few dollars behind Gene Littler. I'll tell you, old Miller's playing some golf. I'll bet right now that he wins one of the major titles this year—the Open or the Masters or the PGA.

A few years ago, after Miller took the early lead in some tournament in Texas, he walked into the locker room, and somebody said, "How'd you do, X?"

"I'm not X anymore," Miller said, very seriously. "I'm Super-X."

He really is, now.

Guess who shot the best round of anybody in the wind today? Right. The Old Sarge—Orville Moody. He started off kind of quiet in this tournament, with rounds of 70-70-72, but today, in his type of weather, he shot a 68 and jumped up into a tie for third.

Every time I've seen him lately, I've said, "Lookin' for the wind to blow, Orville?"

And he's always said, "The harder, the better."

I'm just not asking him anymore.

My roommate here, Steve Reid, earned about five hundred dollars, but Coody didn't do anything much, Colbert missed the top fifty again, and Crawford missed the cut. Dave Hill came in two strokes behind me, so I don't feel bad at all about talking him into staying.

I'm flying home tonight, and it's really going to be great to see Patty and the kids again. I've been touring without them for three weeks now, and it's just no fun for me or for them. I'm going to go home and take it easy and enjoy my family and not lift a golf club for a whole week.

March 10 / Louisville   My father met me at the airport at one o'clock this morning, which was a nice surprise. Pro told me I should've taken a week off sooner, that I had to be getting stale, but I told him I wish I had a little more confidence in my ability so that I could take more weeks off without worrying about everybody passing me by.

I took Patty to the doctor this afternoon—she's getting close, but we don't have any exact date—then took the kids driving around in the country, looking at the farms and horses, a lot prettier sight to me than fairways and greens.

I had a wonderful home-cooked meal tonight, and I'm afraid my diet's going to go right down the drain this week. I hate eating in restaurants and diners all the time, and Patty's going to be fattening me up all week so that probably, by the end, I'll look like the pregnant one.

It just feels so good to be home. I'm going to lie on my rear end all week and watch television and pay a few bills and kind of let the world go by. I'm going to do nothing until I get so sick of it that I want to leave, that I want to get back to the tour. When I'm anxious to get back to the tour, then I'll be ready to play my best golf.

March 17   I didn't actually play any golf all this week, but the last couple of days, I did practice a little. I hit a few balls, and Pro studied my swing and was very pleased with it. He thinks I'm swinging as well as I ever have, so at least I know that's not my problem.

I've been watching the Pensacola Open this week a little closer than I normally watch a tournament when I'm off. The final round's been rained out for two straight days now, but after three rounds, Jimmy Colbert's leading by a stroke, Deane Beman's second, and Dick Crawford's tied for fifth, and I've got kind of mixed feelings.

I'm really glad to see my friends doing well, but at the same time, down deep, I've got to be honest and admit that it hurts to see fellows winning money I could be winning. When you feel in your own heart that you can play better than certain fellows and you see them winning tournaments, it just kind of tears you up inside. I guess that's why I shouldn't read the papers when I'm not in a tournament. These are my friends—the people I like—and yet, somehow, I'm hurt that they're doing well and I'm not playing. I don't think it's jealousy—at least, I hope it isn't—but I guess it's something close to that. It's not a feeling I'm proud of, but it's there.

One thing's for sure: I don't envy Jimmy Colbert the pressure he's under. It's bad enough to suffer through one night, leading after three rounds of a tournament. To suffer through three nights is murder.

Patty's not too happy about me leaving tomorrow. She feels I should stay home and wait for the baby to arrive. We saw the doctor this morning, and he said the baby probably won't come for another two weeks, so I feel I'm doing the right thing, going back on the tour and trying to provide for my family. I was home for the birth of the first two children, and I won't be for this one, but I hope I've got enough confidence in Patty and my relatives to know that everything'll be all right. I hope I don't panic and withdraw in the middle of a tournament and run home.

I'm anxious to get back on the tour. I've picked up a new golf bag from Hillerich & Bradsby. My mind's rested. My body's rested. I want to start winning a little money.

March 18 / Jacksonville   Patty was crying when I left this morning. It's the hardest thing in the world for me to go on tour and leave my family behind, but it's part of this life I've chosen and I've got to accept it. Patty knows how much the tour means to me, how much it means to her and the children—she's an understanding wife, and she makes a lot of sacrifices—but I'm positive the day I quit the tour will be the happiest day of her life.

On the plane to Jacksonville, I sat with Bob Goalby. Bob's a strange individual, very blunt, very outspoken, and because of this, nobody feels lukewarm about Bob; they either love him or hate him. Bob and I got to talking about the caddy situation, particularly about that caddy, The Baron, who shot off his mouth in Orlando. He's been kicked off the tour, and I think it was the right move. Bob said The Baron got more publicity for his attack on the players than Bob got for winning the Masters last year.

Bob was laughing, but underneath he's a little bitter, and I think he has every right to be. Bob won the Masters in the famous score-card incident, when Roberto de Vicenzo was penalized for signing the wrong score. Instead of the Masters finishing in a tie between Bob and Roberto, Bob won by a stroke. Unless you're Nicklaus or Palmer, you don't get many chances in your career to win a major tournament, and when your chance comes along, you've got to grab it and capitalize on it. Bob's big chance was scarred by that score-card incident. The press just wrote about poor Roberto and practically ignored Goalby. It's a shame he's always going to have to live with that.

When we got to Jacksonville, the airline couldn't find our golf bags. I wasn't too upset; it was raining, anyway. I checked into my motel to wait for my roomie, Steve Reid, to come in from Pensacola, and I lay on the bed and relaxed and, probably because I'd just left Goalby, I started thinking about the Masters. I want to win that tournament so badly. I told myself I'd just limber up these next two weeks in Florida, get my game in good shape, then sharpen my competitive instincts at the Greater Greensboro Open in North Carolina and, finally, reach a peak for the Masters.

I started playing the Masters in my mind, remembering each shot I'd hit on each hole at Augusta during the last four years. Anybody who says he doesn't start thinking about the Masters this time of year is a liar. It's just too important. I know that while I'll be playing in Jacksonville, Miami, and Greensboro, I'll be thinking of Augusta and how I'd perform the same shots on the Masters course.

My mind wandered to Arnold Palmer, which is kind of logical when you're thinking about the Masters. I read in the papers today that Arnie says his hip has stopped bothering him, that he's cured and ready to go. Arnie's had a bad hip the past year or two, but I think his troubles on the golf course go a little deeper than that. I'm afraid he's just a little over the hill. When you're a professional athlete and you turn forty, which is what Arnie'll be this year, you're not at a physical peak anymore. Besides, he's a millionaire many times over by now, and I suppose that when you win everything there is to win, you lose your desire, your hunger. I can't speak with any authority about that, because I haven't been there.

I heard this afternoon that Jimmy Colbert won at Pensacola, and Deane Beman finished second, and Dick Crawford and Steve Reid both placed in the top ten. I'm really happy. Now that I'm back on the tour myself, I don't feel any jealousy at all, and I'm just tickled for all of them. I can't wait to see Jimmy to congratulate him. He won it in style, too. After waiting through two days of rain, with the pressure building up every minute, he went out and shot a 67 today and beat Deane by two strokes. Jimmy'll be floating all week.

Late this afternoon, I got kind of lonely in my room, so I strolled outside and saw Bob Rosburg and told Rossy I'd buy him a drink in the saloon. We walked into the motel bar, and we spotted George Blanda from the Oakland Raiders and Daryl Lamonica from the Raiders and Alex Karras from the Detroit Lions. Rossy knew them, and we all sat down together and talked about football and the Super Bowl. I'd never met any of them before, and I was awed, the way I always am when I meet celebrities from other sports, when I meet real athletes.

March 19 Marty Fleckman was standing near me on the putting green this morning, and the guys were teasing him with a new nickname. They're calling Marty the "Easter Bunny" because he's hitting the ball so long and so wild that every time he drives he has to go on an Easter-egg hunt to find the ball in the woods. Marty's a good boy, and he took the kidding pretty well, but I know his game must really be bothering him.

Marty's got a world of potential. He led the 1967 U.S. Open for three rounds as an amateur, and he won the 1967 Cajun Classic, which was only about his third or fourth professional tournament, and he just missed the top sixty last year. But so far this year he's won only a few hundred dollars and he's missed the cut seven times in nine tournaments. He wouldn't be human if he weren't worrying.

I saw Gary Player before I teed off, and Gary was fretting, as usual, about how his body just couldn't adjust to the change in time. He came over from South Africa last week for his first U.S. tournament of the year and his body was in such bad shape he could only finish in a tie for fifth at Pensacola. Gary'll worry for about the first three or four weeks he's over here, and he'll probably finish in the top ten every week.

I had the world's most one-sided kind of pro-am team today, a fifteen-, sixteen-, and seventeen-handicapper, and they all could've used about thirty pops. But they were nice fellows, and even though I picked up my ball and stopped keeping any individual score on the back nine, I had a pretty good time, getting the feel of the course and trying out a few little gimmicks here and there. After the round, I went straight to the practice tee, which is kind of against my religion, and I hit the ball well. My game's going to come around quick.

Jimmy Colbert was on the practice tee, just bubbling over. He's exempt for a year now, and he's got a good start toward the top sixty, and he's won a spot in the Tournament of Champions next month, and he's about as happy as a fellow can be.

When I got back to the motel, I called Patty and talked to her for a while and talked to Danny, and he said he'd see me after his nap. I'm starting to miss them again already.

I'm paired with Dow Finsterwald and Jerry Barber tomorrow, two former PGA champions who have club jobs and don't play the tour full time these days, and I'm looking forward to it. We won't have much of a gallery, and they'll move along good, and I'll enjoy myself.

March 20   When I got to the course this morning, I decided to wear my black-and-white golf shoes, instead of the plain black ones I wear most of the time. I remembered that the few good rounds I'd shot in the past two or three weeks, I'd shot with the black-and-whites on. I hope I'm not getting superstitious; I've got enough problems without that.

On the practice tee, I couldn't hit one decent shot. I hit the ball as badly as I've ever hit it in my life. On top of that, once I started to play, I discovered that my five-iron was missing. I knew I had to get out the old first-aid kit and patch up my game, just try to keep the ball in play and go for pars and not try any of those fancy shots that real professional golfers are supposed to be able to execute.

I did a good repair job. I shot a 69, and when I came off that practice tee, if anyone had offered me a 71 or 72 for the day, I'd have grabbed it. I didn't think there was any way I could shoot three-under today.

One thing I noticed today was that my mind was really clear, that I knew what I was doing all the time. I was aware I was on a golf course. I was aware I was trying to sink a putt, and if I missed, it stung. I didn't have the dull feeling I'd had the last couple of weeks before I went home. I hope I've learned a lesson. I'm not going to play eight or ten weeks straight anymore. I know that in the long run I'll earn more money by taking an occasional week off than by pushing myself all the time.

Playing today with two former PGA champions, I couldn't help thinking how the exemption rules for the tour could stand some updating. Right now, all PGA and U.S. Open champions have lifetime exemptions that qualify them for almost every tournament. I can understand the reasoning—these fellows have contributed a lot to the growth of golf—but at the same time I know that professional golf is the only major sport that allows people to compete out of nostalgia. Could you imagine Joe DiMaggio playing in a World Series today or Sammy Baugh playing in a Super Bowl? I have as much respect for tradition as anyone; in fact, I love to play occasionally with some of the real old fellows who can tell me what golf was like in the 1920s. But I don't think they should be playing every week; it's not even fair to them. Of course, some of the older fellows who happen to have lifetime exemptions still bring a great deal of talent to the tour. A Tommy Bolt or a Sam Snead or a Dow Finsterwald could get hot any week and finish in the top ten; those fellows could qualify without having lifetime exemptions.

I played some bridge this afternoon with Steve and Dave Hill and Tony Jacklin and Bert Yancey, and then we went out and got some dinner and watched the college basketball championships on television. I called Patty and she said that she can feel something moving around and she thinks the baby's going to come in the next few days. She sounded all excited. I guess I'm excited too. I'd like to have a whole houseful of little Beards.

March 21   As I reached the practice tee this morning, a guy came up to me and handed me a message to call Methodist Hospital in Louisville. The note said not to be concerned, nothing pressing. I was really happy. I figured Patty had gone into labor and she was going to have the baby soon and everything was just fine.

I called the hospital and I couldn't reach Patty. I asked if my mother was there, and I couldn't reach her. Finally, I got through to a nurse on the maternity floor, and she told me that Patty had gone in to have a cesarean section, that the baby had flipped over sideways, making the cesarean necessary. If I'd been thinking straight, I would've told myself that a cesarean's a very common operation nowadays and that we had a very competent doctor and that there was nothing to worry about. But, instead, I started to imagine all kinds of things.

I thought maybe there were some problems that nobody wanted to tell me and Patty was going to die or she was going to be sick and the baby was going to die, and I was going half out of my mind. I called my father, and Pro said he'd go right down to the hospital and see what was happening and then he'd call the golf course and have a message brought out to me wherever I was.

"Fine," I said. "I want to know the story from head to toe, and I want to know it as fast as possible."

I was tempted to withdraw right then and hurry on home, but I figured there was nothing I could do to help. I told myself I'd better stay here and play golf and win some money and then go home this weekend and everything'd be all right.

After I'd played one hole—we started on the back nine, and I birdied the tenth—Marcia Colbert, Jim's wife, ran up to me with a message from my father telling me that everything was fine, that we'd had a baby girl named Jennifer Lynn, and that both Patty and the baby were perfect, no complications, nothing to worry about.

I went ahead and played a pretty good round of golf, except for my putting. I've never putted so poorly in my life as I have the past few months. I had, honestly, twelve makable putts for birdies today, all of them ten feet or less, and I made only two of them. Still, I came in with a 70, which put me five-under for the tournament, only a stroke behind the leaders. Six different people were six-under for the tournament, including Arnold Palmer. Maybe Arnie's not quite all the way over the hill yet.

As soon as I got off the course, I called home and found out Patty's coming along fine, and the baby's fine, and my other two children are having fun with my parents. I'm a happy man tonight. I've got everything to be thankful for.

March 22 I woke up feeling great, thinking about my wife and the baby, and then I opened up the front door and saw the wind picking up. It just about broke my heart. I'm so sick and tired of playing in the wind.

The day went the way I expected. I struggled to shoot a 74, but if nothing else, I think I came to some understanding of what the wind does to me. My game always has been, and always will be, based on tempo, the ability to swing smoothly and within myself, not to rush or try to overpower the ball. When the wind starts blowing, I have a tendency to tighten up, to swing too fast or too hard, to try to force the ball into the wind. I lose my tempo, and once I've lost that, I've lost everything.

My partner today was Ray Floyd, a big old boy from North Carolina who was a rookie in 1963, the same year I was. Ray beat me out for rookie of the year, mostly, I think, because the voting was held before I won the Frank Sinatra Invitational. Ray had won the St. Petersburg Open early in the year—he was only twenty at the time—but, after winning the Sinatra, I finished way ahead of Ray on the money list.

Raymond's never quite achieved his potential out on the tour, and a lot of people think it's because he's got too many distractions. He does like to have a good time.

I think you can divide the players on the tour into five different categories. One is the out-and-out swingers, almost all bachelors, who drink and date and get all the good-looking broads, and do it all out in the open. Two is the guys who do the same thing, more or less, but do it quietly so that no one hears about it, especially their wives. Three is the guys who like to drink a little or run around a little, but don't make a career out of either. Four is the guys who rarely have a drink, who want ten to twelve hours of sleep every night, and who don't have too much on their minds except golf. Five is the out-and-out saints, who don't do any drinking or chasing or swearing, who just go to church and play golf and watch a little television.

Raymond definitely falls into the first category, just as definitely as Kermit Zarley, for instance, falls into the fifth. I'm kind of in the middle—I'm not much at running around, but I can handle my Scotch on occasion—which is where the majority of the guys are.

I'm not saying that Raymond is a drunk or anything like that. It's just if he's got a choice between going to bed early by himself or going to a party, he's going to the party. Yet he still takes his golf seriously, and he's still got a beautiful game. He's won only one tournament since our rookie year, but I'd put my cash on him winning another one tomorrow.

Ray really handled that wind today. He shot a 68 and moved into first place, a stroke ahead of Gardner Dickinson and DeWitt Weaver.

After the round, I went to visit Dick Hart's trailer. Dick is one of my closest friends, even though I don't get to see him too much anymore. He tried the tour full time for a while, but he decided that he could fulfill his responsibilities to his family better by holding a club job. Now he comes down to Florida each winter, plays a few tournaments, then heads up to his club near Chicago. Dick and I have been partners in the PGA team championship the past couple of years, and I have tremendous respect for him as a golfer and as a person.

I've also got a debt to Dick. I've always been a notoriously bad bunker player, and last summer, when I was playing in the Western Open outside Chicago, Dick told me he'd found a sand wedge that was absolutely the best he'd ever seen. He took me out to his pro shop and dug around and whipped out this ancient R-90 Wilson wedge, which had to be fifty years old. "Try this," he said.

It was the worst-looking club I'd ever seen, but, somehow, I could see that it had some potential. I took it into a bunker and hit a few shots and turned to Dick and said, "This is the club for me."

I've been a better bunker player ever since. I don't know if it's just psychological or what. All I know is that Dick Hart's beat-up old wedge has saved me a lot of strokes.

March 23   I was paired with Tommy Shaw today, the first time I've played with Tommy in four or five years. I haven't even seen him play in all that time. I had a vague memory that I wasn't too impressed by his game, and I was curious to see if it had really changed a lot or if he had just won by a fluke at Doral. After Doral, he'd missed the cut two weeks in a row. Tommy didn't show me too much today—he shot a 75—but I think I'll reserve judgment on him for a while. He won Doral against a pretty good field.

If I didn't accomplish anything else today, I believe I hit upon what's going to get me back into my winning ways. That's my concentration. I just haven't had my good concentration for a year now. I've been worrying about the holes I've already played and the holes I'm going to play, instead of concentrating on just one thing, the shot I'm about to hit. I suspect that the great golfers play each shot as if it's the only shot they're going to hit the rest of their lives.

About two-thirds of the way through my round, I realized that I had closed my stance on my putts. In the past, I've always putted with an open stance, and apparently, without even knowing it, I'd closed up this year. I opened up the last six holes and made a couple of ten-footers and a kind of scary three-footer, and even though I missed a six-footer for an eagle on the final hole, I came in with a 71. I moved up into the top twenty and earned close to $1,500. Dick Hart won himself a little money here, about six hundred dollars, and Jimmy Colbert finished in the top ten and won more than $2,500.

By the luck of the draw, Palmer and Nicklaus were paired today, and they must've had thirty thousand people following them. You could hear them screaming and yelling and jumping all over the course; when either Arnie or Jack made a good putt, it sounded like a billion horses thundering up and down. The ground vibrated ten holes away.

Arnie had a good day and finished tied for sixth. Gary Player, who says he's still waking up in the middle of the night because his body hasn't adjusted to the States, tied for third, and Raymond Floyd, who says he's been going to bed at night, won the championship in a play-off with Gardner Dickinson.

We had more wind today than we'd had all tournament, so, naturally, old Orville shot a 68. He's slipping, though. Two guys actually shot better scores than he did, and neither of them was from El Paso.

I'm flying home tonight to see Patty and the new baby. We've been married just a little over three years now, and we've got three children. I may not win a lot of tournaments, but I do all right in that department.

March 24 / Louisville   I spent most of today in the hospital with Patty—she and Jennifer'll be home by the end of the week— then stopped at H & B and had them make some little repairs on my drivers. I'm heading back down to Miami tomorrow for the $200,000 National Airlines Open, the second largest purse of the whole year.

March 25 / Miami   I'm really anxious to get back to the old rut, traveling with the family in the station wagon, hearing the kids crying, changing diapers, feeding bottles, all that stuff. I miss it. It's not much of a life for a family, but as far as I'm concerned, it's a lot better than being out here by myself, wondering what they're doing and who's getting hurt and everything else.

When I got into Miami tonight, I was dead tired. I wanted to go right to sleep, but I ran into Jack McGowan, John Lutz, and Randy Glover, who were looking for a fourth for bridge. Old Frank couldn't resist. I told Charlie Coody, who's my roommate here, to go ahead and go to sleep, and I went and played bridge.

I feel badly for Randy Glover. He was one of the up-and-coming young players on the tour—from 1965 through 1967, he averaged more than thirty thousand dollars a year in prize money—then last year his back started acting up, and his earnings slipped to less than twenty thousand dollars, hardly enough to break even. He told me tonight that he's going to have an operation on his back. He's just twenty-seven, and his career may be finished. I know professional golf isn't a very strenuous sport, compared to football or basketball, but I swear we have more back injuries than anybody else.

March 26   We're playing the National Airlines Open at the Country Club of Miami, and the course is too young to be in first-grade condition; I imagine it'll be great in four or five years. I've always argued that we ought to play right down the middle of Saigon if the price is right, but I'm starting to change my mind. We've reached the point now where we can be a little bit selective. Even if this tournament is for $200,000, we'd all be a lot happier if the course were as impressive as the purse.

I've got to admit that one thing here is really first-grade, and that's the girls helping out the tournament committee. Most of them are stewardesses, I guess, and they're driving little golf carts around, ferrying us back and forth between the clubhouse and the practice tee, which is a good distance away. I've never seen so many attractive girls in my life. The one who drove me this morning started talking to me and she said, "Oh, the golfers are so handsome. I really enjoy this work."

"Yeah," I said, "but, you know, our guys are getting married left and right. There aren't too many bachelors left."

"Oh, I don't care," she said. "The married ones are better."

I didn't know what to say to that. I knew she sure didn't mean me.

I didn't do anything much in the pro-am today, but it didn't make any difference because we got rained out before everyone finished. That meant that all the pros would share the prize money.

The way we've been seeing rain this year, we ought to go into the rain-making business. Any place that's suffering from a drought just has to sponsor a professional golf tournament, and we'll come in and do our little Indian dance, and the rain'll pour down.

We had a little extra excitement today, because one of the pro-am foursomes included Joe Namath, Jackie Gleason, Arnold Palmer, and some doctor from Hawaii, a millionaire who gave ten thousand dollars to charity for the privilege of joining the other three. Namath and Gleason were playing a grudge match—they'd been needling each other in the papers for the past couple of weeks—and the loser had to give five thousand dollars to charity. Namath beat Gleason pretty easily—they got in nine holes before the rain—but they both had fun, shouting insults and hamming it up for the gallery. They had thousands of people following them.

I'm all in favor of a little sideshow like that every week. It draws people who might not come to golf tournaments otherwise, and in the long run that's got to be good for me.

I've got a touring caddy working for me this week, one of the better ones, a fellow named Paul Bentley, who's caddied for Coody quite a bit. Charlie and Paul had some kind of run-in—over cash, naturally—so Paul became available and I hired him this week. He knows his job. In the rain today, I didn't feel much like walking off yardages, and Paul had already done it, so I just checked a few of his and found they were as accurate as I could get. Paul's really something. He buys a new notebook for each tournament and draws each hole on a separate page. Then he draws in the green and the traps and the water hazards and indicates all the yardages.

There's another caddy, a guy who works for Steve Reid sometimes, who actually uses plastic overlays, like the overlays on military maps, and he marks all the measurements down to half yards, which is kind of ridiculous. If I'm 139 yards from the pin or 140 or 141, I'm going to hit the exact same shot. I'm not a machine.

The practice of walking off yardages is a fairly new one. I know guys have been doing it since I came on the tour six years ago, but it started only a little before then. As far as I know, Walter Hagen and Bobby Jones and even Ben Hogan and Byron Nelson never walked off yardages.

Some pros still don't. A few years ago, according to a story I heard, Tommy Bolt was playing one day with Bob Shave, who is very intense, very dedicated, the kind who measures his yardages to the exact step. Bolt's never taken a yardage in his life; he plays by feel. They got to about the third hole, and Shave hit his drive, then pulled out his little black book and stepped off the distance between his ball and the tree he'd used as a marker. He made some mental calculations and figured out exactly how far he had to go to the pin and then hit an iron and just blanked the flag all the way and sailed right over the green. Bolt turned to Shave and said, "You know, son, if you didn't have that little book, you'd be in a helluva mess, wouldn't you?"

We lost a bridge player today. Dave Hill got suspended. The explanation I heard was that he abused a PGA official. He got all hot about some slow play at Jacksonville—Dave hates to be slowed down—and blew up and swore at the official.

I don't imagine the suspension'll last too long. Davy's got to write a letter of apology and pay a fine and then, I hope, he'll be reinstated. Davy's got a temper, but he's one of the finest people I've ever met, kind, generous, a helluva guy. It may sound corny, but if I die tomorrow, I'll be happy because I met Dave Hill.

Here's the latest on my diet: I've been real good lately—still staying away from the potatoes and the bread—and yet I'm back up to 190. Steve Reid says that next Lent I should give up Cokes, Scotch, and macaroni.

March 27   I played today with Jack Nicklaus and "The Chinese Pro"—Dudley Wysong, who got his nickname from his last name. I've never seen Nicklaus play so badly as he played with me today and at Doral. I don't know what's going on with him, whether he just doesn't care or he's thinking only about the Masters or what. All I know is he's not playing his game of golf, and that leaves more money for the rest of us.

Nicklaus shot a 73 and he was lucky to get that. Wysong shot a 77. I don't know what's the matter with him, either. He's been in the top sixty for four straight years—he's my age, exactly fourteen days younger than me—and he should be near his peak. But, instead, he's having all kinds of troubles. He's finished in the top forty in only one tournament so far this year.

I had a pretty good round. I was using my open putting stance, and I felt like I knew what I was doing, like I was stroking the ball right. I parred seven of the first eight holes routinely, on in regulation and two putts, and I picked up one birdie, with a six-foot putt on a par-five. I came to the ninth, a long par-four, and had to hit a two-iron off the tee. Robert Trent Jones designed this course, and he's supposed to be one of the greatest golf architects in the world, but I've never played a course of his that I liked. It's ridiculous, laying out a long par-four so that you can't hit a wood off the tee.

My tee shot left me with a four-iron to the green, and I kind of hooked it. The ball bounced off the green into a trap. I climbed in with that old sand wedge of mine and popped it right up next to the cup. Nicklaus's eyes popped, too. "Frank Beard hit that shot?" he said.

"Hell, yes," I said. "I've been practicing."

"Can't believe it," Jack said, shaking his head. "I can't believe Frank Beard hit that shot." Then he put on a British accent and said, "Nice splash-out, Frank," the way the English players talk.

I saved my par at nine, then birdied the tenth and eleventh holes. On the twelfth, a narrow fairway that Trent Jones dreamed up, I pushed my drive off a little to the right. On most courses, I'd be in the rough, but here I'm in a creek. I dropped a new ball, hit a low hook around a tree, reached the green, then sank a thirty-footer for my par, just when I thought sure I was heading for a double-bogey. I couldn't help thinking that that's the sort of thing that happens when you're going to win a tournament.

The next hole, a par-five which is laid out so that you're wasting your strength if you bother to hit a driver off the tee, I hit my second shot into the creek. The ball was on the edge of the water, so, instead of taking a penalty stroke, I hit a wedge out, then chipped onto the green, and missed an eight-footer for a par. I was happy to get out with a bogey.

On the fourteenth, a par-four, Nicklaus, Wysong, and I all had to hit two-irons off the tee, thanks to Trent Jones again, and I got a routine par. After I birdied the fifteenth to go three-under, I really messed up the par-five sixteenth. I hooked my tee shot into a bunker, and the ball bounced out and went in behind some trees. I hooked a three-iron out of there, over the creek and into some deep rough. Then I hit a sand wedge to within six feet of the cup and sank the putt for a birdie—without ever touching the fairway.

"I haven't seen you this hole," Nicklaus said, after I sank my putt. "What'd you make—six or seven?"

"Nick," I said, "don't worry. I'll laugh all the way to the bank."

I came in with a 68, which put me in a tie for third place, and I'm really happy. It's the old Frank Beard. Maybe I'm going to win my first Florida tournament ever. The only guys in front of me are DeWitt Weaver, who's erratic, and Sam Snead, who's fifty-six and hasn't won a tournament in four years. I'm in good shape.

Some people I'd met down here took me to dinner tonight, and on the way, we stopped at the motel for me to change into a suit. Coody was there, so the people invited Charlie along. "Fine," he said. "I'm hungry." He probably figured we were going around the corner or something.

We wound up at the Palm Bay Club, which is where Ray Floyd and Doug Sanders and Miller Barber stay, and, of course, Charlie and I don't quite fit in that set. The service was a lot slower than the crowd, and Charlie, who's not used to being up after ten o'clock, began chomping at the bit. He was real subtle. He kept saying, "C'mon, Frank, let's us go to Howard Johnson's and get one of those

Ho-Jo colas and a cheeseburger." He's teeing off at 8:48 tomorrow morning, and I knew he wanted to get to bed at 8:48 tonight.

We finally got served—capon instead of cheeseburgers—and Charlie gobbled down his dinner, said he didn't want any coffee, and dropped little lines like "Do cabs come out this far?"

I managed to get Charlie home before midnight, but I know if he shoots a bad round tomorrow, he's never going to forgive me for keeping him up so late.

March 28   I got up at six o'clock this morning and woke up Coody, who was sleeping like a baby. After a good breakfast at Howard Johnson's, Charlie said he felt great. "Can't beat the service here," he said.

When we left the restaurant, the wind was blowing up strong. "Charles," I said, "this is going to be a bad day."

I've got to admit it: I got a lot of help today from my caddy, Paul Bentley. We consulted on distances and on clubs, and he gave me good advice. I believe in paying for what I get, and this week I'll be paying Paul a little extra, no matter whether I come in first or fiftieth.

Nicklaus, Wysong, and I played the back nine first, and I made all my five- and six-footers and managed to get through there at even-par. Jack putted terribly—at one point, he sank a two-footer and said, "That's the longest putt I've made in a few weeks"—and Dudley really tried to make up for that 77 he shot yesterday. He had a good round, a 70, but it wasn't good enough for him to make the cut. Big Jack shot a 75 and missed the cut, too.

I concentrated on my putts, studying the line, like I always do, from four directions, front, back, and both sides. I took a lot of time, shifting my eyes from the ball to the hole to the ball to the hole as many as seven and eight times before I felt ready to putt.

When we reached the eighth hole, our seventeenth, I was just one over par. For the first time all day, I three-putted to go two-over. I walked to the ninth tee feeling disgusted. I was facing the hardest hole on the course in my opinion, a 435-yard par-four, and

I knew I could easily get a bogey and come in with a 75. I'd have wasted my opening 68.

I'd hit a two-iron off the ninth tee yesterday. You don't have too much choice. It's a direct dogleg left with out of bounds on the right and a big bunker about 240 yards out on the left. The fancy shot, the technical shot, would be an iron at the bunker with a little fade into the fairway.

I turned to my caddy. "Paul," I said, "by God, I'm sick and tired of all this. I'm playing everybody's game but my own. I'm not Hogan. I'm not Dickinson. I'm not Bolt. I'm not going to play any more cute little shots. Give me my driver."

I stood up and hit a Frank Beard shot. I aimed at the out of bounds and hooked the ball smack into the middle of the fairway. I left myself about 180 yards to the green. With the wind blowing right to left, I was faced with another fancy little shot. The professional thing to do was to take a little more club than normal, cut the shot into the wind, let the direction of the wind cancel out the direction of the shot, and land nice and soft. That's the professional thing to do, and I knew I couldn't do it.

"Paul," I said, "I'm not going to play any more of those cut shots, those hold shots, the canceling vectors, and all that bull. I'm going to play it the way *I* can." I took a three-iron and hooked a low shot over the trap on the right front of the green and landed on the green and rolled up about eight feet from the cup.

I felt like a million dollars. I was finally playing Frank Beard's game. "Paul," I said, "if I make this putt, we're going to win this tournament." And I knocked it right into the middle of the hole. I'll tell you, I felt so fired up I just wanted to run right to the first tee and play the third and fourth rounds today.

Bob Murphy, who'd shot a 66 today, was leading the tournament at nine-under, and with my 73, I was only three-under, but I didn't care. I felt I could go out and shoot me a pair of 67s or 68s the next two rounds and overtake Murphy and everybody else.

Charlie Coody shot a 74 today, which wasn't great, but at least he made the cut, so he won't be too angry with me for keeping him up last night. Steve Reid missed the cut, and he had some good company—Nicklaus, Yancey, Goalby, Sanders, and Weiskopf.

In the locker room, I saw Nicklaus, and I thought I might be able to give him a little tip on his putting. I mentioned that he was picking up his putter when he drew it back. The rule is to bring the putter back low and slow.

"I know," Jack said. "I know I'm picking it up. But when I don't pick it up on Bermuda grass, I catch it." Jack shook his head. "I don't know what to do about it," he said. Jack didn't sound really depressed, the way I get sometimes, but he wasn't happy, either.

I never thought I'd see him having trouble with this game.

March 29 The hardest thing for me today was to call home. I spoke to Patty and I spoke to my folks, and I know it hurt them even more than it hurt me to tell them I shot a 76 today. Pro was bewildered. He doesn't think I should ever shoot a round that bad. Patty could tell from my voice that I was upset, so she got upset, too. At times like this, I wish I were a bachelor, without any family, so that I wouldn't feel like I was letting so many people down.

I played like Joe Blow today. I hate to keep talking about the wind, but it was unbelievable it was so bad. I couldn't do a thing right. Every time I made the slightest mistake—hit the ball just a little too long or a little too short—I caught a bunker or a creek or a tree or some kind of trouble. I was lucky to get in at 76. On one par-five, I had to chip in to get a par.

It looks to me like Bob Murphy's going to win this National Airlines Open. He's got a three-stroke lead, and I don't think anybody can catch him, the way he putts.

Coody shot a 71 to move past me by a stroke, and later, back in our room, he wanted to discuss our rounds. I love Charlie—there's nobody on the tour I like better—but, frankly, I wish I were rooming with Steve Reid tonight. Charlie's too intense about his golf; he wants to analyze it all night. When I'm with Steve, he just says, "What'd you shoot?" and I tell him and ask what he shot, and that's it; we drop the subject right there. I've got to get my mind off golf away from the course, but Charlie likes to review every stroke. I suffer enough playing the round; I don't want to hear about it again.

March 30   At Mass this morning, I prayed for my golf game. I didn't pray for a 67 or anything like that. I prayed just to be able to relax and get a little insight into my general problem. I'd like to be able to figure out why I'm not functioning the way I should.

Something's definitely wrong, and I can't put my finger on it. If I were broke or my wife was divorcing me or I had a headache, I'd know what's bothering me, but it's nothing like that. It's something so deep and indirect that I just don't know what it is.

I've got no problems, really. I've got three healthy children. My wife's fine. My investments are all going well. My bank balance is good.

Even my golf game's in decent shape. I'm hitting the ball as well from tee to green as I ever have and, despite all my moans and groans, my putting's not that bad. I should be on top of the world, just eating up these tournaments, and I'm not.

I went out to the course and, just the opposite of yesterday, when I was all charged up and raring to go, I felt kind of submissive today, like I was ready to accept whatever happened. I retreated into my shell and played a conservative game and ended up with

Frank Beard's Record

TOURNAMENT	1ST ROUND	2ND ROUND	3RD ROUND	4TH ROUND
Doral	71	73	74	71
Citrus	71	69	70	75
Monsanto		DID NOT PLAY		
Jacksonville	69	70	74	71
National Airlines	68	73	76	72

a conservative 72. I finished around fiftieth and earned $480. I tried right down to the end, concentrating as hard on a six-foot putt on the eighteenth as I did on the first (and missing both of them), because I know every stroke means a few hundred dollars, and I still remember what happened to George Archer in 1964. George missed the top fifty—only the top fifty got exemptions then—by about $1.98.

I played with a fellow named Herb Hooper today. I spent a lot of time with Herb my first year on the tour. He had a pretty good game, but he never did a thing, and he just drifted off the tour and got married and took a club job. Herb shot a 70 today and beat me by a stroke. He seems more relaxed with the security of a job.

At the end of the round, I gave my caddy one hundred dollars. Paul worked five days for me, so I wound up paying him about fifteen dollars a day plus five percent of my winnings, a lot higher than the ten-and-three the touring caddies always demand. Paul was worth one hundred dollars to me this week, and I probably would've given him that if I'd won anything from two hundred up to a thousand dollars.

Bob Murphy blew his three-stroke lead today. He shot up to a 76, and young Bunky Henry, who was kicking extra points for the Georgia Tech football team just a couple of years ago, came along and won his first tournament. For the fourth time in five weeks,

TOTAL SCORE	FINISH	PRO-AM EARNINGS	INDIVIDUAL EARNINGS
289	T 43	$30.00	$ 442.50
285	T 18	—	1,207.77
284	T 17	—	1,450.00
289	T 46	89.29	480.00

we had a first-time tournament winner, and three of them—Henry, Colbert, and Shaw—weren't even in the top sixty last year. I could've had a hell of a parlay betting those three guys. Pretty soon, I'll be the only guy out here without a 1969 victory.

I certainly didn't perform in Florida the way I'd promised. I played four tournaments, never finished in the top fifteen, and never won more than $1,500 in a tournament. It was miserable. I did better than that in California.

I don't feel very confident heading up to Greensboro. I just hope I can straighten myself out a little and get ready for the Masters.

First, I've got to figure out what's wrong with me.

4

Who
Am I Fooling?

TOURNAMENT	SITE	PURSE	DATES
Greater Greensboro Open	Sedgefield Country Club, Greensboro, North Carolina	$160,000	April 3– April 6
Masters	Augusta National Golf Club, Augusta, Georgia	186,975	April 10– April 13

March 31 / Greensboro   I am absolutely pooped tonight. I got up at six o'clock this morning to catch a flight to the Bahamas to play in a pro-am at the club Gardner Dickinson represents. A bunch of us went—Trevino, Jacklin, Player, Murphy, Littler, Goalby—and we took a chartered DC-3 from Miami, drank champagne for breakfast all the way down, then played happy. I played with Bruce Fleischer, the youngster from Miami who won the U.S. Amateur championship last year, and I'm glad he's an amateur. He hits the ball a mile, and he hits it straight.

After we played, Goalby, Littler, and I hitched a ride back to Miami in a little private plane, owned by a fellow we know. I hesitated before getting in but, finally, decided to try it. If my wife knew I flew in a private plane, instead of waiting for the charter, she'd probably divorce me.

We had a bumpy, but pleasant flight, ate dinner at the Miami airport, then flew into Greensboro tonight. I just staggered to my motel room.

I noticed a story in the papers yesterday about a pro named John Schlee. I know John slightly. He tried the tour briefly in 1964, dropped out, then came back full time in 1966. That year, he earned more than twenty-one thousand dollars, finished second in the Minnesota Classic, made the exempt list, and was named golf's rookie of the year. He looked to me like he might have a pretty good future.

But he slumped and missed the top sixty both in 1967 and 1968. This year, he's kind of fallen apart. He's entered all of the last eight tournaments, he's averaged 75 strokes a round, and he hasn't made the cut even once. In the past three years, John told the newspaper-man who wrote the story about him, he's earned seventy thousand dollars and spent seventy-two. He said he's tried the tour both on his own and with a sponsor, and either way, he hasn't liked the arithmetic. Now he's going to look for a club job.

The story reminded me that I'd started on the tour with a group of sponsors, ten successful businessmen in Louisville. "We want to give you a chance on the tour," they told me. "We want to help get you started." They agreed to put up ten thousand dollars—a thousand apiece, five hundred in cash and five hundred in notes—and I could draw out of that for my expenses. In return, we split all my winnings—half to me, half to them—after expenses. The contract was for two years, with an option for them to renew for three one-year periods.

I had to dip into their account only for a few months before my earnings passed my expenses. My first full year on the tour, I won about eighteen thousand dollars and, living pretty frugally, being a bachelor and all, kept my expenses down to about ten thousand dollars. At the end of the year, I was ahead four thousand dollars, and my sponsors were ahead four hundred apiece.

The next year, I earned about twenty-three thousand dollars, and my expenses went up to about thirteen thousand dollars, so I got five thousand and the sponsors got five hundred each. At the end of the second year, I went to them and thanked them and said I was ready to make it on my own on the tour. I told them I really appreciated their help in getting me started, but now I wanted to be independent.

They said no. They said they had an option to renew—after the first two years, the split shifted to two-thirds to me, one-third to them—and they intended to renew. I couldn't believe it. I honestly thought they just wanted to help me. They were all well to do, and more than one of them had told me that as soon as I had some security, they'd let me go. I didn't think they considered me an investment. I should've known better because once, at some gathering, my father overheard the wife of one of the sponsors saying, "Having Frank's better than having a racehorse." Pro got so upset, hearing me discussed like a piece of property, that I thought he was going to hit the lady.

Legally, I had to live up to the contract. Over the next three years, I earned about $230,000, and maybe fifty thousand dollars of it went for expenses. That left me with $120,000 profit, and my sponsors with six thousand dollars apiece. All in all, they ended up with about seven thousand dollars each, which I don't think had any effect on their standards of living.

I don't hold anything against those men—I still see some of them every now and then, and a few of them are very close friends—but I learned a lesson. They were businessmen, and I was a schoolboy. I learned that business is business, and friendship is friendship, and you shouldn't confuse the two.

As tired as I am, I just don't feel like going to sleep. The same thing keeps running through my mind: the Masters. I'm having trouble thinking about anything else.

April 1   When I started hitting on the practice tee this morning, I began thinking, "There it goes to the fifth hole at the Masters. There it goes to the ninth hole at the Masters." Every shot was just as if I were at Augusta. I should've skipped Greensboro this week and practiced for the Masters.

In the clubhouse, after I finished practicing, I took a look at the latest Ryder Cup list. The Ryder Cup is a match that's played every other year between a group of American professionals and a group of British professionals. They've been playing these matches for forty years, and all the great names have competed—Ted Ray, Henry Cotton, and Dai Rees for England; Hagen, Sarazen, Nelson, Hogan, Snead, Palmer, and Casper for the United States.

To be a member of the Ryder Cup team, you have to have been competing for at least five years, and this is the first time I've been eligible. The United States is going to take twelve men to England this year, and the players are selected on a point system. The points are based on performances from the first tournament after the 1968 PGA championship through the 1969 PGA championship. Right now, I'm eighteenth on the list, so I've got to put on a little rally if I'm going to make the team. It's always been one of my goals in golf to represent my country in the Ryder Cup matches; next to winning the Masters or the U.S. Open, I think it's the greatest thrill a professional golfer could have.

I bumped into Dave Hill in the locker room. His suspension has been lifted. He wrote a letter of apology and paid a fine and missed only one tournament. "They treated me fairly," Davy said. "I'm just glad to be back. I didn't miss the golf so much as I missed the bridge games."

Davy returned to the bridge table tonight and picked up a little change, most of it mine. Maybe if I'm losing in cards, I can start winning in golf.

April 2   I couldn't make any putts in my pro-am round today, but I hit the ball about as well as I can. When I wanted to hit a little cut shot, I hit a little cut shot, and when I wanted to hook one, I hooked one.

I think my whole game'll be coming together about the end of this week and then reach a peak when I get to Augusta.

It's difficult for me to remember that I'm playing in Greensboro because almost everything seems to set off thoughts of the Masters. I noticed today that Bert Yancey, who missed the cut in Miami last week, withdrew from the pro-am here. I know what's happened to Bert. He's gone into his annual pre-Masters fog.

Bert's approach to the tour is unusual, to say the least. He's pretty well off financially, so he doesn't seem to worry much about making money from week to week. Most of the year, he doesn't demonstrate any great intensity. But as soon as one of the major tournaments approaches—the Masters or the Open—Bert begins to burn. He is totally dedicated to winning one of those titles. He played in his first Masters only two years ago, and he led the field at the end of the first round. He led the field at the end of the second round. He was tied for the lead at the end of the third round. And he finished third. In 1968, in his second Masters, Bert finished third again. The same year, in the U.S. Open, Bert led the field all by himself for three rounds, then slipped to third. He's got to break through soon.

Before my round today, I chatted with Charlie Sifford, and Charlie was kind of depressed. Each year, the Masters invites the six players who—not eligible for invitations in any other way—have scored the most Masters points, which are based on performances since the preceding Masters. When Charlie won the Los Angeles Open at the start of this year, he moved up among the top six in Masters points, and an awful lot of us were rooting for Charlie Cigar to become the first Negro to be eligible for the Masters.

But since the L.A. Open, Charlie hasn't done too well, not a single top-ten finish. About the only way he can become eligible now is to win the Greater Greensboro Open, and the odds are pretty heavy against that. But Charlie did shoot a 67 today, one of the best rounds in the pro-am. I'd love to see Charlie win here, just to find out how the Masters people would react. I wonder whether they'd extend him an invitation or snub him. I won't know the answer until Charlie qualifies.

I can't wait for the Masters. For one thing, the tournament itself means so much to me, and, for another, it's the last tournament I'll play for a long time without my wife and kids around. I spoke to Patty and Danny tonight, and I told them that right after the Masters, I'm coming home for a week. Then I'm packing them all up in the station wagon—the baby, too—and setting off on the tour.

I'm looking forward to having my family with me just as much as I'm looking forward to winning the Masters.

April 3   Marty Fleckman's still having trouble with his game, and he's getting upset about his nickname—the Easter Bunny. When he went to his locker this morning, he picked up his box of golf balls, opened it up, and found, instead of balls, a dozen painted Easter eggs. Marty exploded. He didn't find the eggs amusing at all.

Lionel Hebert and Bob Charles were my playing partners today, and I couldn't ask for a better pair. Bob's both quick and quiet, and Lionel always gives me the biggest kick, watching him fit in his little shots, trying to execute every shot perfectly. Lionel works so hard on his game he always looks amazed when he makes a mechanical mistake. The other day, somebody told me he was playing with Lionel, and on a long par-three, Lionel took a two-iron, stepped up, and hit the ball so fat he tore up the turf and splattered mud all over himself. His shot was right on line, but the ball fell thirty yards short of the green. With mud dripping from him and from his two-iron, Lionel shook his head. "I just never learn to take the right club," he said.

We all played about the same game today. Lionel shot 71, Bob shot 70, and I shot 69. I played one of my better rounds from tee to green and missed eight or ten putts from twelve feet or less. It could've been a 64 or 65 easily, but I'm not too unhappy. If I can shoot me four 69s, I'll pick up a good check here.

My diet's not doing too well. I haven't had any bread or potatoes in weeks now, and still I'm up close to 195 pounds. It's frustrating. I don't know what's bothering me the most this week—my belly, my putting, or my bridge cards.

April 4   I had an early tee time today, and when I got to the course, it was cold and a little windy and raining, making it thirteen weeks in a row that we've had rain fall on our tournament site.

The rain quit soon after I teed off, and a fog set in. It was hard to see the ball off the tee and it was hard to see the ball hit the green, and I had to use more club than usual because fog has a tendency to hold a ball up.

Everything was stacked against me. I was even wearing my black shoes, and I knew that every time I'd worn them lately, I'd shot a bad round. I just plain decided that I was going to overcome both the weather and the superstition, the black skies and the black shoes, and shoot me a good round. And I did. I shot a 69, and for a real change, I putted beautifully. Hebert and Charles and I teed off on the back nine, and on the tenth hole, our first, I sank a fifteen-footer for a birdie. I figured right then I had my putting problem licked.

But then, on the next hole, I three-putted from twenty feet, and suddenly, I was lower than a snake's belly again. I'd gotten so pumped up from the birdie on ten that the three-putt on eleven had a doubly depressing effect. I felt like jumping in the lake right near the eleventh green. In other years, these things never bothered me so much. Maybe because we're playing for more money now, or maybe because I'm tired, but whatever the reason, I felt totally let down. I could've given up right there, but, instead, I gave myself a little pep talk. "The hell with it," I told myself. "I'm gonna try and regain my old attitude and get moving again."

The talk worked. I had twelve pars, three birdies, and a bogey on the next sixteen holes, sinking a fifteen-footer for one birdie and a twisting downhill four-footer to save a par. My second straight 69 brought me up into the top fifteen, only four strokes behind the leader, Dave Marr, and two strokes behind the second-place group.

When I got to the clubhouse, I saw Harry Toscano, the young boy I'd played with at the beginning of the year in the Southern Cal Open. He was wearing a cast on his right wrist. Yesterday, standing on the practice tee, Harry'd been hit by a shot hooked off the tenth tee. The ball broke his wrist, and he'll have to wear the cast for six weks. I feel sorry for Harry. Just the other day, he told me he'd changed his grip and was really starting to hit the ball. Now he's out of action for a few months, and in all likelihood, his chances for a successful career on the tour are gone.

I noticed that Bert Yancey missed the cut by a stroke today. I'm sure he doesn't mind at all. He'll probably just hustle down to Augusta and start getting used to breathing the Masters air.

I'm in a good mood tonight. I played a strong round in bad weather and in my jinx shoes. I'm over my superstition. I may even wear those black shoes next week when I'm winning the Masters.

April 5   Charlie Coody and I drove Steve Reid to the airport this morning. Steve missed the cut here, and he's heading home to spend his first week off all year with his family. He needs a good rest.

On the way back from the airport, I stopped for gas. "I'll pay for it," Coody said. He's been driving with me all week.

"Forget it," I said. "Just buy me dinner tonight."

"Hell, no," said Charlie, looking at my waistline. "I'd rather fill the car up than fill you up."

I've got to do something about that diet.

I saw in the morning paper that Charlie Sifford had a pretty rough time yesterday. He and a couple of spectators got into a shouting match—I don't know what it was all about—and they yelled things at him, like "Miss it, nigger" and "Fall down, nigger." Charlie's used to abuse—he's told me about letters he's received warning him not to enter certain tournaments or he'd be shot or his house'd be blown up—but he hit the ceiling yesterday. Charlie missed the cut and missed his last chance to qualify for the Masters this year. The strange thing about Charlie having trouble here is that Greensboro, as I recall, was the first tournament in the South to welcome him.

I'll tell you, it's easy to get a little touchy here in Greensboro. They've got three tough spots—around the seventh, sixteenth, and eighteenth holes—that are set up almost like picnic areas, and some of the fans sit there all day long, guzzling beer and eating hot dogs. It's certainly a minority who get raucous, but those few discourage a lot of players from coming to Greensboro each year.

I had my own share of problems today. Soon as I saw the rain and wind this morning, I knew it was going to be another one of those Saturdays for me. I was psyched out.

It didn't help any to be paired with Sam Snead. Sam can be pretty humorous in the clubhouse spinning his hillbilly tales, but it's no fun out on the course listening to his excuses for every shot that goes wrong, especially when he's shooting 72 and I'm on my way to a 76.

Over the past seven tournaments now, I've averaged slightly worse than 73 strokes each Saturday round. In comparison, I've averaged 69.4 strokes each Thursday round and exactly 70 each Friday round. That's a helluva difference; it's the difference between being one of the leading money-winners and being one of the pack.

Today, I three-putted the first, second, and seventh holes, then hit a shot out of bounds on the eighth and took a double-bogey, and I was finished. I parred in, but I'd dropped from the top fifteen clear out of the top fifty, and I'm just plain disgusted. I'm disgusted with the weather, I'm disgusted with the crowd that cheered every move Snead made, I'm disgusted with my putting, and most of all, I'm disgusted with myself, with all my damn excuses, all my alibis. You'd think I'd grow up and stop feeling sorry for myself. I've been told that adversity makes a man out of you, but all it's doing right now is beating the hell out of me.

April 6   When you tee off at 9:30 on a Sunday morning, like I did today, you know you're not playing well. The highest scores tee off first, and there were only four or five twosomes in front of young Jim Hardy and me.

It was rainy and windy again, and my Sunday average for the last six tournaments was 72, so I was almost psyched out again. But I concentrated on winning a decent check, and I shot my third 69 of the tournament. If my other round had been a 69—not a 76 —I would've finished in the top ten. Instead, I finished just out of the top thirty and earned something between $800 and $850.

I used one of the regular touring caddies this week, and when we finished, I paid him ninety dollars, which, for six days of work, was a little better than ten-and-three. He blew up. He said he deserved $150 or $200, and I told him to leave me alone before I got angry. I cannot understand these touring caddies. If I'd told him in advance I was going to give him ten-and-three, he'd have thought I was the greatest guy in the world, but when I end up giving him more than ten-and-three, he starts crying. Sometimes I wish we had robots carying our clubs. It'd be a lot less trouble, and probably better conversation.

The tournament ended up in a four-way tie, among Littler, Boros, Moody, and Weiskopf, and Littler won the play-off on the fifth extra hole. Gene's now won more than eighty-six thousand dollars this year—more than he's ever won in a full year before—and we've finished only a third of the tour. I'm really happy for Gene; nobody deserves success more than he does.

I was also happy to see today that Deane Beman finished in the top ten and earned enough Masters points to qualify for Augusta.

I've got my own little competition going. Besides trying to get a place on the Ryder Cup team, I'm trying to win an exemption from qualifying for the U.S. Open. The fifteen leading money-winners since the last Open automatically qualify, and right now I'm fifteenth and Arnold Palmer's sixteenth. I sure want to beat him out. If I don't, I have to go out and qualify, just like a rabbit.

As we were getting ready to leave Greensboro—I'm driving down to Augusta tonight with Tommy Aaron and Charlie Coody—Lionel Hebert was asking around the clubhouse if anybody had made a plane reservation for him.

"Hey, Liney," somebody yelled. "Just take a couple of Miller Barber's pills and you can fly down without wings or motor."

A lot of guys laughed—we're always kidding Mr. X about popping pills—but Lionel didn't. "Don't joke with me," he said. "I just finished bogey, double-bogey. I'm not in a laughing mood."

April 7 / Augusta   The azaleas are in bloom, the cherry trees are blossoming, and this little old Southern town is coming to life, just like it does every year for one week. It's hard to be depressed in this kind of setting, but I've got to admit I'm a little worried about myself.

I saw a money list today, and for the first time since San Diego, I've dropped out of the top thirty money-winners. Over my last five tournaments, I've averaged less than nine hundred dollars a tournament in official money, and if I did that poorly over a full year, over thirty or thirty-two official tournaments, I'd be right on the borderline of making the top sixty. I hate to even think of the possiblility, but if I don't wake up soon and start winning some money, I could actually lose my exemption. I don't really think that's going to happen, but I'm a worrier. Suppose I were to get hit on the wrist by a ball or twist my back or get a cyst on my ribs. Old Frank could be in bad shape.

That's enough worrying for this week. I'm just happy to be in Augusta, playing in the Masters. There's an air of excitement, almost a glamorous feeling, that I haven't felt all year.

I'm staying in a private house—Mother and Dad'll be joining me Wednesday—which is the only way to stay in Augusta. The prices here during Masters Week are ridiculous; the motels triple their normal rates, and a room can cost $250 for the week easily. We're paying less than that for two nice rooms in a private home only a few blocks from the Augusta National Golf Club.

I've got a courtesy car—almost all the contestants get them this week—and when I drove to the club this morning, I felt, as always here, like I was stepping back into the Old South. The clubhouse looks like it belongs on some big old plantation, and everything reeks with tradition.

The dominant color here is green. The official badges are green, the pins are green, the course is green, the refreshment stands are green, and the number-one green is that green coat they give to the Masters champion.

I played in my first Masters in 1965, and I was absolutely awestruck. It must've taken me three hours to move from the registration desk out to the practice tee. I walked around and stared at everything, all the different comfortable locker rooms, all the photographs of Bobby Jones and Ben Hogan and General Eisenhower, all the people I'd only heard about and read about before.

That first year, I was lucky enough to get into a practice match with Henry Picard, Ralph Guldahl, and Herman Keiser. Picard had won the Masters in 1938, Guldahl in 1939, and Keiser in 1946; and among them, with their permanent invitations, they'd played more than 160 rounds in the Masters. These were people my father had been reading about before I was born. My round with them went faster than any round I've ever played in my life, it was so fascinating. They mentioned trees that had been knocked down by lightning and mounds that had been leveled, and they kept saying things like "Now here's where I hit the shot that cost me the Masters in 1937" or "Now here's where I made the shot that won me the Masters in 1939" or "Now here's where I had a putt to beat Nelson and it just slipped off the edge." And then Picard or Guldahl would line up the same putt and stroke it again and it'd slip off the edge again, and he'd shake his head sadly.

For me, it was like participating in history. It was like being a modern big-league baseball player and batting against Walter Johnson or being a modern professional football player and tackling Red Grange. It was beautiful.

After I picked my locker this morning, I went out and found the caddy who'd been assigned to me. He told me his name was Fireball and he'd caddied for Doug Ford for about ten years at the Masters. I figured Fireball had to be either very good for Doug to use him that long, or very bad for Doug to fire him. When I played a practice round with Doug later, he told me that he'd just gotten too old for Fireball, that he didn't have a chance to win anymore, and that Fireball wanted to try his luck with a younger player.

Fireball's not too frisky himself. He's about fifty, and he's very quiet. "I learned to caddy by keeping my mouth shut, Mr. Frank," he told me. "If you don't want to ask me any questions, I'm not gonna give any answers."

"I'll put you to the test tomorrow," I said, "and see how many distances you know. If I know more than you, then I'm not going to bother you, and if you know more than me, I'm not going to bother myself. If we both know about the same thing, then we'll put our heads together and maybe we'll win this thing."

"That's just fine with me, Mr. Frank," he said.

Fireball works hard and doesn't show much emotion. I checked a couple of distances with him this afternoon, and he seemed to know what he was talking about. Maybe Fireball and I can strike up some kind of ten-year relationship.

I played my practice round with Ford, Doug Sanders, and Jerry Pittman, and even with a double-bogey, I shot a 67. I had a fistful of birdies and hit the ball pretty good. I've got no complaints at all about my game today. It's coming along right on schedule.

There's a saying in golf—"Horses for courses"—and if any course is built for me, it's this Augusta National. I'm a natural hooker, and almost all the dogleg holes here dogleg to the left. I just kind of bend my old hook around the dogleg and set myself up pretty. The fairways are nice and soft so that I can spin my irons off them. The only problem is the greens. They're holding the ball good now, but toward the end of the week, they'll get firm and I'll have some trouble holding my irons. I tend to hit the ball kind of hard into the greens.

This is absolutely one of the most beautiful golf courses in the world, but basically, it's not a very difficult course. I remember the first time I played the course, I was kind of disappointed; I'd heard so much about how hard it was to score well in the Masters, but I didn't find the course very demanding. There's no rough and no out-of-bounds, and you don't have to be Superman to reach the par-fives in two. I shot a 68 the first competitive round I ever played here, and last year, in the second round, I shot a 65, without anything higher than a four. If you brought a young boy in here and blindfolded him and didn't tell him he was playing the Masters course, he'd think it was pretty easy and shoot a good score.

The problem is that you don't play here blindfolded.

The single factor that makes this golf course difficult is the knowledge you're playing in the Masters. You start thinking about the green jacket and the past champions and the millions of people watching on television and the hundreds of photographers and reporters, and all of a sudden, you get frightened by a little creek you wouldn't even notice in a normal tournament. You start to think about how much it means, in money and in prestige, to be the Masters champion, and the fairways shrink and the greens break five or six different ways, and a tame golf course turns into a lion.

You can lick this course with your normal game—if you ever calm down enough to play your normal game.

This really ought to be an easy tournament to win. The field here, frankly, is one of the weakest we play in all year. The Masters generally starts with some eighty or ninety players, the smallest field of the year (except for a few special events, like the Tournament of Champions and the Alcan). I wouldn't mention the small field if it included the best eighty or ninety players in the world, but it doesn't. Just about half the field doesn't have any chance to win; some of the players are too old and some are amateurs and some are obscure foreign players. Of course, you do get about the twenty best players in the world—and you rarely get all of them together in any other tournament—but you don't have the kind of players who can suddenly emerge from the pack and beat anybody. For instance, Tom Shaw and Bunky Henry, who whipped all the big names in the Doral Open and the National Airlines tournament, aren't here. They didn't qualify.

It's an easy course, an easy field—and a murderous tournament.

I played a little bridge tonight at Bert Yancey's rented house, but it wasn't like our usual bridge games. We couldn't get our minds completely off the golf course. Between hands, questions kept coming up like "What do you play on eleven?" and "What do you think about the green on twelve?" You can't escape it.

Ordinarily, as I'd be getting ready to go to sleep, my mind would be on my family. But right now it's on the Masters and the golf course, and all I can think is it sure would be great to win.

April 8   When I got up this morning, I went over to Yancey's for breakfast. Bert's deep into his Masters fog now. He's got diagrams of the course and topographical charts, and he studies them every morning and every night. He spent breakfast asking me my opinions on certain difficult holes, comparing my strategy with his. Bert's obsessed, and maybe I am, too.

As I walked into the clubhouse, I ran into Gene Sarazen, and I thought to myself, "Here comes Gene. He's going to tell me about his double-eagle again."

In the 1935 Masters, Gene Sarazen hit probably the most famous shot in the history of golf. On the par-five fifteenth, he hit his second shot, a four-wood, 220 yards right into the cup. The double-eagle enabled him to finish in a tie for first place, and then he won the play-off from Craig Wood. Gene never tires of talking about that shot.

"Gonna hit any more double-eagles this year?" I asked Gene, who's in his late sixties now.

"I just hope I'll be able to walk thirty-six holes," he said, "before I miss the cut."

Gene made the cut in 1963 my rookie year, when he was *sixty-one* years old.

A lot of the former champions were strolling around in their green jackets, guys like Cary Middlecoff and Jackie Burke and Jimmy Demaret and Claude Harmon. They might as well wear the jackets here, because they can't wear them anywhere else. When you win this tournament and get a green jacket, you don't take it with you. You have to leave it on a rack in the jacket room of the Augusta clubhouse, and you can only wear it when you're here.

I played a practice round with Jerry Pittman—he doesn't play the tour full time, but he qualified for the Masters by placing seventh in the U.S. Open last year—and I worked on a few special shots, like getting across the water to the greens on the par-fives, testing my range from different spots. I played as well as I could've hoped. My whole game's starting to fall in place, and my confidence keeps growing and growing.

Later, on the practice tee, a sportswriter came up to me and asked me what a victory in the Masters would mean to Frank Beard. He wanted me to put a price tag on it. For a fellow like me, I told him, I don't suppose the Masters would mean more than $100,000 or $200,000 over the next few years. But for a guy's who really set up to take advantage of a victory, who's got a clothing line and a club line and all kinds of endorsements, it could easily be worth half a million. I'm not jealous. I'd like to win, anyway.

I hit a bag of balls, then worked on the putting green for a while. Putting's the whole key to Augusta. The greens here are contoured differently from any other golf course in the world. They have their own unique humps and bumps and slopes and valleys, and some are fast and some are slow, and you have to treat each one of them individually. The late Tony Lema used to say to me, "You can have all the drives and all the iron shots, but just let me know how to negotiate those Augusta greens, and I'll beat 'em all."

To win the Masters, you've got to make your share of putts—and somebody else's too. You've got to eliminate your three-putts and sink a few of those crazy twisting putts and you've got the course whipped. Nothing mysterious about it. Nothing tricky. Just try it.

One of the myths of Augusta is that the caddies here are the best in the world. From my experience, it just isn't true. I think most of the caddies here have never caddied in any tournament except the Masters. They try hard and they're awfully polite, but they don't have too much knowledge of the game of golf. At least my old friends, the professional touring caddies, know how to carry your clubs and clean them and stay out of your line and rake the traps.

Old Fireball, my caddy, is pretty good, at least on the basic things like toting the bag and cleaning the clubs. But I tried a few more distances on him today, and when I had to be 175 or 190 yards from the green, he said, "Just a good 150." Doug Ford had a caddy today who didn't know what shoulder to carry the bag on. I swear he never saw a golf course before this week.

This town is getting as cluttered as New York City. People are pouring in from all over—plain golf fans, equipment salesmen, promoters, con men, hustlers, and more press than you ever saw in your life. I'll tell you what the press situation's like: the reporters are asking *me* questions. You know there's a lot of competition to see Arnie and Jack and the other big boys when the reporters have to start talking to me.

April 9   Tommy Aaron and I played a practice round this morning with Charlie Coody and Lou Graham. Charlie and Lou have rented a house here in Augusta, and they're paying seven hundred dollars for the week, but they've got five people coming in from Abilene, Texas, to share the place. It'll end up costing only about a hundred dollars a person. Tommy and I decided to play a little joke on Charlie this morning.

As we were walking down the tenth fairway, Tommy said, "Charlie, did you see that message posted for you in the mail room?"

"What message?" Charlie said.

"The one from those people who were supposed to come down here," Tommy said. "They're not going to be able to make it."

Old Coody turned blue and purple, and I think he almost swallowed his tongue. The thought of him and Lou having to split seven hundred dollars just about killed him. Tommy and I couldn't stop laughing.

Charlie's at his absolute best at lunchtime here, with the free lunches they give the players. At just about every other tournament, we pay for our meals, and Charlie always asks the price of every single item and what comes with each item, and then he figures down to the last penny what's the best buy. Here, he just prances right in and orders strawberries and ice cream and cake and soup and salad and a steak sandwich. The last time Charlie had a steak sandwich was when his father took him out to lunch.

We had to clear off the course by two o'clock—in the afternoon, the course got its final grooming—so we just played the back nine today. It's the more subtle, the more demanding of the two nines, but once you learn how to play it, you can probably score better there than on the front nine. It requires patience and experience, and then you can solve it for birdies.

The tenth hole is a great golf hole, a downhill dogleg to the left that plays around 450 yards usually; it's a driver and a five-iron. The eleventh hole's often called the hardest on the course. It plays around 425 yards, and it's a slight dogleg to the left with a huge lake guarding a narrow green. It's a heartbreaker. Bruce Devlin was leading this tournament last year and on his way to the championship when he made a quadruple-bogey on the eleventh. Four strokes less, and Bruce would've won the Masters.

The twelfth hole is just a little bitty old 150-yard par-three, but for me, it may be the hardest hole in the world. The green isn't any wider than a bowling alley, and there's a creek in front that looks to me like a river. There are a couple of bunkers in back, and if you don't hit that green just right, soft and easy, forget it. If anybody's offering, I'll take three pars and a bogey on that hole right now and feel like I've gotten away with murder. Palmer once lost the Masters with a bogey on this hole and once won it with a par out of the bunker. Gary Player blasted into the cup from behind the bunkers in 1961, the year he won the Masters.

The thirteenth is a par-five, about 470 yards, but it's no problem, just a driver and a four-wood and two putts for a birdie, as long as you don't let it intimidate you. If you get scared, the creek in front of the green is sure to snatch you. The fourteenth's a routine par-four, and the fifteenth's a 500-yard par-five, with a lake to frighten you, and the sixteenth, seventeenth, and eighteenth are just good solid golf holes that'll give up birdies to the proper shots. I really don't anticipate any trouble.

After our round, I spotted Jack Nicklaus smiling and laughing, and that scared me a lot more than the course did. If Jack's ready to play, nobody can beat him on this course. If ever a course and a man were built for each other, it's Augusta and big Jack. But last year he failed to make the cut, and maybe the rest of us will be that fortunate again. Nick's got to be the favorite every time he steps on this course.

Some of the reporters who don't know too much about golf are asking all of us what score we think'll win here at Augusta. It's a ridiculous question. We don't know where the tee markers are going to be, or where the pins are going to be, or whether the wind's going to blow or whether it's going to rain, and there's no good answer. Just in the past four years, the winning scores have ranged from even par, 288, to seventeen-under, 271, which is a pretty big spread. It reminds me of the story of the old Scottish caddy who was asked one year what score would win the British Open on one of those tough English courses, and he said, "Oh, maybe three hundred. Or, if the wind blows, maybe four hundred."

I saw Roberto de Vicenzo today, and the Gay Gaucho's still smiling. He's got no bitterness toward Bob Goalby, who beat him here in the scorecard incident last year, or toward Tommy Aaron, who marked down his score wrong, or toward the Masters committee. "The rules are good," Roberto told me. "I make a mistake."

Then Roberto walked over to the pairing sheets for tomorrow, and he noticed that the sheet was marked Thursday, **April 9.**

"What is today?" Roberto asked Charlie Coody.

"I don't know," Coody said, and he turned around and asked someone else, who told him that today is Wednesday, April 9.

"But, look," said Roberto. "The pairings say tomorrow is April 9."

"It's just some kind of mistake," said Coody.

Roberto looked at Charlie very gravely and said, "The man who did that ought to be disqualified."

I'm nervous tonight. Anybody who says he isn't nervous the night before the Masters is pulling your leg. Mother and Dad are here now, and Pro's more nervous than I am. He's an addict, a real golf addict.

I still remember the night before my first Masters. I was literally shaking like a leaf.

Now I'm only shaking inside.

April 10   I've been kidding myself all week, and I'm too old for that. I've got to face up to it. I'm just not hitting the ball well.

Bruce Crampton, the Australian, and I had a ten-o'clock tee time, an ideal hour. There was no wind, no rain, just an overcast sky, an ideal day. Your depth perception is much better on an overcast day than a sunny day.

I had no excuse today, not even my putting. I didn't three-putt a single hole, and on the back nine I took only twelve putts. (I parred both eleven and twelve, the toughest holes for me.)

And, still, I shot only a 72.

I had four birdies and four bogeys, and on every bogey I just plain hit a bad shot—a bad two-iron, a bad nine-iron, and two bad drives hooked into the trees.

Crampton shot a 69. He played beautifully, and if he'd made a few putts, he'd be right out in front. Billy Casper's leading at 66, and I'm tied for about twenty-fifth. I'm three strokes behind an amateur, Bruce Fleischer, and one behind a man in his late fifties, my old friend Herman Keiser.

After my round, I went to the practice tee and worked for two hours with my father. Pro's the only person I ever go to for help, and he told me I was aiming way too far to the right. When you aim too far to the right, you have to pull over the top of the ball to get it back on target, and this accentuates a normal hook. Pro got me to aim more at the target, and before we finished, I was hitting the ball well. He thinks he's got me straightened out, and I think so, too. I hope I'm not kidding myself again.

I played scared today, and when you play scared, you get a scared score—a 72. I didn't take my own advice. The only way to win at Augusta, I've been telling myself, is to forget that you're playing at Augusta. But when I stepped on that first tee today, all I could think was this is the Masters. I was almost shaking.

I played bridge tonight with Bert Yancey and his wife and

father-in-law, and we didn't even mention golf. Bert shot a 69 today, so he's in good position, and he's not looking for any more advice, especially not from somebody who shot a 72.

I'm not quitting. I'm ready to go out and shoot a 65 tomorrow, just like I did in the second round last year.

April 11   On the practice tee this morning, I was fantastic. I tried opening up my stance and realigning myself the way Pro said I should, and I could do nothing wrong. "It's gonna be a Frank Beard day," I told my father.

Once I left the practice tee, it was a Frank Beard day all right, the kind I've been having all year. I got to the first tee and my playing partner, Tommy Horton, a young British Ryder Cupper, was nowhere in sight. The officials looked for him and paged him, and I got fidgety and more fidgety waiting. Finally, about ten minutes late, Horton showed up. The tournament committee asked him if he'd had any problem getting to the course or if he'd been delayed for any good reason, and he said no, he just lost track of time in the clubhouse. He was penalized two strokes, which he felt was fair.

When we finally teed off, I got off to a decent start. I three-putted the fifth hole for a bogey, but it was no disgrace. The pin was tucked away in an inaccessible corner. Then, on the sixth hole, I hit a seven-iron, landed about eighteen inches short of the cup, and rolled up to within one inch of a hole-in-one. It was the closest I'd ever come to an ace in competition.

I finished the front nine even-par for the round and for the tournament. I parred the tenth hole with a fantastic chip shot out from under some trees, and then I faced the two killer holes. On eleven, I hit a big drive, then took a two-iron and just stroked it perfect. It may have been the best golf shot I've executed in three years, the perfect swing, the perfect trajectory. "Frank," I told myself, watching the ball sail at the flag, "you just can't hit a shot that good."

I was right.

The ball landed just six inches short of the green, which is built into a little knoll, and instead of bouncing up and toward the cup, it rolled back down into the lake. I took a double-bogey. Then I missed a two-footer on twelve, and I was three over par.

Old Frank kept plugging away. On the long thirteenth, I hooked my drive around the bend, then knocked a four-iron onto the green, and just lipped out a putt for an eagle. They give out beautiful glassware here for eagles and for aces, and I'd come within an inch twice.

I came in with a 74 for 146, and 148 made the cut. Forty-seven golfers survived the cut, including Herman Keiser. Casper and Bruce Devlin tied for the lead at 137, so, realistically, trailing by nine strokes, with almost thirty people in front of me, I know it's pretty difficult for me to win this tournament. But I won't give up until someone's in the clubhouse Sunday afternoon with a score lower than mine. If I shoot a pair of 66s or 67s, I could still pull this thing out.

If I can't win, I want to make sure I finish in the top twenty-four. Everybody in the top twenty-four comes back next year, and it's the easiest way to earn an invitation. I've finished in the top twenty-four three of the four previous times I've played here.

Just after I finished, I saw Bob Goalby, and while he wasn't too happy with his game—he'd made the cut at 146, too—he was elated by the way the gallery's been treating him. He's been getting standing ovations at every green and every tee.

In all the other tournaments since the Masters last year, Bob's taken a lot of razzing and even some booing from the fans, but he told me the fans here have made up for everything. He said he almost cried on one green yesterday when the crowd gave him a standing ovation for five full minutes. It made him feel, for the first time all year, like he really was the defending Masters champion.

When I got back to the house tonight, I called Patty and told her how close I'd come to winning her some glassware. She just about had a heart attack hearing about it. Well, maybe I can win her something tomorrow.

April 12   The first person I saw in the clubhouse today was Johnny Owens, my accountant from Louisville. He'd come to see the Masters, and he'd happened to bring my tax returns with him.

He showed me the forms and I found out that my taxes for 1968 were a whole lot less than I'd anticipated. It was the perfect way to start the day.

Then I went to the mail room and found a beautiful letter:

Dear Mr. Beard:
I'm very sorry that you won the Masters last year the way you did. Everybody is calling you a cheesecake champion, but I've followed you for many years and I know you are a true champion. You would have won a play-off last year. I hope you win again this year. Good luck.

A fan of yours

It sure is good to have a real fan.

I shot a 70 today and moved back into the top twenty. I played the best round I've had in a long time, and I could've shot 66 or 67 easily. But any time you birdie both the eleventh and twelfth holes —with putts of twenty feet and ten feet—you've got no right to complain.

My playing parner, Takaaki Kono from Japan, shot 68, and if he'd made a few putts, he'd have shot 62 or 63. He's one of the best foreign players I've ever seen, and all I can say is thank God he's playing in Japan and not here or he'd be taking a big bite out of our purse money.

Casper's leading at eight-under, one stroke in front of George Archer and two ahead of Tom Weiskopf and Miller Barber. I don't think anyone's going to catch Billy, but the one with the best chance is Weiskopf. He's young and strong, and he's got the kind of game where he could shoot a 66 or 67 on this course and overtake Billy.

After I finished, I did some of the color on the CBS radio broadcast. I did a pretty good job for a rookie. When I'm too old to walk around the course, in two or three years, I'd like to get into radio and television work.

I saw Palmer in the clubhouse and asked him if he were going to play in the Tournament of Champions next week and in the Byron Nelson Classic the following week. I'm fifteenth on the money list since the last U.S. Open, and Arnie's sixteenth, only $4,500 behind me. The top fifteen are exempt from qualifying for the Open.

"Why don't you just skip the Tournament of Champions and the

Either those kids surrounding me collect rare autographs or they couldn't find Arnie. My bunker game showed startling improvement in 1969, but my putting didn't always make me happy. When you're snake bite, you're snake bite.

It's easy to spot my wife on the golf course.
She's always the one walking next to me in the maternity dress.
Patty must have a great sense of humor to be able to smile
when we're traveling the tour with Jennifer, Randi, and Danny.

WIDE WORLD PHOTOS

Growing up in Dallas, I played football (I'm just to the left of No. 11) and baseball (third from the left in the front row), and my sports hero was my brother, Ralph, an All-American basketball player. But I ended up playing golf, with lessons from the Pro, my father, and smiles from Mom.

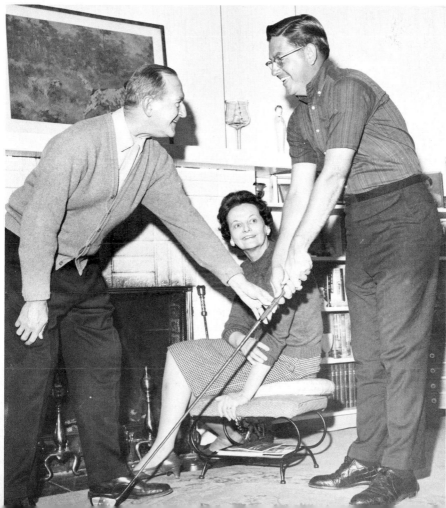

Louisville COURIER-JOURNAL and TIMES

My game always has been, and always will be, based on tempo . . .

...the ability to swing smoothly and within myself, not to rush.

Dave Hill: my rival for the money

Charlie Sifford: Charlie Cigar

Lee Trevino: Smiling Super Mex

Billy Casper: usually calm

When I wasn't rooming with Patty in 1969,
I usually roomed with Charlie Coody (top, saving the
expense of a new ball) or Steve Reid (below, celebrating his
first tour victory). I hardly ever saw
Jack Nicklaus and Arnold Palmer, except on the golf course.

I had some thoughts about winning the U.S. Open in 1969,
but while I faltered, the Old Sarge, Orville Moody
(top, refusing a chance to re-enlist),
overtook Super X, Miller Barber (below, making his sign).

*You can't tell whether I hit a good shot or not
by my face or Ben Hogan's. I don't show much emotion on the course,
but next to Ben, I'm a regular carnival. In my opinion,
Hogan's the best golfer of all time. Tom Weiskopf,
in the background, is going to be one of the great ones.*

The stakes sure went up in ten years from the time I won a cup in a local Louisville tournament. I can't quite figure out why I look happier with the cup than the check. That's my mother with me when I was nineteen. I don't know who those other girls are.

WESTCHESTER GOLF CLASSIC

Frank Beard

FIFTY THOUSAND

Nelson?" I said. "If you go on home, they'll give you an invitation to the Open, anyway."

Arnie laughed. "I'll show up for those two," he said. "I don't want to have to qualify any more than you do."

You'd think the king'd take it easy on me once in a while. Somebody ought to give old Frank a break.

April 13   I played with an American today—first time all week—my old college friend, Tommy Aaron. Tommy had himself a good day, shot a 70, and moved up into the top ten.

I figured I needed a 72 or 73 to finish in the top twenty-four, which was all I was really aiming for, and after I got through five holes, I was two over par and talking to myself. "C'mon, Frank," I said. "It's going to be a lot easier to try on these last thirteen holes than to try for the next eight or ten months to qualify for the 1970 Masters. You want to work for the next two hours or you want to give up now?"

My answer was to birdie the eighth and tenth holes and come through fourteen at even par. Then, on, fifteen, a birdie hole, I knocked my second shot over the green and into a lake and wound up taking a bogey. I parred the next two holes; then, on eighteen, stroked my first putt eight feet past the hole and missed coming back.

I staggered in with a 74 for 290, the highest total I'd had for seventy-two holes all year. I was ready to shoot myself because I thought for sure I'd blown my chance to make the top twenty-four. I walked into the scorers' tent and up to Joe Black, a PGA official.

"What's gonna make it?" I said.

"You're in," Joe said. "Even if everybody still out on the course comes in under 290, you're in the top twenty-four."

I was ecstatic. Qualifying again for the Masters was all I cared about at that point. As it turned out, I finished in a tie for the nineteenth through twenty-third places, so that even if I'd shot one stroke higher, I would've made the top twenty-four.

Jack Nicklaus came in at 291, a stroke behind me. He's in trouble.

Since his victory in San Diego two months ago, Jack's won only thirteen thousand dollars. For anybody else, that'd be great, but for Jack, it won't hardly pay for fishing bait.

The scores were high today—Masters pressure. Don January shot an incredible 66, and Trevino and Beman shot 69s, but they were the only ones under 70 all day. In the first three rounds, there'd been twenty-one rounds under 70, an average of seven a day.

I worked on the CBS radio broadcast, and I got more excited about the finish than I did about my own play. About the time I finished my round, I heard that Charlie Coody had sunk an eagle putt on the thirteenth hole to move into first place, three-under for the day and eight-under for the tournament. Casper had just about ruined his chances with an unbelievable 40 on the front nine.

I was really rooting for Charlie, and after he bogeyed fourteen and birdied fifteen, I thought he had the tournament won. He was one shot ahead of everybody with three holes to play, and as thing developed, if he'd just parred the last three holes, he would've won the Masters and the green coat and everything that goes with it.

I don't know exactly what happened to Charlie—I haven't had a chance to talk to him—but he must've been feeling tremendous pressure. You just don't get into a position like that and not feel pressure.

The only time Charlie ever won a tour event was five years ago,

Frank Beard's Record

TOURNAMENT	1ST ROUND	2ND ROUND	3RD ROUND	4TH ROUND
Greensboro	69	69	76	69
Masters	72	74	70	74

the Dallas Open, and he hadn't even finished in the top three in any full tournament in more than a year. Poor Charlie bogeyed sixteen, bogeyed seventeen, and bogeyed eighteen. He was through. He finished fifth, one stroke behind Casper, Weiskopf, and George Knudson, two strokes behind George Archer.

I was happy to see George win—he's one of the exceptional players on the tour—but not as happy as I'd have been if Charlie had won. If old Charlie had won the Masters, he might even have bought me a steak sandwich next week.

I couldn't get a plane out of Augusta that'd make connections into Louisville tonight, so I'm going to drive home with Mother and Dad. I feel badly about letting them down and letting Patty down. Pro said I looked like I was playing in a stupor today. I guess I'm just overgolfed.

The first major tournament of the year is over, and I sure didn't do much. I'm really wondering about my golf game. I picked up a couple of thousand dollars here, official money, so my official earnings for the year are now around twelve thousand dollars, and my total earnings are just a little under twenty thousand. I'm probably somewhere around fortieth on the official list.

I've always been a slow starter—I've never won a tournament played earlier in the year than the Masters—but this is ridiculous.

What's wrong with me? Why can't I get the ball in the hole?

TOTAL SCORE	FINISH	PRO-AM EARNINGS	INDIVIDUAL EARNINGS
283	T 31	—	$ 819.20
290	T 19	—	2,100.00

5

How to
Two-putt from
Eighteen Inches

TOURNAMENT	SITE	PURSE	DATES
Tournament of Champions	La Costa Country Club, Rancho La Costa, California	$150,000	April 17– April 20
Byron Nelson Classic	Preston Trail Golf Club, Dallas	100,000	April 24– April 27
Greater New Orleans Open	Lakewood Country Club, New Orleans	100,000	May 1– May 4
Texas Open	Pecan Valley Country Club, San Antonio	100,000	May 8– May 11
Colonial National	Colonial Country Club, Fort Worth	100,000	May 15– May 18

April 18 / Louisville   After a few quiet days at home, just paying my bills and talking my semiannual physical—the doctor told
me I'm fine except for one thing; I didn't really need him to tell me
I'm too fat—Pro and Patty sat me down and gave me a little talking
to. "You can play a lot better than you've been playing," Pro said.

"Frank," Patty said, "you can be the best golfer in the world.
You can be number one if you just try."

Pro and Patty both felt that I'm not setting my goals high enough,
that I'm not pushing myself, that I'm content just to make a good
check each week. They're both on my side—I know that—but they
were saying that I've been too lazy, that I haven't worked hard
enough.

I'm going to give it a try. I'm going to practice more than I've
ever practiced before. I'm setting myself new goals.

But I don't know about number one. I don't know if I can aim
that high.

April 20 / Dallas   I backed our two-year-old station wagon up to the door of our home in Louisville yesterday morning and loaded up. I dumped my golf bag in the well, then stacked five suitcases across the back—one for me, one for Patty, one for Danny, one for Randi, and a little one for Jennifer. I tossed in my shoes, a bag of toys, a bassinet, a box of Pampers, a few bottles of Enfamil, some road maps, and a bag of sandwiches, cookies, and candy, and Cokes. Then we spread out a blanket in the back for Danny and Randi to play on, piled all the children into the car, and took off for the glamorous life of the golf tour.

As we pulled out of our driveway, I turned to Patty and said, "Could you imagine Arnie or Jack traveling like this?"

They probably flew over us in their private planes on the way to Dallas.

We drove all day yesterday and all day today, looking like a jungle safari, and sounding like one, too, with the children screaming and crying. I felt like screaming a few times, too. I'll never forget the time in Canada, the night before the opening round of a tournament, Danny was up all night with a fever, crying and fussing. Finally, I went into the bathroom, spread a blanket out in the tub, and tried to sleep there. I ended up sleeping on the bathroom floor.

It's no picnic, traveling with the family, but traveling without them is worse. Just to be able to get a hug from Danny every night and a kiss from Randi is worth all the crying and the trouble.

I'm sitting in our motel room in Dallas right now, and it looks like a junk shop. There are clothes all over the place and suitcases and books and diapers and irons and everything else. I suppose we'd be a little more comfortable if I took two motel rooms, but I just can't see wasting that money.

April 21   First thing this morning, I looked at the newspaper to see how Arnie did in the Tournament of Champions. He stuck it to me. He finished strong, tied for third place and won ten thousand dollars. Now he's almost five thousand ahead of me in our race for the final exemption for the U.S. Open, and the only way I can possibly overtake him is by finishing in the top three here in the Byron Nelson Classic. I'm going to give it a run, but I'm not overconfident. I haven't placed in the top three in any tournament in almost nine months.

After breakfast, I went out to the Preston Trail Golf Club, one of the best and most beautiful courses we'll play all year, and I ran into Charlie Coody and his wife, Lynette. I told Charlie how hard I was pulling for him to win the Masters.

"I had it all locked up," he said. "All I had to do was finish and it was mine." Charlie shook his head.

"You gave it a good try," I said.

"Next time I get in a position like that," Charlie said, "I hope I'll be able to handle it a little better."

Charlie seemed a little downhearted, but he didn't look like he was going to cut his throat or anything. Then he went in to register, and I talked with Lynette, and she told me Charlie really took it a lot harder than he was showing. "It just wasn't like him," Lynette said. "He looked and acted as if he'd been horsewhipped. I never saw him like that before. I almost wish he'd never had a taste of the chance to win. I know he's man enough to throw it off, but right now he wakes up every morning with a little scar on his face, and I can't help but see it."

"He'll snap out of it," I said. "Charlie's a great fellow, and he knows now that he can win a big one. He came so close this time. The next time, he'll handle it all right."

I went and hit three buckets of balls, a lot more than I usually hit, then played a practice round with Crawdaddy, Hound Dog, and the Garbage Man—Dick Crawford, Gay Brewer, and Jack McCowan. Everybody calls Gay "Hound Dog"; his facial features do kind of resemble an old bloodhound. Gay's a Kentucky boy with a hillbilly twang; when he sounds like he's saying he hit a "foreign," he's actually saying he hit a four-iron. Jack McGowan's been trying the tour on and off for almost ten years, and although he's won about $120,000 in the past five years, he's won only one regular tour event. He's called the Garbage Man, I've been told, because once, in a tournament several years ago, his ball landed in a trash pile, and he just went in there and flailed away, scattering trash everywhere.

After my round, I put in about half an hour on my putting. I think I've figured out what I've been doing wrong lately. When I'm putting well, I keep my hands on a line perpendicular to the line of the putt; that gives me a smooth pendulum stroke. But recently I've slipped into a crouch, which brings my hands closer to my body and spoils the perpendicular line. I hope I've got that straightened out. I'd like to start sinking a few putts.

April 22   I can't remember the last time I dreamed about golf— or anything else, for that matter—but this morning I woke up with a nightmare. In my dream, I couldn't make a putt. I couldn't get the ball to the hole. I don't know why. I was hitting them straight. I wasn't flubbing them. But the ball wouldn't go in the hole. It was the worst dream I've ever had in my life.

I guess my putting's bothering me more than I'll admit—and I'll admit it's bothering me plenty.

April 23   I've got a local youngster caddying for me here, a wonderful boy, just the type I always look for, polite, punctual, and neat. There's just one thing wrong: he doesn't know anything about caddying. I've got to explain the fundamentals to him.

Every time I get a caddy who doesn't quite know what he's doing, I'm reminded of the caddy I had one year in Palm Springs. He wasn't only incompetent; he was drunk every minute. I was on him all the time, telling him what to do. Midway through the third round, he fired me. I didn't fire *him*; he fired *me*. "I'm one helluva caddy," he said, "and nobody can talk to me the way you've been talking to me. Just give me my money. I'm through."

I was so startled I paid him off. And I still had nine holes to go. Father Jack Jones from Louisville had come out to watch the tournament, and he walked over to me and said, "If it's not against the rules, what if I caddy for you?"

"You don't want to do that," I said.

"Sure I do," he said. Father Jones is an absolute golf nut.

"Okay," I said. "We've just got nine holes to go, so throw them over your shoulder."

"Just give me a minute," Father Jones said.

The next thing I knew, Father Jones had run over to the caddy yard and started asking some of the old-timers about the finer points of caddying. Then he soaked a towel and came out to the tenth tee and cleaned off all my clubs. "Let's go," he said. "I'm ready now."

We went nine holes together, and Father Jones took it as serious as anything he'd ever done. You'd have thought he was saying Mass he was so serious out there on the golf course.

I don't have Father Jones to rescue me this week, so I'll have to put up with the boy I've got. Sometimes I think I ought to take back all the harsh things I've said about the touring caddies. At least they know their job.

I may have to take back all the things I've said about the pro-ams, too. I had three pretty good partners today, and besides having fun, we shot twelve-under as a team and I shot 71 on my own ball. Our team finished first, which meant four hundred dollars for me, and I tied for fourth in the individual competition, which meant another $250. I've won close to five thousand dollars in the pro-ams this year, so I think I'd better start looking forward to Wednesdays instead of dreading them. In fact, if you figure it out per hole, I think I'm earning more money in the pro-ams this year than I'm earning in the tournaments.

April 24   I spent the day today with two good friends, Steve Reid and Jack Montgomery. We're all staying at the same motel, so we ate breakfast together, drove to the course together, and played the opening round together.

I'm really happy to see Jack back on the tour so soon after his rib operation. When he went home for the operation late in February, we heard that he wouldn't be able to play for at least three months. I was afraid that he wouldn't have a chance to make the top sixty, that he'd lose the exemption he worked so hard to earn last year.

But Jack's back now, earlier than anyone expected, and he's got the perfect attitude. "I'm not going to worry about a few bad shots or missing a couple of cuts," he told me. "Anything I win in the next six weeks is pure gravy. I didn't think I'd be earning a penny before June."

Jack got pretty tired today, but you can't have major surgery and lay off walking that five or six miles we walk every day and not get tired. He hit the ball well and came in with a 73, which is no disgrace on this course. I think Jack's going to get himself back up into that top sixty and become one of the really outstanding players on the tour.

Steve didn't play at all well today. He's just going to have to give up any thoughts of ever making any money on the tour till he learns to control his temper. And I mean really control it, not just hold it in, but throw it out and divorce it from his entire system. He shot 75 today, and his temper must've cost him at least three or four shots. I've been lecturing him about his temper for years, but he's like an alcoholic; he can't kick the habit.

The thing that kills me is that Steve works so hard on his golf game, harder than most people work on anything in their whole lives. He won about $3,500 in the Tournament of Champions last week and moved up into the top sixty, but he's at a real danger point now. The one-year exemption he got for winning the 1968 Azalea Open ran out this week, so from now on, Steve's got to begin qualifying again. That's going to make it that much tougher for him to make the top sixty.

It's not just the pressure of qualifying itself that's so bad; once you do qualify, you've got to gear your game toward making the cut so that you won't have to qualify the following week. In the first two rounds, while the other guys can aim for the flag and think about birdies, you've got to be more cautious and think about pars. In those first two rounds, if you're not exempt, you know a bogey's going to hurt you more than it'd hurt a guy who doesn't have to worry about qualifying.

The last person I saw before I teed off today was Arnold Palmer. By coincidence, he drew a starting time for today and tomorrow right behind mine. As I walked to the first tee, Arnie gave me a look and one of his majestic grins, like he was saying, "Well, buddy, did I put it to you last week at the Tournament of Champions? I'm down here to beat you out of that U.S. Open spot."

We played the back nine first, and the crucial hole for me was the second one I faced, the eleventh, a par-three with water running along the right side of the green. I decided early this week that I was going to gamble a little and go after holes like this instead of shying away from them. I got up on the tee and I knew that if my swing didn't come off just right, I was going to smack the ball into the water. It was a psychological challenge. I aimed right at the edge of the water, and my shot held the line and came up eight feet from the cup. I knocked it in for a deuce.

For sixteen holes, I was two under par, but then I lost my concentration and finished bogey-bogey for an even-par 70. Arnie came in a few minutes later with a 69.

The king doesn't let up.

April 25   The wind blew up like crazy this morning, and I thought, "Oh, God, here I go, down the drain again." But when I sank a twenty-five-foot putt for a birdie on the second hole, I stopped worrying so much about the wind. Then I holed a twenty-footer for a birdie on six, and after bogeying the eighth hole for the second straight round, sank a ten-footer for a birdie on thirteen, which put me two-under for the day.

Old Arnie was playing right behind me, and I kept turning around and giving him the evil eye. He couldn't see my face, but I was sort of saying to myself, "Stick that in your kilt, Palmer." I knew that every time I sank a putt, he had to see it and groan and moan a little.

On fourteen, I must've been thinking about Arnie, and I went to sleep. After blasting out of a bunker, I missed a three-footer and took a bogey. But I came right back and sank a five-footer for a birdie on fifteen and a four-footer for a birdie on sixteen, then parred in for a 67, my lowest score since Phoenix, more than two months ago. I couldn't be much happier with my putting, and my bunker play's getting better and better.

I'm three-under for the tournament and tied for the lead—with Bruce Devlin and Bert Greene, the powerful young boy I played with in Miami—and, even better, I'm seven strokes ahead of the king. Arnie shot a 75 today; I guess he didn't have much fun watching my birdies.

One of my two playing partners was happy today, and the other was Steve Reid. Jack Montgomery kept calm all day and came up with a fantastic chip shot on eighteen to make the cut right on the button at 148. But Steve blew his top again. He three-putted a couple of times, lost all control of himself, came in with a 77, and missed the cut. Now he's got to start qualifying all over again. I don't know when he's going to learn.

After my round, I went into the press tent. The press really wanted to be talking to Arnie about his troubles or to Trevino, who's just two strokes off the lead, but they had to give me a little time today, just to ask me the form questions, where I got my birdies and what I hit and things like that. While I was talking, they were straining their necks looking for Arnie or Lee.

As I came out of the press tent, a television reporter walked up to me and said, "Come on over. We want to do a little interview with you. We're just going to do ten minutes with Arnie and then we'll take you."

"Stick it in your kilt, buddy," I said. "If you've got Arnie, you don't need me."

I didn't really say that, but I thought about saying it. I was upset, and I did give the television man a look that meant, "If you want the leader of the tournament, you can have me now, or you don't get me at all."

I know I shouldn't act like that, but I can't help it. Sometimes I get sick and tired of playing second fiddle to Arnie and Jack and all the other big boys.

April 26   Just before I teed off today, Orville Moody came over and congratulated me on my 67 yesterday. "You beat me by four strokes," Orville said. "You're the new wind man."

I laughed. "Not yet, Sarge," I said. "Just give me a few lessons, and I'll be right up there with you."

The wind blew up again today, but I was more worried about my old Saturday jinx than about the weather. I had a lot going for me today. One of my younger sisters, Judy, a nun who teaches school down here, walked the full eighteen with me. Some of the spectators must've been wondering what a nun was doing at a golf tournament, but my sister really knows the game. Judy started playing golf when she was a junior in high school in Louisville, and by the time she was a senior, she was shooting regularly in the 70s from the men's tees. She gave up the game right after high school when she went into the convent, but I'll bet she could still give me a good match. (My one other sister, Marianne, is a nun, too. She got her master's degree at twenty-two and her doctorate at twenty-three and now heads up the science department of a university in the Congo.)

I picked up a couple of quick birdies today and moved two strokes ahead of the field, then faltered and shot a couple of bogeys to slip back to even-par after twelve holes. I parred in from there for a 70, but I should've shot a 67. I had birdie putts of six feet, three feet, and four feet on the fourteenth, fifteenth, and sixteenth holes, and I missed all three.

My playing partner today, Bob Charles, moved into a tie for first place. He shot a 67 to go four-under for the tournament, a stroke ahead of me. I'm absolutely convinced that Bob is the most under-rated player in the world today. I never cease to be amazed by how straight and accurate he is, what a wonderful short game he has, what a great putter and great thinker he is. We must've shook up a few people when we went into the scorers' tent after our round. I played right-handed and signed my scorecard left-handed, my natural way. Bob played left-handed and signed his scoreboard right-handed, his natural way. I sure don't blame him for switching over to playing left-handed; he's got the whole market locked up on endorsing left-handed clubs.

As far as I'm concerned, Bob's the man to beat tomorrow. He's tied with Lee Trevino, who also had a 67 today. I paid another visit to the press tent today, and when I got there, Lee was up in front of all the reporters. I squeezed in next to him, and Lee looked at me and said, "What are you doing here, Beard? I'm not finished talking yet."

"I know, Lee," I said, "but I've got to get home in three hours."

Lee gave me a hurt look, and I said, "Trevino, why didn't you take off this week? You won yourself seventeen thousand dollars last week in the Tournament of Champions. Why didn't you go home and rest?"

"My wife's got a broken wrist," Lee said, "we got a ten-week-old baby, and our dog's pregnant. I came out here to rest."

I saw that Arnie shot a 69 today, so he's three-over for the tournament, six strokes behind me. He's somewhere around tenth place, and if he moves up a couple of notches tomorrow, he'll win about three thousand dollars. He's not making it easy for me. I've got to come in first or second to be sure of beating him out.

I don't feel too tense tonight. I don't have the pressure of leading the tournament, just the pressure of having to finish high and beat Arnie. My body's tired, but my mind's relaxed. I want to win tomorrow, but if I don't, at least I know now that my game's good enough to win.

And I'm confident of one thing. With Charles and Trevino at four-under, Bruce Devlin and me at three-under, Bruce Crampton at two-under, and nobody else under par, I've got a helluva chance of coming in low North American.

April 27   When I got up this morning, the big stud pro golfer with a shot at winning the Byron Nelson Classic, I started stuffing toys and suitcases and diapers into the station wagon, jamming everything in. I swear we had more stuff than when we started the week. I don't know whether we buy or it just materializes. I checked us out and paid the motel bill, which came to about $175, not too bad for two adults and three children for seven days.

Patty dropped me at the course, then dropped the kids at a nursery so that she could walk the course with me. I had a whole fan club today. On the putting green, both Terry Dill and Charlie Sifford came over and offered me putting lessons. They'd watched me miss a couple of key putts on television yesterday, and they were just trying to be helpful, trying to give me a little tip as to what I'd been doing wrong in case I hadn't caught it myself. They wanted to show me they were pulling for me.

On my way to the first tee, a young fellow, twenty-two or twenty-three years old, wearing a Coca-Cola driver's uniform, ran up to me and said, "Mr. Beard, could I bother you just for a second?"

"I'm kind of in a hurry," I said, "but what can I do for you?"

"Well," he said, "I was watching you practice, and whenever you hit your bad ones, your body was getting out in front of your hands and your hands were falling way behind it and it gave you kind of a whiplash. If you'd just slow your body down a little bit and let your hands catch up, you'd eliminate all those bad shots. Just stop lagging your hands behind your body."

I was absolutely stupefied. I thought I was supposed to be the professional, and here was a young kid in a Coca-Cola uniform telling me how to hit the ball just before I teed off in the final round of the Byron Nelson Classic. I couldn't believe it.

I played with Lee Trevino, the first time we've been paired all year, and before we teed off, somebody asked Lee if he'd gone to church this morning. "No," Lee said. "I don't believe in going to church. But if I keep putting the way I've been putting lately, Kermit Zarley's going to have him a convert. He's going to have me going to his Tuesday-night Bible classes."

On the fourth hole, after three pars, I missed a thirty-inch putt—just two and a half feet—and took a bogey. I got mad as hell at myself. "Now, c'mon, Beard," I told myself. "Let's play some golf."

I started hitting some unbelievable shots, but just like in my dream the other night, I couldn't get the ball in the hole. On the fifth hole, I had a six-foot putt for a birdie. On the sixth, I had a ten-footer for a birdie. On the seventh, I had a four-footer for a birdie. And on the ninth, I had another ten-footer for a birdie. I missed every single one of them. I wasn't getting to the hole. It had rained this morning, and they hadn't been able to cut the greens, and I think it threw everybody just a little off.

After nine holes, I had a 36, one over par, and I was in front of Trevino, who shot a 39. It's really fun playing with Lee, and I envy him his easygoing attitude, but sometimes I think if he'd be just a little more serious and spend a little less time gabbing with the gallery and concentrate on his shots instead, he might be one of the best players to come along in a long time. But you never can tell. Every man's different, and I guess if Walter Hagen had been a clean liver, no drinking and no partying, he might never have broken 80.

I started on the back nine even with Bob Charles, but two strokes behind Bruce Devlin, who'd shot a 34 going out. On the twelfth hole, looking for a birdie, I gambled on my drive and just caught the edge of the left-hand rough. I found my ball in one of the worst lies I've had all year. It looked like somebody had done a war dance there and had left a big heel print. I messed up the shot. I took a bogey and fell three strokes behind Devlin.

Then, on the thirteenth, I missed a ten-foot birdie putt. On the fifteenth, a long par-five, I chipped my third shot up eighteen inches from the cup, practically a tap-in. But I didn't get careless. I lined the putt up, hit the ball exactly where I was looking—and missed. The ball hit in the hole, bounced out, and sat there, sticking out its tongue at me. I had to settle for a par. I was still one-under for the tournament, still three shots behind Devlin, and then, playing right in front of me, Bruce bogeyed the sixteenth. He almost didn't get away with only a bogey. His drive landed right under a tree, and he had to straddle the ball and hit it back out through his legs into the fairway.

By then, Trevino and Charles had shot themselves out of contention, and Devlin was sharing first place, at three-under, with Bruce Crampton, who'd birdied four out of five holes through the sixteenth. I was two strokes behind. If I'd made that eighteen-inch putt, I'd have only been one stroke back.

I didn't quit. I parred sixteen—Trevino hooked his drive into the boondocks and hollered, "There it goes, heading for Marlboro country"—and then sank a six-foot putt for a birdie on seventeen.

Crampton bogeyed the eighteenth hole, and I drew even with him. Then, standing in the fairway after my drive, I watched Devlin sink an eight-foot putt to save his par. I knew I needed a birdie to tie him. Just as I reached for my club, I saw Palmer's jet fly overhead. He'd finished with a 69 for 282, tied for eighth place, which was worth close to three thousand dollars in prize money. He wasn't even staying around to see whether I beat him out or not. It must've been my imagination, but I felt he was kind of razzing me with his jet.

I took a three-iron and I didn't hit it too well. I came up about thirty feet short of the hole.

I knew I had to make the thirty-footer to tie Devlin. I studied the green, then stepped up and hit the ball right on line. I thought

I'd hit it hard enough, but I hadn't been able to gauge the greens all day. I stopped five feet short. Devlin had the championship, his first tournament victory in three years, his first since he'd changed his style of play.

Suddenly, before I could even feel let down, a bunch of thoughts started going through my mind. If I missed my putt, I'd fall out of a tie for second place with Crampton, I'd give up about four thousand dollars, and I wouldn't win enough money to beat Arnie out of that U.S. Open spot. My whole week would've been wasted.

I was facing the same kind of putt I'd been missing all day. I didn't spend much time fiddling over it. I lined it up, hit it good and firm, and watched it roll right into the hole. I finished two-under, tied for second place, won $9,250, and—by a margin of about $1,200—beat old Arnie out of the Open exemption.

I guess I just wasn't aggressive enough to win the whole tournament today, and I suppose I should feel disappointed. Hell, if I'd made that eighteen-inch putt on fifteen, I'd have forced Devlin into a play-off.

But I feel great. I feel better than I've felt on a Sunday night all year. I accomplished every goal I set for myself this week—playing good golf and beating out Arnie—except winning. I worked hard all week, and I'm going to work doubly hard next week.

I'll tell you, I'm going to win a tournament sometime in the next three weeks. You can mark that down as a cinch.

April 28 / New Orleans   Our five-hundred-mile ride to New Orleans today was a three-ring circus. We had pee stops and Coke stops and gas stops and food stops, and screaming and yelling, and I told Patty that all she needs to really enjoy life on tour is another hand.

We're staying with some friends here—a couple named Derbes and Louise Brandon—and even though I don't ordinarily like to stay with people during a tournament, this ought to work out perfectly. The Brandons are lovely people—they won't bug me about golf —and their children will sort of keep an eye on ours. Besides, it never hurts to save a few bucks when you get a chance.

I ought to pick up a few bucks, too, playing here. The last three years in the New Orleans Open, I've finished first, third, and seventh and collected about thirty thousand dollars.

I've got only one complaint with New Orleans: with all the great restaurants, I know my diet's going to hell—if it isn't there already.

April 29   I spent most of the morning getting a haircut, dropping off the laundry, and picking things up at the drugstore. You've got to do these things on tour, unless you've got a personal valet, like Doug Sanders used to have. But Frank Beard is Frank Beard's valet.

When I got out to the course, I swear it was just like being on the girls' golf tour. They're always hugging and kissing each other when they win a tournament, and today people were patting me on the back and congratulating me for finishing second in Dallas as if I'd had a baby or something. It was no big thing; for God's sakes, what we're supposed to do is play well.

A bunch of the pros were all excited about me knocking Arnie out of the Open exemption, and there's a lot of speculation about whether or not he's going to try to qualify. I really can't quite figure out why the guys seem so tickled about me beating Palmer. It's not that they dislike Arnie; I guess it's just that everybody likes to see the king get knocked on his earlobe once in a while.

I've got to admit I'm feeling kind of cocky this week. I've got my confidence back, the feeling that all I have to do is show up and play my game and I'll go home with a big check. I'm getting back in my old rut, my two- or three-thousand-dollar-a-week rut. I'll tell you, it's a nice rut to be in.

April 30   Billy Maxwell came up to me this morning and asked me if I'd play in an exhibition on June 9, the Monday before the U.S. Open. He offered me a thousand-dollar guarantee, which is good money, but I told him no. I'm starting to point toward the

Open now. That's my next target, the next major tournament, and I want to spend that Monday in Houston, polishing my game for the Open.

We're always kidding Billy about his temper, and I suppose he's been fined and suspended for his language as much as anybody on the tour. He told me a story today about a tournament in Texas several years ago when he got fined two hundred dollars for using obscenity during the first round. When he showed up for the second round, Jimmy Demaret was standing on the tee wearing red ear-muffs. "Your language is too much for my delicate ears," Demaret said.

I went out and played my pro-am round with three nice guys, and even though we were twelve-under, we didn't win anything as a team. But I shot a 66 on my own ball, tied for first in the individual competition, and earned about $450. I'm really starting to enjoy Wednesdays.

My putting on the first nine today was just plain incredible. I sank four birdie putts from twenty feet and another one from eight feet and came in with a 31. My putting touch disappeared on the last nine, but it didn't bother me. I'm ready. I'm not going to be patty-caking it this week. I'm going out and winning this tournament. Starting tomorrow, I'm charging.

May 1 Old Frank Beard turned thirty today, and I went out and gave myself a 67 for a birthday present. I'm not leading the tournament—Kermit Zarley and Lee Elder shot 66s—but I'm right up there, the way an old stud tour veteran should be.

I felt kind of ancient teeing off because I read in the paper this morning that Jack Nicklaus said his age was catching up to him. Jack is twenty-nine years old. He started playing the pro tour a year ahead of me, but, really, he's been just like a professional golfer for fifteen years. He started playing in all the national amateur tournaments when he was a teen-ager, while us old country boys were playing in high-school events.

Old Jack shot a 74 today. Maybe his age is catching up to him.

My round was not a Frank Beard round at all, not like yesterday when I had twelve pars and six birdies. Today, I let it all out and gambled and scrambled and shot myself only eight pars, one eagle, six birdies, and three bogeys. I sank ten-foot, twelve-foot, and twenty-foot putts for birdies, and a twenty-five-footer for my eagle. I should've come in with a 66, but I went and three-putted the last hole, missing a little old two-footer for my par.

It's just about two years now since I won a tournament, and I've got a feeling the drought is over. I'm happy to see Zarley and Elder doing well. Kermit's been struggling this year; he's been on a weight-lifting kick and he thinks now that it's hurt his game. Lee's in a little slump, too, but he's the heir apparent to Charlie Sifford as the finest Negro golfer on the tour. I like them both, but they better look out for old Frank.

I'm feeling good about everything. I've got me a touring caddy here, a fellow named Alec, and he's very intelligent and very capable. Maybe I've been a little narrow-minded about the touring caddies; maybe I haven't given them enough credit. After my experience with that local boy in Dallas last week, maybe I'm ready for a real professional caddy. One time today, I was caught between hitting a real big nine-iron or a little eight-iron, and even though I'd kind of made up my mind to hit the nine, I turned to my caddy and asked him, "What do you think?"

"Well," he said, "I like the nine, but you really got to hit it."

He knows my game. He knows my thinking. He may make me change my whole philosophy about touring caddies.

I'l say one thing for the touring caddies; they're a lot smarter than some of the sportswriters. One of the local sports editors is waging a real war against George Archer. George is the defending champion in the New Orleans Open, but he's not playing this week. He sent word that he burned his hand on a cigarette and got a blister and can't swing a club. This sports editor said today that even if Archer really is hurt—and he doubted it—George had a moral obligation to come down here and watch the tournament because he's the defending champion and the new Masters champion.

I never heard anything so ridiculous in my life as expecting a man to travel three thousand miles from his home in California just to watch a golf tournament. Some of those writers are beyond belief.

Only one thing puzzles me a little: George doesn't smoke.

May 2   I had a late tee time today, but Patty saw to it that I didn't waste the morning. She had me chasing around town looking for diapers and baby milk and picking up the laundry, and then she pushed me into buying some new slacks. I got ten pairs, and as far as I'm concerned, that'll last me forever. But I know that six months from now Patty'll be yelling at me again to buy some more. I guess I do have a responsibility to look halfway decent, but it just seems like wasted cash to me.

By the time I got to tee off, the early starters had come in, and I looked at a scoreboard and saw that Davy Hill was leading at nine under par. I set myself a goal of ten-under. I don't usually watch anybody else's score, but I did today, and I got right to work on beating Davy. I started on the back nine and birdied the tenth hole with a thirty-footer and the eleventh hole with a fifteen-footer. On the thirteenth, I came within two feet of a hole-in-one and knocked that in for my third birdie in four holes.

I finished the round with thirteen pars and five birdies for my second straight 67. I'm ten-under for the tournament, one stroke ahead of Dave Hill. For the first time this year, I'm all alone in first place after two rounds of a tournament.

The cut came at 143, one-under, and seventy-seven golfers are still in the competition, all within nine strokes of me. The list of players who missed the cut was pretty impressive, including Jack Nicklaus, Doug Sanders, Bruce Crampton, Tom Weiskopf, Charlie Coody, Ken Still, and Bert Yancey. I bumped into Bert afterward, and he wasn't at all concerned about missing the cut. As far as he's concerned, if we played just four tournaments a year—the Open, the Masters, the PGA, and the British Open—he'd be happy.

Patty and I had dinner tonight at a local convent with a few nuns and Father John Moore, the priest who married us back in October, 1965. Father Moore's a great golfer and a great friend of mine, and every time we're in New Orleans, we get together with him.

I'm ready to charge again tomorrow. To hell with pars and trying to play conservatively. I'm going to go out and shoot me another 67.

May 3   I played today with a fellow named Jack Harden, a club pro from Houston who just slipped into the tournament as an alternate when George Archer withdrew. Harden shot 68 and 67 the first two rounds and tied Dave Hill for second place.

He'd never been in contention in any tournament before, and naturally, he was just as nervous as could be today. He stepped up and bogeyed the first three holes and took himself right out of contention. Then he settled down and finished with a 74, two-over, but he'd lost any chance of winning the tournament.

If I was ever going to run away with a tournament, I should have done it today. I must've had ten makable putts for birdies, and I missed six of them. What hurt even worse was that I missed an eighteen-inch putt for a par on the fourth hole. It was nothing more than a little tap-in, but I marked my ball, cleaned it off, looked at it from all four angles, took my stance, and just as I drew back my putter, the crowd around the sixth green, which is right behind the fourth green, let out a big roar. I almost jumped. I missed the entire hole. I didn't even touch the corner.

I came in with a 69 and now I'm tied for first place with Dave Hill, who shot a 68. We're both thirteen under par and three strokes ahead of the rest of the field. Davy's been in kind of a slump lately. He won about twenty-two thousand dollars the first two months of the year, but in the past two months—with his suspension and a disqualification and some minor ailments—he's won only three thousand dollars. With my second-place finish at Dallas last week, I passed Davy on the money list for the first time all year.

Davy's a good friend of mine, and an excellent player, and I hope he breaks out of his slump—any time after tomorrow.

I'm nervous tonight, nervous because I'm so close to winning a tournament. I feel like a hungry man getting ready to dig into a thick steak. Winning a tournament means so much. It's twenty thousand dollars in the bank and twenty thousand on the money list, and it's a lot more than that. It opens up so many doors. It gets me into the Tournament of Champions. It gives Bill Boone a great deal more leverage than he has now trying to set up endorsements and exhibitions for me.

I want to win so bad I can taste it. I wonder if fellows like Palmer and Nicklaus and Casper, who've won so many tournaments, get this feeling when they're close to winning another championship. For somebody like me—I've won only six tournaments in my career—it's like a kid waiting for a new toy at Christmas.

I'm kind of pooped physically, and I hope I'll be able to channel my nervousness tomorrow and use it as an asset, use it to make the adrenaline flow a little. I've been under the pressure of leading or being close to leading for seven straight rounds of competition now, and it's wearing me down some.

Well, this is when I find out whether or not I'm made of championship fiber.

May 4   How the hell can a man finish second two weeks in a row on this tour and be anything but happy?

And that's just what I am tonight—anything but happy.

I still don't believe what happened today. I still don't believe I could have given away a tournament like I did today. I played just as well as I can play the first three rounds here, and today I played even better. And I lost. I gave it away. I don't want to believe it.

I was nervous this morning, as nervous as I've ever been in my life, but I was determined, too. I told Patty I was going to go out and win this thing today. She believed me. I believed me, too.

The first five holes, I picked up routine pars—down the middle, on the green, two putts. The sixth hole, a par-five, I got on in two and two-putted for a birdie. Then I parred the next three holes, two-putting from twelve to fifteen feet each time, and I made the turn at one-under for the day, fourteen-under for the tournament.

Dave Hill was second, still at thirteen-under, and Larry Hinson had moved up to third. Hinson's the young boy I played with at Orlando two months ago, the boy whose left arm is shorter than his right as the result of polio. Larry started today at eight-under, but by the time I'd finished nine holes, he'd finished thirteen and he was twelve-under for the tournament.

On the tenth hole, I hit a good drive down the middle of the fairway, and—I feel like a man describing his own execution—when I reached the ball, I found it sitting in a little hole full of clover. It was worse than being in the rough. I was 175 yards from the green, and I had absolutely no idea what the ball would do when I hit it. I guessed that the ball would fly out of the clover, so I took a six-iron. I usually hit a six-iron about 160 yards, so I figured that even if the ball flew, I'd come up a bit short of the pin, in good position. I hit the ball right toward the stick—right at the stick—right over the stick. I went way over the green, almost into a creek behind the green. I'd hit the six-iron at least 190 yards, and it just about broke my heart. I wedged back up and left myself an eight-foot putt for my par. The putt stopped on the lip. I had a bogey, and I'd lost my one-stroke lead. I almost got sick to my stomach.

I made up my mind I wasn't going to quit without a fight. On the next hole, a long par-five, I sank an eight-footer for a birdie, and then I parred five holes in a row, all regulation two-putts from fifteen to twenty feet. I was back in front. I was fourteen-under, and Larry Hinson was in the clubhouse at thirteen-under. Dave Hill had slipped to eleven-under, and he was out of contention.

All I had to do was par the last two holes, and I had my first tournament victory in two years. I was a cinch. I'd bogeyed only one of my previous fifty-two holes.

I took a three-iron on the seventeenth, a par-three, and instead of going for the pin, which was on the left, I favored the center of the green. I wasn't going to get greedy and go for a birdie; I was willing to settle for a par. You get the same money if you win by five strokes or by one. I made the green and left myself a long putt, maybe forty or fifty feet. I stroked it just right. The ball hit the hole dead in the center, jumped out, and rolled eighteen inches behind the cup. I marked my ball, replaced it, lined it up from every angle, took my stance, took my grip, took my time, didn't hurry it, didn't jump at it, didn't try to steal anything, and the next thing I knew, the ball was past the hole. I'd missed.

I wanted to jump in my car and leave. I didn't want to play the last hole.

On the eighteenth, I faced a pretty tough hole, a hard-driving hole that I'd bogeyed on Thursday. I hit a real good drive. Then I couldn't make up my mind whether to hit a six-iron or a seven. Finally, I took the seven. I blanked the flag out all the way and came up fifteen feet short, not quite enough club. Still, I didn't feel too bad. I was almost certain to get down in two, and I had a shot at making the putt to win the tournament. I hit probably the best putt I've hit in two years. It caught the inside of the cup on the left, caromed to the back, and popped out two inches behind the hole.

I tapped in my two-incher, and Larry Hinson, whose caddy wore number one on his back all week, and Frank Beard, whose caddy wore number thirteen, went back to the fifteenth hole—for the benefit of the TV cameras that were set up there—and started a play-off.

I'd been in a play-off only once before—against Lee Elder and Jack Nicklaus in Akron last year—and I'd lost out quickly. But I wasn't nervous today. I was dejected. I kept telling myself that I shouldn't be in a play-off, that I should have won the thing outright.

On the fifteenth, a par-five, Hinson hit his drive into the rough, then caught a tree with his second shot and bounced off into the rough again, behind a pair of cypress trees. He looked like he was dead, but he sliced his third shot onto the green and two-putted for a par without ever touching the fairway. I'd birdied the hole Thursday and Saturday, but I hacked my way to a par, too.

We both got routine pars on the sixteenth, then moved to the seventeenth, where I'd three-putted only an hour earlier. Larry put his tee shot on the edge of the green, about twenty feet from the pin. I hooked my shot onto the fringe, about twenty-five feet from the pin. I hit first, trying to chip the ball in, and I was a little strong. My ball rolled four or five feet past the cup. Hinson putted up to within a foot of the cup, a tap-in.

That was it. I missed my putt, he made his, and it was all over. I handed the tournament to Larry Hinson on a silver platter, a gift from Frank Beard.

The only way I could possibly lose today was to give it away, and I did it. I had everything going for me—good course, good weather, even a good caddy (I paid him $350 for the week)—and

I blew it. I've got no excuses. Judging from the past two weeks, the biggest weakness in my game right now is eighteen-inch putts.

As bad as I feel, I can't help thinking that if I had to lose, I couldn't lose to a better fellow than Larry Hinson. He's a dedicated, determined, clean-cut young man, just the kind of boy I like to see winning on the tour. He's only twenty-four, and he's been on the tour for exactly a year now. He won more money today than he'd won in the whole past year.

Patty and I had the saddest dinner tonight. We stopped on the way home from the course—the kids were with a baby-sitter—and we sat alone, just the two of us. I didn't have anything to say. I couldn't get out of my depression. You just don't get many streaks like I've had in the past two weeks. You just don't get that many chances to win tournaments. It made me sick the way I'd wasted my chances.

Patty tried to cheer me up. She talked about our kids, about how lucky we've been, about how we've got our health and money in the bank. "There's always next week," she said.

Next week seems a long way away tonight.

May 5 / San Antonio   It was a long, long trip from New Orleans, long in miles and longer because of what happened yesterday. I believe it was one of the worst things that ever happened to me. I can't think about anything else. I can't think about the Texas Open this week or about the U.S. Open next month. All I keep seeing in my head is that damn putt I missed on the seventeenth green.

The one other thing I think about is eating. During the drive here, we had to stop two or three times just to fill up my big fat stomach. It seems the worse I play, the more I eat. It must be some kind of complex, like I'm trying to punish myself.

My diet's gone to hell. I'm up to two hundred pounds. I've just plain given up.

If I can't discipline myself on a small thing like food, how the hell can I ever control myself on the golf course?

May 6   All the guys were teasing me today about blowing the tournament in New Orleans, about the old man giving it away to the kid. Some people were sympathetic, and some pointed at my stomach. Frank Boynton came up to me and said, "Frank, I thought I saw the money list in the paper this morning, and you were first. I made a mistake. It wasn't our money list. It was a list of corporate earnings for the last five years."

Boynton said the leading corporation had earned about twenty-nine billion dollars in five years, so, naturally, he thought he was looking at my winnings.

I felt a lot better today than I did yesterday. I felt better, I guess, because I got a look at the real money list for the golf tour. Old Frank can stop worrying about making the top sixty. I'm in right now if I don't play another tournament all year. With the $11,400 I earned for finishing second in New Orleans, I've won about thirty-three thousand dollars in official money this year. On the total money list, including pro-ams and unofficial tournaments like the Hope and the Crosby, I'm over forty-one thousand dollars and I'm up to fourteenth place, the highest I've been all year. I'm only thirty dollars behind the thirteenth man, Ray Floyd, and only ten thousand dollars behind the fifth man, Billy Casper. If I have a good week here, I can shoot into the top ten easily.

As I was leaving the course today, after playing a practice round with Boynton, Deane Beman, and Steve Reid (who skipped New Orleans last week and had to qualify here), I saw Larry Hinson. Larry is bubbling over, just as I knew he'd be. The real enjoyment of that first tour victory comes during the following week. All kinds of people are going to be congratulating him all week, and fans are going to be asking him for his autograph for the first time, and sportswriters are going to be writing nice stories about him. I don't know how the fuss'll affect his golf game, but I know this'll probably be one of the most pleasant weeks of his life.

I'm happy for Larry, and I'm a little jealous.

May 7 Before the pro-am today, I saw Don Massengale on the practice tee, and it just about broke my heart to see the way he's striking the ball. He hasn't won more than a few thousand dollars all year, and he just doesn't have a chance of getting up into the top sixty. I can't understand what's happened to his game. Three years ago, he won two big tournaments—the Crosby and the Canadian Open—and now he's only thirty-two years old, and he looks like he's finished. He's not making enough money out here to pay expenses. I'm afraid he's going to have to go look for a job.

My pro-am string finally ran out—no team money and no individual money—but I had a good excuse. One of my amateurs owns a go-go place here in town, and he had three of his employees following him around. I don't know whether they were dancers or waitresses or what, but they were wearing the tightest slacks I ever saw. It looked like we had three *Playboy* playmates-of-the-month chasing our foursome. I think I lost a little concentration.

I got away from the course early and hustled back to our motel. This place is really a pro's paradise. Half the families on the tour must be staying here. We've got kitchenettes and a play area for the kids and a swimming pool, and all the guys have been out playing with their kids, tossing a football around, and all the wives have been out, too, tossing the gossip around. They like to keep close tabs on the husbands whose wives aren't here this week.

We had a little accident tonight. Danny slipped off the slide that runs into the swimming pool and fell about ten feet and hit the cement and got a big lump on his head, a lump on his arm, and some scratches. Fortunately, he was wearing one of those foam life preservers, and that kind of cushioned his fall. He seems to be all right, but, just to be safe, we're taking him to see a doctor in the morning.

Sometimes I wonder what I'm doing, making my family lead this kind of touring life. A year ago, Danny came down with the mumps one day, and we had to drive several hundred miles that day for me to get to the next tournament on time. When we finally reached our motel and hunted up a doctor, Danny was running a 105- or 106-degree fever. He was a sick little boy.

Why am I out here on this tour?

I don't know. I know I don't feel like playing golf this week.

May 8   I took Danny to the doctor this morning, and he's going to be fine as soon as his bruises heal. If he hadn't been wearing that life preserver when he fell, the doctor said, he might have killed himself. I can't wait till I give up this touring life.

By the time I got to the course, shortly before noon, it was raining and hailing so hard that the tournament committee had canceled play for the day. I was happy. I need a little rest.

Charlie Coody, Dick Crawford, Jack Montgomery, and I and our wives all went over to Shakey's and had us some pizza for lunch. Then we went back to the motel and spent the afternoon playing cards.

I got to talking with Coody, and poor Charlie hasn't gotten over the Masters yet. "Just can't get it off my mind," he told me. "I had it. I was so sure I was going to win I was thinking about who I had to call back home in Abilene. I was even thinking about who I ought to get to represent me for business deals. I had it all locked up. The only thing I forgot to do was go ahead and win."

After the rest today, I feel like playing golf tomorrow. I got to pick up a little money here to knock off some of the room rent and some of the food bills and some of my wife's big-time hairdressing bills.

May 9   No matter how you add it up, no matter what the course or what the conditions, this is a putting contest out here. It's not who plays the best or thinks the best or gets the most breaks who wins the big money. It's the fellow who makes the most putts.

And I made the least today. I hit sixteen greens in regulation and, every time, I had a putt of twenty feet or less for my birdie. I missed fourteen of those putts; I made one from twenty feet and one from six inches. On the two greens I missed, I chipped up and had six-foot putts for my pars and blew both of them. I finished at even-par, 71.

From tee to green, I'm hitting the ball better than I ever have in my life. I feel like I can win any tournament anywhere. That lesson my father gave me at the Masters has really paid off. Pro hit the nail right on the head. I'm aiming more at the target these days and hitting down on the ball instead of hitting over it, and everything's working out just perfectly.

I'm getting plenty of lessons this week—in the mail. I guess there must've been millions of people watching television who saw me miss those short putts in Dallas and in New Orleans, and a lot of them have written to me, offering me little tips. According to the letters, I'm either crouching too low or standing too straight, bringing the putter back too slow or too fast. I suppose some of the people are right, but I can't figure out which ones. I like getting that television exposure, but I wish it had been a little more favorable.

I had a late tee time today, so before my round, I took it a little easy and chatted with a bunch of the guys. Doug Sanders asked me for a putting lesson. He was using three different putters on the practice green, and maybe four different grips and six different strokes. He is never going to make another putt if he doesn't stop fooling around. He used to have one of the best putting strokes on the tour, but now his confidence is shot. I tried to get him to go back to his old stance today, but either he disagreed with me or he couldn't remember the old stance. Poor Doug hasn't done a thing all year, and I'm really afraid he's in deep trouble. I hate to see it.

On the practice tee, I watched Jack McGowan hitting, and I swear the Garbage Man has got to be one of the most underrated pros on the tour. He didn't really start playing the tour till he was in his thirties, and he's almost forty now, and the press doesn't pay any attention to him, and the public doesn't, but the golfers know him. He can really strike the ball, a fantastic player who can break out and win a tournament anytime.

Orville Moody played early today, and he came up to me just before I teed off and told me he'd shot a 74. "The ol' weather fouled me up," Sarge said.

It was an absolutely beautiful day, no rain, no clouds, no wind, just the kind of weather Orville hates.

Steve Reid finished early, too, and he came in with a 67. His score held up all day, and he's leading the tournament. If he can just hold on to his temper, maybe Steve can win some money here and get himself a solid position in the top sixty.

In the clubhouse, I saw that one of the PGA officials had posted the standings for both the Ryder Cup team and the Vardon Trophy. After my two strong weeks, I'm up to ninth place in Ryder points, and with a few more decent finishes, I'll wrap up a place on the American team. In the Vardon rankings, I'm running fifth among all the pros, averaging exactly 71 strokes a round. Gene Littler's the leader at 70.23. Last year, with an average of 70.66, I finished second behind Billy Casper.

Tonight, the Coodys, the Crawfords, the Montgomerys, and the Beards went out for a fancy Mexican dinner aboard a boat cruising along one of the canals running through San Antonio. It was a nice change of pace, a pleasant, relaxing evening with no mention of golf.

I guess life on the tour isn't all bad.

May 10   One of those beautiful sportswriters really took off on me this morning. He wrote about how the professional golfers are all stuck on themselves and refuse to cooperate with the press, and he listed me and Tom Weiskopf and Lee Trevino and Jackie Burke as special offenders. He thought he was being humorous, talking about how we'd only answer questions if our attorneys were present, but I didn't find it very funny. He said that he didn't need Burke for stories anyway, that Jackie was too old to be recognized by anybody. I think if Burke gets his hands on the guy, he'll kill him.

I know we need the press out here, but sometimes they get a little carried away. They can't seem to make up their minds whether they're God or Arnie is.

When I got to the course, I ran into Charlie Sifford, and old Charlie was dressed in the greenest outfit you ever saw, from green socks right up through a green hat, everything but the cigar. "Charlie," I said, "where the hell did you get that outfit?"

"Don't you know I'm Irish?" he said.

The PGA announced this morning that it had pulled twenty-seven Approved Tournament Player cards. The ATP cards are held by players—not Class A members of the PGA—who qualified at the PGA school; the cards are subject to review every six months. If you haven't maintained a fairly respectable scoring average and won a few checks and played in enough tournaments, you lose your card, and you're not eligible to play in any more tournaments unless you go through the school again or bide your time and become a Class A member. I looked at the list of the twenty-seven who lost their cards today, and to be perfectly blunt, they all deserved to lose their cards. They have not done a thing out here. Personally, I feel that many, many more cards should be pulled. There are just too many players out here who are wasting their time and their sponsors' money, taking up places that might be filled by a young fellow who could become a good golfer. We've got to work something out soon, or every Monday we're going to have three or four hundred guys trying to qualify for five spots in the tournament. We'll end up scaring away some potentially good players.

For the second day in a row, I couldn't sink a putt. I shot 72, one over par, and with 143 after two rounds, I'm tied for something like twenty-fifth place, six strokes behind the leaders. Doug Sanders is one of the three guys tied for the lead; all I have to do is write a fellow off, and he starts playing great golf. Steve Reid shot even-par today, and he's just one stroke off the pace.

I've got mixed feelings about my own game. I'm happy with the way I'm playing and unhappy with the way I'm scoring. This is a game of streaks and cycles, and when you're on a hot streak, you have to capitalize on it. Because sure as hell it's not going to last forever.

May 11 / Mexico City   I got up at five o'clock this morning and played thirty-six holes of golf in San Antonio, and now I'm in Mexico City. Sometimes I wish I'd gone into accounting. Then I look at my bankbook and I say to myself, "No, I don't."

We had to play thirty-six holes today because of the rain-out

Thursday—there was a commitment to televise the final round today—and I'm glad we got it out of the way. The day after tomorrow, I'm playing Lee Trevino and Julius Boros here in Mexico City in the first round of the 1970 Shell Wonderful World of Golf. If we hadn't wrapped up the Texas Open today, I would've had to fly to Mexico City tomorrow and play the Shell show without a practice round; I don't like to do that when there's a lot of money at stake.

I kissed Patty and the kids good-bye this morning—Dick Crawford's wife, Diane, is going to drive with Patty from San Antonio to Fort Worth tomorrow—and got a lift to the golf course from Al Balding, a Canadian who was one of the most consistent money-winners on the tour ten years ago. Then he came up with the golfer's disease, some kind of back trouble.

As much as he hated to, Al gave up the tour and took a couple of club jobs, one for the summer and one for the winter. About a year ago, he had an operation on his back, and afterward he felt he was swinging better than ever. He decided to quit both of his jobs and go back on the tour at the age of about forty-five. He was giving up a lot of security for a big gamble, but his wife and his family backed him up one hundred percent. They knew he'd been unhappy off the tour. "I'll tell you, Frank," Al said today, "no matter how I do out here, I'm happier than I've been in a long time." He was like a kid with a new toy; it's hard to get this tour out of your system.

I played with Trevino in San Antonio today, and, I swear, he is an absolute nut. He went around all day chatting with the crowd, laughing, smiling, and at the same time, shooting a 67 and a 68, moving up from about twentieth into a tie for third. I don't know how he does it; if I started gabbing like Lee, I'd shoot 100. He's a phenomenon.

Lee was telling me today about the luckiest shot he ever hit in his life—a shank, an absolutely atrocious shank on the last hole of the last round of the Houston Champions International last year.

"How the hell can a shank be a lucky shot?" I said.

"Well," Lee said, "de Vicenzo and I were tied for the lead going to the last hole, and Roberto was on in two when I shanked my second shot. He got a par and I got a bogey. I saved myself about a million dollars."

I figured Lee was setting up some kind of joke.

"You see," he said, dead serious, "there was a guy waiting to sign me up for a bunch of endorsements if I won the tournament. He would've tied me up for years at pretty low rates. But when I lost, he didn't sign me. The next week, I won the U.S. Open, and that's been worth a million dollars to me."

Lee made the day pretty enjoyable, and my golf game wasn't too bad. Actually, I could've made a fantastic move today, right up into the top ten, if I hadn't fallen apart on four holes.

During the morning round, after fourteen holes, I was three under par, heading for a 68. Then I bogeyed, parred, and bogeyed, and came to the last hole only one under par. I reached the green in two, maybe thirty feet from the hole, and I hit a miserable first putt. I went ten feet past the cup. Then I left my second putt six inches short.

I walked up, and I didn't exactly backhand the ball. I just kind of tried to drag it to the hole. My putter hit behind the ball and barely moved it maybe an nich. I ended up *four-putting* for a six. I never did anything like that before in my life. I've always preached against carelessness. I've criticized people for signing the wrong score and backhanding two-inch putts and all that plain dumb stuff. And then I turned around and did the most stupid possible thing today. As things turned out, it didn't cost me too much money, thank goodness, but it hurt me plenty to think that I did something I've been crusading against all my life. It was like Billy Graham going out and committing a sin.

I wound up with a 72 in the morning, then shot a 69 in the afternoon, and finished in the top twenty-five. I earned between eight and nine hundred dollars, which is better than nothing. In the afternoon round, I played exceptionally well, even though I did manage to come up with one of my new specialties: on the fourth hole, I missed an eighteen-inch putt.

I stayed around the course long enough to see the finish, and for a minute I though I was watching a replay of myself. Jack McGowan came to the eighteenth hole with a one-stroke lead over Deane Beman. All the Garbage Man had to do was sink an eighteen-inch putt, and he'd win his first tournament in five years. He missed.

He was so hot with himself you could have cooked an egg on his head.

On the first play-off hole, Deane sank a twenty-foot putt for a birdie and won his first professional title. I felt as happy for Deane as I felt sad for Jack. When Deane came out on the professional tour two years ago, after ten years as an outstanding amateur golfer, I really didn't think he was going to make it. I thought he was a little too short off the tee, and I thought he was a little too cocky. I was wrong. Deane just worked and worked and worked and made himself into a fine tour golfer.

Tommy Aaron, Dave Hill, and Trevino tied for third place, and Steve Reid, with two steady rounds of 70 today, tied for sixth and won about $3,500. Doug Sanders came in right behind him.

Trevino and I took off for Mexico City together, and during the plane ride, Lee found himself a couple of rich-looking Mexicans. They asked him why he was going to Mexico City, and he said he was Lee Trevino and he was going to play a golf match. They'd never heard of Lee, but they said that if he wanted a match, they knew a pretty good player they'd be willing to bet on, for about ten thousand dollars.

Lee's eyes got as big as half-dollars. "You're on," he said.

"No checks," they said. "It's got to be cash."

"Hey, I'll find the cash," Lee said.

Finally, a stewardess or somebody told the two Mexicans who Lee was, and they backed out of the match. Lee almost had himself two beautiful pigeons.

May 12   I've got to be the world's worst tourist. Once I leave the United States, I'm lost. I'm just spoiled, I guess. I love Mexican food in Houston, but I can't stand it in Mexico City; and I've heard so many stories about people getting the *turista,* I'm afraid to drink the water. I'm living on Cokes. At least they're bottled and they're clean.

Well, nobody forced me to come here. I just couldn't pass up all the money. Shell puts up for its show. The winner of this opening match among Trevino, Boros, and me gets seven thousand dollars, the second man gets five thousand, and the third man gets three thousand. The winner's also guaranteed another seven thousand dollars for his next match, the semifinal match, even if he loses.

I guess it's worth coming down here, but I can't wait to get back to the United States and turn on the tap and get myself a little drinking water.

May 13 / Houston   Before we teed off in Mexico City today, Lee Trevino told Boros and me that he felt sick, that he had caught some kind of virus. Even Lee had to laugh: Old Super Mex was the only one of us who'd come down with the *turista*.

We started the match, and Lee's pains kept getting worse and worse. As we were walking down the seventh fairway, he just about passed out. The Shell people had to stop the match and bring Lee back to the clubhouse and send him to the hospital. He had some kind of food poisoning.

After about an hour's delay, Julius and I played out the match alone. It was pretty dull until the eighteenth hole, and then I knocked in a seven-footer for a par and beat Julie by a stroke.

Both of us wanted to make the four-o'clock plane to Dallas, and because of the delay when Lee got sick, we knew we were cutting it tight. We got a Mexican driver to take us from the course to the airport, and he never went under a hundred miles an hour. We reached the airport exactly at four o'clock. The plane was still on the ground, but the gate was closed, and the airport people wouldn't open it for us.

Julius and I checked around and found out there were no more flights to Dallas today, but we could get an evening flight into Houston, then a morning flight out of there to Dallas. We had several hours to kill, so while we sat around the Mexico City airport and ate dinner and had a few drinks, I finally got to know Julius. I'd always thought of him as being reserved and not having much to do with anybody but his close friends, but he really took me in tow and started telling me stories about the old days on the tour. Julius has been on the pro tour for twenty years, and after his first year, he's never been out of the top fifty money-winners. I really had a good time talking with him. And I couldn't help thinking that in 1952, about the time I first picked up a golf club, Julius Boros won the U.S. Open.

May 14 / Fort Worth   Boros and I flew into Dallas this morning, then drove over to Fort Worth. I stopped to see the family— I hated being away from them for even two days—then hurried over to the Colonial Country Club for the pro-am.

I'm ready to take back everything bad I've said about pro-ams. My foursome's gallery this week even topped last week's go-go dancers. One of my partners was a young guy, and all his friends came out, and all their girl friends came with them. They looked like college girls, and they wore tight leotards and short-shorts, and I'll tell you, Wednesday is getting to be sight-seeing day for me.

I even won a couple of hundred dollars with a fourth-place finish in the team competition and a 69 on my own ball. A 69 for me on this course is just incredible. I think I've consistently scored higher here than on any other course in the world, including Akron and Flint and the U.S. Open courses. Last year, I shot 72, 78, 70, and 79 here, a total of 299, my highest score of the whole year.

There's no good reason I should have so much trouble here, unless it's because this is where I saw a big golf tournament for the first time. In 1952, when we were living in Dallas, Pro brought me over to the Colonial Invitational. I'd just turned thirteen, and the holes looked much bigger then, much more fearsome. I was awed watching Hogan and Snead and Demaret and Mangrum, and it kind of shocks me that now I'm playing the same course as a professional against some of the same fellows I watched seventeen years ago. In fact, I'm paired tomorrow with Tommy Bolt, who finished third here in 1952.

During the round today, rain held up play for a while. We went into the locker room during the delay, and Palmer and Nicklaus and a few others were sitting around, shooting the bull. Arnie looked at me and said, "Hi, Frank, how you doing?"

It was the first time I'd seen him since all the publicity about me beating him out of the Open exemption. I looked at him kind of sheepishly, he looked at me the same way, and a couple of reporters eyed both of us pretty carefully. I think they thought we were going to draw guns. It was a funny confrontation.

This tournament is one of the favorites among the players because we get treated like kings here. The tournament people set up nurseries for our kids. They make motel reservations for us. And they let us sign for all the free meals we want. Charlie Coody's probably going over to the clubhouse for eight meals a day.

I'm going home after this tournament. I'm pooped, Patty's pooped, and the kids are pooped. I was so tired last week in San Antonio that I didn't spend more than ten minutes a day on the practice tee. I probably won't practice much here, either. I'm overgolfed again.

May 15 It turned out to be a typical Frank Beard day at the Colonial Country Club today. I shot 73 and I was never in the ball game. I guess I've shot 73 a thousand times here, and I had to scramble to make my 73 today. I can't say whether my putting was good or bad, because I almost never got myself in position to putt for a birdie. I think I was chipping more than I was putting.

I played with Tommy Bolt, who is twenty-one years older than me, who turned professional when I was seven, and he beat me by two strokes. He is unbelievable. He keeps groaning about the "flippy-wristed college kids" who are making all the money on the tour, but Bolt may still be, at fifty-one, one of the two or three finest strokers of the ball we have on the tour. He's so smooth.

It was a pleasure to play with Tommy, partly to watch him and partly to listen to him. He's called "Thunder" Bolt and "Terrible Tommy" and "Tempestuous Tommy," all in honor of his famous temper, and there's one story about him that's probably been told more than any other golf story. Supposedly, in the middle of a round one day, Tommy turned to his caddy and said, "What do you think I ought to hit?"

"A three-iron," the caddy said.

"A three-iron!" Bolt said. "My God, son, I can see that it's only 130 yards from here to the green. How the hell can you say it's a three-iron?"

"Because," said the caddy, "that's all you've got left in your bag."

Tommy's past his club-breaking and club-throwing days now, but he still puts on a good show for the gallery. He's the Ted Williams of golf. When the crowds razz him, he sticks his tongue out at them, yells at them, and cusses at them. He carries on a running war with the press, too. "Sportswriters can't even get your age right when you're old," he told me today. "Three, four years ago, a fellow wrote in the papers that I was forty-nine. I was forty-eight, and I chewed that fellow up and down and told him I didn't mind him getting what I said wrong, but he could've at least got my age right.

" 'I'm sorry, Tommy,' he told me. 'It was a typographical error.'

" 'Typographical error, my butt,' I said. 'It was a perfect four and a perfect nine.' "

After my round, I ran into Ben Hogan in the clubhouse, which, from my point of view, is like an average big-league baseball player coming face to face with Babe Ruth. In my opinion, Hogan is far and away the greatest golfer who ever lived, and there isn't anybody in second place.

I was glad to see Ben, even just to say hello and wish him well. He told me he's recovering from a shoulder operation and hopes to start playing a little golf soon. I first met Hogan when we were paired together in the U.S. Open in San Francisco in 1966. He was already fifty-three years old, but he could still stroke the ball; the following year, he shot a 66 in the Masters, the lowest round of the whole tournament.

Later, I played an exhibition with Ben and spent an evening sitting and talking with him, and I found that the image I had of him, the image that had been built up by the press and by the players, too, was all wrong. He was full of warmth and humor, eager to talk about his days on the tour, easy to listen to. He had mellowed, I'm sure, in the years since he'd stopped winning tournaments regularly.

I've got my own theory about Hogan. I think that one day, when he was in his twenties, he flat decided he was going to be the greatest golfer that ever lived, and for the next twenty years, he shut everything out of his life except golf. I don't think it was his natural way, but he put himself in a box, from the moment he approached a golf course until the moment he left, and nobody and nothing could penetrate that box.

Hogan paid a big price to be the best—he gave up social life, friendships, everything; he dehumanized himself—and I think he always knew how big the price was. Now, with everything proven and competition behind him, I think he's trying to make up for all the years he lost. He's returned to his natural, friendly ways.

He was my first hero in golf, and he still is.

I drove home from the course today with George Knudson, and I was a little surprised by the way George was driving. He was driving with two hands, no glass in either hand. I had a Scotch in my hand. "Where's your glass?" I asked George. He likes an occasional nip, just like I do.

"I'm giving up drinking this week," George said. "I'm in training. Not going to touch a drop."

George's willpower may not be tested for too long. He shot a 74 today, and he's going to have to improve tomorrow if he wants to make the cut. My old friend Chuck Courtney's leading the tournament with a 66, just a stroke off the course record. But, I'll tell you, he's not going to keep up that kind of golf. I'll give odds right now that when the tournament's over, there won't be more than two or three fellows under par.

May 16   I was so tired this morning I couldn't even loosen up on the practice tee. I hit three wedges, three five-irons, and one driver, and I hit them all so bad I was embarrassed. I couldn't get them over the rough in front of the tee.

I gave up. I called my caddy in and sat down and rested a few minutes and then dragged myself to the first tee. I figured the Colonial Country Club was going to eat me alive.

Then I birdied the first two holes and ended up with a 68.

I'm one-over for the tournament now, only five strokes behind the leader, Bert Yancey, who shot a 65 to tie the course record (set by Ben Hogan seventeen years ago). There's a group of fellows tied for second place at 138, and I'm about tenth or eleventh.

All I want to do now is win a nice check here and then go home and sleep for a week.

May 17   The same man who shot a 68 yesterday played with the same golf clubs today and hit the same golf balls on the same golf course and shot a 76. I never hit one decent shot the whole day. If my putting hadn't been sharp, I would've shot an 86.

The way I was playing, I wouldn't have done any good on a pitch-putt course, but Colonial was really a monster today. The wind was blowing and the course was wet from an overnight rain, and some of the scores climbed out of sight. Old Arnie shot an 80, Tony Jacklin shot an 81, Jimmy Colbert shot an 82, and Bert Yancey jumped up twelve strokes in a day, from 65 to 77. Tom Weiskopf and R. H. Sikes, playing together, both shot 82s, and afterward, R. H., a good old Arkansas country boy, said to me, "I'll tell you how bad we were. On one hole, Tommy took an eight and didn't lose his honor."

Usually, if you shoot a 76 in the third round of a tournament, you fall clear out of sight—like I did in Greensboro six weeks ago—but today I just dropped about twenty places. Bruce Crampton shot an amazing 69 and tied for first place with Billy Maxwell They're both two-under for the tournament, and I won't be at all surprised if nobody ends up breaking par here. I'd bet my money on little Max tomorrow. It's like David and Goliath, the way he handles this big course.

I played with Don January today—he shot 70 and moved into a tie for fourth place—and before we teed off, he asked me, "Frank what the hell happened in New Orleans?"

"What the hell do *you* think happened?" I said. "I had an eighteen-incher, and as good a putter as I am, I can't miss an eighteen-inch putt. There's just no way. The only conclusion I can come to is that I choked."

It's been two weeks now, and that damn thing is still on my mind. I'm really getting psyched out. I'm beginning to think that I'll never win a tournament again, that I can't do it, that I don't have the intestinal fortitude.

I'm really down, but I guess I'm not the only one. George Knudson came knocking on my door tonight. "Got any Scotch?" he said.

"I thought you gave up drinking for the week," I said.

"I did," George said, "and I'm seven over par. Do you have any Scotch?"

I gave George a big glassful. I hope it helps. It hasn't done me any good this week.

May 18   Before we went to sleep last night, Patty turned to me. "Frank?" she said.

"Yeah, honey?"

"I watched you today and I think you're doing something wrong."

"Sure, honey," I said. "Get some sleep."

"Frank," she said, "I think you're aiming too far to the right again. It looked to me like you were pulling over the top of your shots."

Patty doesn't know much about golf—she's never played the game—but when I came home from the Masters, I'd told her about the lesson Pro'd given me. I guess she understood what I was talking about. She's got a good eye. Once, right after we got married and she knew even less about golf than she knows now, she was walking

Frank Beard's Record

TOURNAMENT	1ST ROUND	2ND ROUND	3RD ROUND	4TH ROUND
Champions		DID NOT PLAY		
Byron Nelson	70	67	70	71
New Orleans	67	67	69	72
Texas	71	72	72	69
Colonial	73	68	76	67

with me and I messed up a few putts. "Why are you moving your legs on your putts?" Patty said.

"What do you mean?" I said.

"I don't know," she said, "but you never moved your legs before."

Thanks to Patty's tip, I figured out that I'd been moving my head, which moved everything else. Soon as I stopped moving my head, I started sinking my putts again.

Patty was right last night, too.

I got out to the golf course and started aiming more at the target again, and I shot a 67—three birdies and fifteen pars, my steadiest round ever at Colonial—and moved out of nowhere all the way up to tenth place. I earned a nice chunk of money, about three thousand dollars.

I could've finished even higher if George Knudson hadn't fired a 66—tying the low round of the day—and come in one stroke ahead of me. I guess my Scotch didn't hurt him any.

My choice to win the tournament—Billy Maxwell—blew sky high and shot a 78. He started the day nine strokes ahead of me and ended the day two strokes behind me, tied with two of my good friends, Dick Crawford and Charlie Coody. They won about two thousand dollars apiece.

TOTAL SCORE	FINISH	PRO-AM EARNINGS	INDIVIDUAL EARNINGS
278	T 2	$641.67	$ 9,250.00
275	2	462.50	11,400.00
284	T 24	—	810.00
284	10	200.00	3,125.00

Old Flip—Gardner Dickinson—won the tournament, and it was an appropriate victory. Gardner has modeled himself after Ben Hogan. He walks like Hogan. He dresses like Hogan. He smokes like Hogan. And today, on one of Hogan's favorite courses, he played like Hogan. Old Flip shot a 66 and came in at 278, two-under for the tournament, one stroke in front of Gary Player. I heard afterward that on Thursday, Gardner had taken an hour-and-a-half lesson from Hogan. The master and the pupil must both be pretty happy tonight.

I'm happy, too, because I'm heading home. I'm going to stay home for two weeks, just skip the next two tournaments. I'm going to try a new approach for me. For the next two weeks, I'm going to work on my game for the U.S. Open. I'm going to eat, drink, and sleep that Houston Champions golf course. I'm going to be as well prepared mentally and physically as I've ever been in my life.

I've had a good swing through Texas. I've enjoyed having my family with me, and I've won about twenty-five thousand dollars.

Now I'm dreaming. I'm dreaming about winning the U.S. Open.

6

The Old
Frank Beard
Charge

TOURNAMENT	SITE	PURSE	DATES
Atlanta Classic	Atlanta Country Club, Atlanta	$115,000	May 22–May 25
Memphis Open	Colonial Country Club, Memphis	150,000	May 29–June 1
Western Open	Midlothian Country Club, Midlothian, Illinois	130,000	June 5–June 8
United States Open	Champions Golf Club, Houston	196,900	June 12–June 15

May 19 / Louisville   I drove all day today, which gave me lots of time to think, and I came to the conclusion that if I hadn't had my family touring with me, I probably wouldn't have been able to stand the past four weeks and I certainly wouldn't have been able to play so well. I'm firmly convinced that you can't reach a peak on the tour until you get married, until you have that stability, until you have those responsibilities that practically force you to play better.

The late Tony Lema was a classic example. He couldn't hit a lick when he was single. Then he got married, and before he was killed in a plane crash, he proved that he was one of the five or six best golfers on the tour.

Of course, you've got to have the right kind of wife. Pat's always encouraging me, always telling me I'm going to do better. Not all the wives are like that. I remember once, after I'd played my first round in some tournament, Patty and I were visiting with one of the other wives, and her husband walked in, fresh from the golf course. "What'd you shoot?" she said.

"Had a 75," he said.

His wife jumped up and started slamming their clothes into a suitcase, getting all packed up so that they could leave the next day after her husband missed the cut. She wasn't exactly inspiring great confidence in her husband.

I'm not saying that the tour can't be a great life for a bachelor. We've got some fellows out here—Johnny Jacobs, Rocky Thompson, and Bob Smith come immediately to mind—who seem to have a good swinging time. They've got the sharp clothes that most of the young boys wear now, they've got their suntans, they've got a few dollars to spend, and there are beautiful girls who pop up at every stop along the tour. I imagine there's a million guys who'd run to change places with one of those bachelor pros.

But none of those guys I mentioned has ever won a tournament. There were twenty-six different golfers who won championships on the tour last year, and of those twenty-six, only one was single— Miller Barber. Of the top twenty money-winners last year, Mr. X was the only bachelor. Of the guys who've done well so far this year, the only bachelors are Miller and Raymond Floyd. I don't know the exact number of bachelors playing the tour, but I'll bet anything that the percentage of bachelors among the golfers who miss the cut each week is a helluva lot higher than the percentage of bachelors among the golfers who finish in the top ten.

I suppose you might figure that the explanation's simple, that with all the beautiful women who hang around golf tournaments, the married men have a big advantage because they get more rest. Well, most of us do, but some of us don't. We've had some funny things happen out here on the tour. One married fellow used to have a girl traveling with him regularly, and she wasn't his wife or even a distant relative. One time he took his girl to the airport to catch a plane to the next tournament, and one of the other players' wives spotted him in the terminal and turned to her husband and said, "Who's that with so-and-so?"

"Oh," said the husband, thinking fast, "that's one of the courtesy drivers the tournament committee provides to make sure the fellows get to their planes all right."

Later, when they were up in the air, the wife tapped her husband on the arm and said, "What a thoughtful tournament committee! Look! That courtesy driver's come along to make sure so-and-so gets off the plane all right."

Another time, down in Texas, one of the married guys called up a girl he knew, and while he was giving her a good pitch on the phone, the operator at the motel made a mistake and hooked a long-distance call from his wife into the same line. The wife listened for a few seconds, then interrupted with a few choice words and slammed down her receiver.

The guy took a minute to figure out a plan, then phoned his wife back. "You crazy?" he said. "That was the daughter of one of my sponsors. She goes to school down here, and she wanted tickets for the tournament. I was just being polite to her to stay in good with the sponsor. Hell, she's ugly, anyway."

The wife ended up apologizing for being so suspicious.

Every now and then, a pro golfer's marriage breaks up, and the other wives all have something to buzz about, but it's pretty rare, especially considering the kind of life we lead and the kind of temptations we face. Of course, a lot of us cut down the temptations by having our wives and families travel with us.

I noticed at the motels in San Antonio and Fort Worth that quite a few of the golfers' wives are pregnant right now. You can always tell when we've had a lot of rain-outs early in the year.

May 27 / New Orleans   My string of victories in the Shell television matches came to an end today. Dan Sikes had me by four strokes after four holes, and I never saw daylight. He won by the same four strokes and picked up ten thousand dollars. I got seven thousand. I not only lost the three-thousand-dollar difference; I lost ten thousand more, the minimum guarantee for getting in the finals.

Dan brought along his own caddy today, a fellow named Perry, paid his plane fare and everything. Perry works for Dan all the time, advises him on every club, studies every putt, and acts like he's Dan's confessor. It's almost like they're blood brothers. We always kid Dan about Perry, but he really believes in him. "The only reason Dan keeps me around," Perry once told Tommy Aaron, "is that whenever something goes wrong, he can blame me. He gets on me, throws clubs at me, and shouts, 'Perry, you can't give me the right club. You can't read a green. You're not worth a damn.' The more he hollers at me, the more he pays me."

I found out today my game needs some work, but mentally, I'm in good shape. I've been off the tour for more than a week now, and I've gotten a good mental rest. Most of the fellows were down in Atlanta last week—Bert Yancey beat Bruce Devlin in a play-off for the championship—and for the first time I can remember, I didn't mind reading the paper and seeing what was going on and who was winning what. I didn't hate it. I was almost interested in it. I hope this is a sign of maturity.

I've played a few practice rounds, mostly with my father and Bill Boone, just staying loose, not worrying about score or anything like that. Pro's been helpful, as usual. I ought to put him on the payroll and take him everywhere with me. He caught something right away. I'd gotten my hands way too low when I was addressing the ball, and after he'd seen me hit a few, he said, "Why don't you move your hands up a little bit?" I did, and everything started to fall into place. Pro's got a fantastic eye for my game. He knows my swing better than I do.

My thoughts are on the U.S. Open. I took out some old magazines the other day and studied the layout of the Champions Golf Club in Houston. I know that course like the back of my hand, but I figured it wouldn't hurt to bone up on it a little. I read some comments on the various holes by golfers who've played well there, and I spent some time thinking about every hole, remembering every shot I'd ever hit there, thinking about the different kinds of shots each hole can demand. I don't think I've ever prepared quite like this. I feel like Bert Yancey getting ready for the Masters.

Bill Boone's been whipping up some pretty good deals for me lately, pulling them out of the woodwork, getting me a thousand dollars here and a thousand dollars there. Bill's done a wonderful job for me. I swear, if I could ever win the Open, this man would make me a fortune.

June 2 / Louisville   I looked at the paper this morning and saw all the money that the boys had won in the Memphis Open, and for the first time in two weeks, I really missed the tour. I saw the way they cut up $150,000, and I thought, "God, I wish I'd played this week."

The only consolation was that a few of my best friends got in there for some big money. Davy Hill won the tournament and thirty thousand dollars, and shot all the way up to fourth on the money list. Charlie Coody tied Tommy Aaron for third place and got his biggest check of the year, nine thousand dollars. Steve Reid shot an incredible 61 in the third round—a new course record, the lowest round of his career, and the lowest round by anybody this year—wound up in fifth place, and collected more than six thousand dollars, the second largest check he's ever earned as a professional golfer. Gene Littler won a few thousand dollars, too, and became the first pro this year to go over the hundred-thousand-dollar mark. Gene had won hardly any money in six weeks, mostly because he'd skipped about five out of six tournaments.

I really expected Bert Yancey to win the tournament. Bert was tied for the lead with Lee Elder going into the final round, but he just fell apart, shot a 76, and slipped all the way out of the top ten. Elder finished second, for seventeen thousand dollars, the most he'd ever won.

Well, I'm ready now to go in and grab my share. I've had my rest, and I've got the perfect attitude. I'm absolutely dying to get back on the tour.

I'm playing in the Western Open this week, and I'm going to concentrate on sharpening my game for the U.S. Open next week. I don't mean I'm not going to be trying to win the Western, but the most important thing is being ready for Houston. In this game, the man who wins the U.S. Open is the man who cashes all the chips. Even for me, it'd be worth half a million dollars.

June / Midlothian, Illinois   I'm off on the road without my family again. Patty's going to join me next week for the U.S. Open, but this week I'm bacheloring it. I'm sharing a room with Steve Reid, and I'll tell you, I can't remember the last time I saw Steve so happy.

Everybody's asking him about his 61, and he's taking great pleasure in reliving it. He had seven straight birdies during one stretch, and with three holes to play—two of them par-fives—he needed three birdies for a 59, which would have been a new record for the PGA tour. Steve thought he had a good shot at it; he told me he lipped out three or four putts along the line, or he would've had the record. Steve's got about twenty thousand dollars on the money list now, and if he can just win himself another couple of decent checks, he'll have that top sixty locked up. Once he gets in, I think he'll stay there. He's worked hard to get this far, and he'll learn to relax, to keep his temper under control. I'm tickled for him.

This Midlothian Country Club, just outside Chicago, is a beautiful course. I love all the courses around Chicago. They're old—built by designers who knew what golf was all about—and they're demanding, but they're fair.

The proceeds from this tournament go into a scholarship fund for caddies, and they run an advanced caddy program here. The youngsters are smart and enthusiastic and really know what they're doing. I've got an excellent boy. I played a practice round today, and after I checked about four or five of his measurements, I didn't have to walk off a step. He'd actually mapped out the whole course, showing exactly how far each big tree, each trap, and each creek is from the green. He even had the pin placements marked down for the practice round. He's a good, clean-cut kid who's going to Notre Dame next year, and we're going to get along just fine.

I spent some time on the putting green after my practice round, and I'm going to find out something about my putting during the next couple of months. If I don't putt well this summer, if I don't putt the way Frank Beard should putt, then I'll just have to face up to the facts: either my stroke is gone—or my nerves are.

June 4   Beyond any doubt, I had the worst pro-am score today I have ever had in my life. We didn't even shoot par *as a team*. For partners, I had a one-handicapper and two eighteen-handicappers, and I'm almost positive the one-handicapper didn't get a birdie all day. I don't think he even had too many pars. I don't know where in the world he got his one-handicap from. Neither of the eighteen-handicappers shot a *bogey* the whole round. Never mind a par or a birdie; they didn't get one bogey between them. And, to tell the truth, the old pro didn't shine today either. I didn't feel much like playing, especially after watching my partners.

They were nice fellows—I can't stress that enough—but they had no more chance of winning a golf tournament than I'd have of winning a bathing-beauty contest. On the sixteenth hole, one of the eighteen-handicappers walked over to me and said, "Well, Frank, you've seen me play for a few holes now. What am I doing wrong?"

My mouth dropped. What do you say? He couldn't break 300, and he wanted to know what he was doing wrong. I could have talked from now to Christmas and not been halfway through.

After the pro-am, I went straight to the practice tee. About ten times as many fellows as usual were out there, and they were working twenty times as hard. We all figure one week of practice is a small price to pay to go to the U.S. Open hitting the ball well.

I think my game's shaping up—that tip from my father about moving up my hands is a big help—and I just want to bring myself slowly to a peak next week.

I got my pairings tonight for the first two rounds here, and I'm not too happy. I'm playing with Nicklaus, who is the defending champion, and Archer, who is the new Masters champion. "Hey, Frank," Steve Reid said when he saw the pairings, "you'll draw a helluva crowd tomorrow if those other two guys can pull their weight."

June 5   Just as I expected, we had a mob following us today, and the fans were split three ways. A third of them were Nicklaus fans, shouting, "Go get 'em, Golden Bear." A third of them were

Archer fans, hollering, "C'mon, Cowboy George." And the other third were anti-Nicklaus and anti-Archer fans, yelling, "Beat 'em both, what's-your-name."

I don't mind telling you, old what's-his-name put on some show today. I beat Nicklaus by five strokes and Archer by eight. I shot a 66, five under par, and Nicklaus said afterward it could've been a 62 or 63 easily. I won't argue with big Jack.

I missed six makable putts—two from ten feet, two from six feet, one from two feet, and one, naturally, from eighteen inches. I can't groan too much, because I sank a twenty-footer, two eight-footers, a six-footer, and a two-footer for birdies, and the only time I came close to making a bogey, I sank a ten-footer to save my par.

Strangely enough, at the end of the first nine, Archer was a stroke in front of me. I was two-under and he was three-under. On the fourth hole, a par-five where I made the long putt for my par, George put his third shot in the fringe behind the green. Then he took an eight-iron and stroked the ball just as if he were putting, and the ball rolled through the fringe, onto the green, and into the cup. George knew exactly what he was doing; he didn't have enough green to loft the ball, and he didn't want to use a putter because the putter could get hung up in the grass going back. So he deliberately putted an eight-iron, and the ball went in for a birdie. The fans started razzing him, thinking he'd been trying to get the shot airborne. "These people have just seen one of the greatest golf shots they'll ever see," George said to me, "and they think it was a miss." He wasn't bragging; he was just disappointed in the mentality of the crowd.

George looked like he was heading for a course record, but on the back nine he took six bogeys while I was shooting three-under. We had a little wait at one tee, and I asked George what was the real reason he'd withdrawn from the New Orleans Open.

"I burned myself lighting a cigarette," he said, "just like I told them. I really did."

"You've got to be kidding," Nicklaus said. "I've never seen you smoke a cigarette in your life."

"Well, I don't exactly smoke," George said, "but every night I light one cigarette and inhale it two or three times. It makes me dizzy and I fall right asleep. That's the way it happened."

Before our round, I happened to see Billy Maxwell on the practice tee, the first time I'd seen him since he shot that disastrous 78 on the last day of the Colonial. I told Billy I thought sure he was going to win that tournament. "So did I, Frank," Max said. "I felt so confident when I went to the first tee, it was almost scary." Billy laughed. "The only other time I ever felt that confident," he said, "was in Dallas a few years ago when I was leading going into the final round. That day, I shot an 80."

Billy played right behind me today and matched me stroke for stroke. He came in with a 66, too, tying me for the lead, and we both went up to the press room for the standard interview. "Look, fellas," I told the reporters, "I kind of feel like talking a little bit today. Let's get all the quotes right for a change."

I talked for about forty-five minutes. I'll be interested to see what comes out in the papers tomorrow.

June 6   I called it. I picked up a local newspaper this morning and read: "Frank Beard was very disappointed in his golf game after Fort Worth and, feeling that he needed some repairs, went home two weeks to practice."

Where in hell did that reporter come up with that? First, I never said it, and second, if he'd done some simple arithmetic, he'd have seen how wrong it was. In four weeks in Texas and New Orleans, I won about twenty-five thousand dollars and I finished with a 67 in Fort Worth on a rainy, windy day. How could I want to repair that? I'd just like to preserve it.

I told the reporters yesterday that I went home after Fort Worth because I was tired, dead tired, no other reason. I suppose everybody else got it right, but when one guy messes it up, he messes it up for everybody. How can I stand up in front of a group of reporters and tell them what I honestly think about a tournament or about a course or about another pro when I know that one guy can't even get a simple quote straight?

My brother, Ralph, told me a long time ago never to get on the wrong side of the press because those guys can make you or break you. I've tried to stick to that, but I'm ready to give up. I'm making a resolution right now. I'm never going to talk to a reporter again, except to say, "I took a driver, a six-iron, and two putts," things like that.

Just before I teed off today, a reporter came up to me and asked me what I thought about Nicklaus' game with the Open coming up. "No comment," I said.

The guy looked like I'd slapped him, but what the hell could I do? Actually, Nicklaus is playing as badly as I've ever seen him play. I can't believe how badly he's playing. Jack complimented me yesterday on my round. "You played as fine a round as I've ever seen anyone play," he said. I would've liked to have reciprocated and said something nice to him, but I couldn't. I would've been lying, and Jack would've known I was lying. He knows he's playing poorly. I don't know whether he's lost his desire or what, but he just can't handle it. I'll tell you right now that Jack Nicklaus is not going to be a threat in the U.S. Open next week. There's no way he can get his game in shape in time.

I'm talking about Jack Nicklaus now. I'm not talking about Joe Blow. There are a hundred professional golfers out here on the tour who would trade all their good games for a few of Jack's bad ones. At his worst, he's better than most of the people, but by his own standards, he's playing miserably.

Suppose I'd said all that to the reporter. I could imagine the headline tomorrow: "Beard Says Nicklaus Is Old and Finished and Can't Hit It a Lick Anymore."

On the first tee, I said to Archer, "You smoke your cigarette last night?"

"Yeah," George said. "I smoked it and fell asleep and then woke up at five o'clock this morning."

"What'd you do?" I said.

"Smoked another," he said. "I'm becoming a real addict."

George and Jack both shot 72s today, and I came in with an even-par 71. I wasn't stiffing my shots today, wasn't blanking the flag with them. I just wasn't swinging the way I did yesterday. The wind blew up a little, and I guess I got scared and decided I had to play conservatively. I made only two bogeys and two birdies, but I thought I was going to get another birdie on my final hole. I had a ten-footer, an easy uphill putt, but just as I lined the damn thing up, I heard, "Click . . . click . . . click. . . ."

I turned around and glared at the photographers, and they quieted down. I got myself organized again, so the clicking really didn't have anything to do with my missing the putt, but I was burning. I felt a little paranoid, like maybe the reporters and the photographers had a conspiracy going against me, just because I wouldn't tell that one guy what I thought about Nicklaus' game.

Old Houndy, Gay Brewer, shot a 67 today and moved into first place at 136, a stroke in front of me. I'm tied for second with Rocky Thompson and Dick Rhyan. I lost my roommate today. Steve Reid missed the cut, and so did five guys who've already won tournaments this year—Dick Lotz, Tom Shaw, Jim Colbert, Larry Hinson, and Deane Beman.

I've been on the road only four days now, and I miss the family already. I told Patty tonight I even missed the kids' crying, and she said she'd be happy to send them up to stay with me.

June 7   When I got to the course today, Al Mengert, a veteran pro, was sitting in the clubhouse, already finished with his round. Al had gone off first today, and because an uneven number of players had made the cut, he'd played all by himself. He finished eighteen holes in two hours and ten minutes. "I made my caddy carry a double anyway," Al said, "just so I'd have somebody else's bag to look at. I thought about playing two balls to keep myself company."

"Al," said Billy Maxwell, "it just goes to prove the old saying: when you play bad, you get bad pairings." Max had followed his opening 66 with a 73 yesterday, but he was still in a good mood. As long as he could count on Johnny Cash being on television tonight, Billy was happy.

I played with Rocky Thompson, and as we teed off, the wind kicked up pretty strong. I started worrying about the wind, and before I knew it, I'd three-putted the first hole for a bogey. I parred the next six holes routinely, and then it started to rain. Then came thunder and lightning, and the officials called a temporary stop to play. Golfers hate lightning, and with good reason. Just since I've been on the tour, we've had three or four spectators killed on the course by lightning. A golf course is so wide open it's got to be a dangerous place in a storm. I've heard that when it starts thundering and lightning, Mason Rudolph throws down his clubs, takes off his metal spikes, and sprints all the way to the clubhouse. I don't blame him.

I was upset about being one over par, and I was upset about being wet, and I was upset about being cold, and I wanted the whole round to be rained out. But after we waited out the thunder and lightning for about an hour, we resumed play. The course was almost underwater, but with a television commitment tomorrow and everybody wanting to get down to Houston for the Open, the officials were dead set on getting this round in.

On the eighth hole, still thinking about my start and the weather, I topped a two-iron and took another bogey. Suddenly, I was only three-under for the tournament, and I could see on the scoreboard that Gay Brewer was eight-under and Billy Casper was four-under, and I started doing a war dance, begging for rain and thunder and lightning and hail and snow and everything.

The dance didn't work. We kept playing. On the ninth hole, I hit a miserable first putt about eight feet past the hole, and I faced a critical situation. If I'd missed that eight-footer and taken another bogey, I could have started packing. I could have headed for Houston, because I would have been finished here. But I sank the putt, and that was the turning point for me.

On the tenth, I sank a twenty-footer for a birdie, and on the eleventh, a long par-three, I pressed my luck and hit my four-wood, my weakest club, and wound up ten feet from the hole and made that for another birdie. After I parred twelve, I chipped in on the thirteenth for another birdie. I was one-under for the day, six-under for the tournament. Gay Brewer had fallen apart, and so had the other leaders. I was back in first place again, one stroke ahead of my playing partner, Rocky Thompson.

Rocky had been playing good, solid golf. He told me he's planning to get married in October, so I guess he's already settling down a little. But while I parred the last five holes, Rocky took a double-bogey on seventeen and a bogey on eighteen and fell four strokes behind.

I came in with a 70 for a three-round total of 207, six-under. Billy Casper, who teed off early and missed most of the bad weather, shot a 68 and moved into second place all alone at 209. Billy almost had to withdraw here. He's got a bunch of allergies—he has his own allergy specialist who goes from course to course and tests their insecticides to determine whether or not Billy can play—and early this week, he had an allergic reaction to some melon he ate. (Cas is on a special diet most of the time, eating things like buffalo meat; the press and the public like to call him "Buffalo Billy.") He had to withdraw from the pro-am Wednesday, and for a while there was a chance he'd miss the tournament. I wouldn't have minded if he had.

I hope I learned a lesson today. I almost ruined my game worrying about the wind and praying for rain and envying the players who teed off early and moaning about being wet and crying about being cold and thinking about everything except my next golf shot. Maturity out here on the tour is learning to accept things as they come. The older fellows like Boros and January wouldn't even have noticed the wind blowing or the rain falling. They would have just gone ahead and played their game. That's what I've got to learn to do.

Here I am again, sitting in first place with one round to go for the third time this year. I need a victory bad. I need a shot in the arm, some real confidence. If I could win here, I could go down to Houston flying on a cloud.

June 8   When I woke up this morning, the rain was coming down so hard I'd have turned over and gone back to sleep if I hadn't had to go to Mass. Just one look out the window—it had been pouring all night—and I knew we wouldn't be able to play. I dressed for church, then stopped in the motel restaurant for breakfast. The woman at the front desk smiled at me and said, "Good luck, Mr. Beard. They're teeing off right on time."

I couldn't believe it. But I called the course, and she was right. I went to church, then to the course, and it looked like a lake. The fairways were drenched and dotted with puddles. The greens were wet, but surprisingly playable, a tribute to their design; they were sloped just enough so that they drained nicely.

If it had been up to me, I would have canceled play for the day, but I've got to give the officials credit. They did a good job making the course even halfway playable, and I can understand their reasoning. The forecast for tomorrow wasn't any better, and nobody wanted to play Tuesday and get down to Houston without enough time for any decent practice before the Open.

Even before I teed off, I knew that in this weather I didn't have a chance of winning the tournament. You can call it pessimism; you can call it giving up. I call it realism. I simply can't play well on wet fairways. I've tried and tried and tried. I've done everything but cheat, and nothing helps.

A long time ago, my father taught me that I should hit down and through my irons and try to spin the ball up. The newer pros have learned to sweep the ball with their irons, to hit them almost like woods. This gives them a much better chance on wet terrain. I'm not alibiing; I'm pointing out a failing in my game. As a pro golfer, I should've learned to compensate by now, but I haven't. I don't have any control on wet fairways; instead of the ball coming out with backspin, it comes out with no spin, sort of like a knuckleball.

Off I went in the rain and the cold, thirty-mile-an-hour wind, wrapped in a long-sleeved shirt and a sweater and a rain suit, knowing I couldn't win. I was absolutely right. Tom Weiskopf and I were the final twosome to tee off, and I bogeyed two of the first three holes. By that time, Casper, playing in front of us, had birdied three out of four. He'd leaped from two strokes behind me to three in front, and for all practical purposes, I was out of the race for the championship.

I decided to charge—not an Arnold Palmer type of charge, a Frank Beard type. When I charge, I don't go for broke; I go for as much money as I can realistically expect to get. After three holes, I realized that the best I could hope for was second place, and I knew the best way to get second place was to shoot pars. I decided not to try to cut across lakes or around trees or take any chance that might save me one stroke or cost me three. I knew that second place was worth about fifteen thousand dollars, and third place about nine thousand, and I wasn't going to gamble for first-place money of twenty-six thousand and risk falling back to the two- or three-thousand-dollar level. I just figured out the odds and decided they were against me.

Unlike some golfers, I know my own limitations. I know I'm not a robot. I know I can't do the impossible. I can't do anything that a good amateur golfer can't do. He makes the exact same shots I make; the only difference is that I make them more often. Anything he can do three times out of ten, I can do seven times out of ten.

I did manage to pick up one stroke on par, to get back to five-under for the tournament, but then I faltered and finished with a 74, three-over for the day, three-under for the tournament.

Casper shot an incredible 67—only three men broke par all day, and he broke it by four strokes—and whipped me by five strokes. I just have to face facts: Billy is capable of doing things on a golf course that I cannot do. I don't feel at all disgraced; he is a great, great golfer, and even if I had shot 70 today, which would have been a small miracle for me, he would've beat me.

Rocky Thompson shot a 69 and moved past me by one stroke into second place, and I think that hurt me more than losing the tournament. If I'd shot all pars after the third hole, after I'd lost hope of winning, I'd have tied Rocky for second and made myself an extra three thousand dollars.

Naturally, I'm a little disappointed that I didn't win, but I can't get particularly upset about the day. If somebody had told me on Wednesday that I was going to earn nine thousand dollars this week, I'd have kissed him. In fact, if I'd been offered a three-thousand-dollar guarantee no matter what I shot or where I finished, I'd have accepted it. I can't even groan too much about the weather. For nine thousand, I'd play in the middle of an ocean.

I've got a lot to be happy about. I moved up close to the top ten on the money list, I think I won enough Ryder Cup points to just about guarantee myself a place on the team, and I brought my Vardon Trophy average down under 71 strokes a round. This game of golf is a business with me, and from a business standpoint, I had a great week.

I'm feeling so content, despite not winning, that I'm reminded of something Patty said to me the other day. "Sometimes," she said, "I think you're afraid to win. You're afraid because you don't want what comes with winning, the responsibilities, the publicity, the attention, all of that."

Maybe Patty's right. I don't know. The toughest person in the world to try to figure out is yourself. You're always rationalizing. Some people might say I played cowardly today, but I say I played realistically. There goes old Frank—protecting his flank again.

June 9 / Houston   Patty and I flew down here today, the first time we've left all three children at home with a baby-sitter. We'll only be away from them for a week, and I hope it'll be a restful week for Patty. I hope it'll be a profitable week for me.

It ought to be. I'm coming off a strong tournament in the Western, and I'm playing a course that suits my game. I finished first in the Houston Champions International in 1967 and seventh in 1968, and during those two tournaments. I shot four sub-par rounds, three even-par rounds, and only one round over par. I'm the only pro who shot 280 or better in the last two tournaments on this course.

In the average weekly tournament, with the normal field, I'd be about a 20–1 shot to win, but in this one, because of my track record, I may be as low as 10–1. I don't think there's more than four or five players who have a better chance than me here.

I know 10–1 shots don't come in too often, but if I'm ever going to pull one off, I'd sure like to do it this week. I'll tell you what it means to win the U.S. Open: it goes up there right next to your name for the rest of your life—Frank Beard, Open Champion. It's just like part of your name, as permanent as if it said, "Frank Beard, Jr."

June 10   This Champions Golf Club is as magnificent and beautiful a golf course as you could ever want to see. Jack Burke and Jimmy Demaret designed it, and they did a fantastic job. The U.S. Open is shifted to a different site every year, and almost always the host club has to fiddle around with its course—add a few bunkers, change a few tees—to bring it up to Open standards. Not this one. This is a true championship course from the first tee to the eighteenth green.

I've put in two practice rounds so far, and as far as I can tell, the course is playing exactly the same way it has for the past four years. The rough is not Open rough. They've let it grow a little, but it's not a jungle, like Open rough usually is. This course doesn't need any extra gimmicks to play long and tough.

For the past two years, the winning score in the Champions International has been 274, and if we don't get a lot of wind, if the weather holds up and the players hold up under the ninety-degree heat, we might see 274 win this tournament. It'd be a new record for the Open.

But, more than likely, the winner will shoot around 276. The course won't be any different, just the stakes. The fact that we're playing in the U.S. Open has to add at least a few strokes to everybody's game.

After my practice round today, I bumped into Dean Eagle, the sports editor of the *Courier-Journal* back in Louisville. "Hey, Frank," Dean said, "I'm picking you to win the Open."

"Yeah," I said, "and you picked Majestic Prince to win the Belmont."

I hope I run better than that horse did.

June 11   I don't know how my game is. I can't tell. I've played three practice rounds now, and I really haven't pushed myself. That's what I always say—I haven't pushed myself—when I've been playing bad golf.

I don't think there's anything seriously wrong, but I did notice today that I was moving my head a little just before impact. I put in a session on the practice tee, concentrated on holding my head steady, and started hitting the ball better.

The heat here is wearing me down, but other than that, I'm in a pretty good mood. I was doing my share of needling today. Larry Ziegler, one of my foursome in the practice round, started telling me that he and his father had been working on his game, and he had come to one conclusion. "My old man doesn't know anything about golf," Larry said.

"Then you both started out even," I said.

Later on, a sportswriter named Art Spander from San Francisco came out on the course and walked two holes with me. I honestly believe that's the PGA record for holes walked by a reporter with Frank Beard. Spander wanted my comments on the course, and instead, I told him what I'd heard Bill Hartack, the jockey, say on television last night. Johnny Carson asked Hartack what he thought of the press, and Bill said, "They do an excellent job considering the fact that they're writing about something about which they know nothing."

I caught a pretty good jab, too. Bill Boone's down here, and he was working on the representative of some clothing company to give me a contract to wear his slacks. The fellow smiled and shook his head. "Frank's a nice guy," he said, "but I'm not going to put my slacks around *his* waist."

I don't blame him.

I swear, if I win the U.S. Open, I will go on a real diet.

June 12   I had good company out on the golf course today. I played with Charlie Coody and with Don Bies, a nice, quiet fellow from Seattle, and our gallery included Patty, Lynette Coody, Father Moore from New Orleans, and Dick Katenberger, who was my Little League baseball coach when I was a youngster in Dallas.

I'm sorry I didn't put on a better show for them. Dick Katenberger was keeping a chart of all my shots, and I wish I'd given him three or four less to mark down. I shot a 72, and after the first round of the Open, I'm just barely in the top thirty.

There's not much danger of my missing the cut, but I'm not much of a threat to the leaders, either. Bob Murphy shot a 66, Miller Barber a 67, and Deane Beman and Al Geiberger had 68s. Skippy Geiberger—he eats Skippy peanut-butter sandwiches during his rounds—is just back in competition after being laid up with some kind of ulcers, and I'm glad to see him doing well. He seems like the calmest, most easygoing guy in the world, but obviously, this game eats him up, too.

Deane's 68 was remarkable for a relatively short driver on this big course. I heard that, on ten different holes, he had to hit wood shots to the green, and he made the green every time. That's going to be hard to keep up.

The way I started, I thought I was going to handle this course as well as ever. I parred the first two holes, then birdied the third to give myself a little cushion going into a dangerous stretch of four holes, the fourth through the seventh.

Then I went and three-putted the fourth hole and lost my cushion and my momentum. I tried to force my way through the next three holes, and it just can't be done. You have to be cool and relaxed. You have to concentrate. I lost my concentration, bogeyed six and seven, and went two-over.

That missed putt on the fourth was the first turning point of the round for me, and the second came on the tenth hole. I faced a six-foot putt to save my par, and I knew that if I missed, I'd be three-over and on my way to a 75 or an 80. I think I would've just given up. But I made the putt, picked up a little momentum, then birdied twelve and thirteen to get back to even-par.

The fourteenth hole, a 430-yard par-four, is the toughest hole on the course, and I let my drive slip and ended up behind a big tree. I thought of laying up and playing for a bogey, but then I told myself, "No, I came down here to win. I'm going for the green."

I turned to my caddy, a fellow named Jessie, a good, capable local caddy, and I said, "If I can make a four on this hole, I'll win this tournament." I meant it. I honestly felt that if I could salvage a par on a hole where it looked like I was going to make double-bogey, I'd have proof that the breaks were going my way. I'd get all charged up.

I tried. I took a four-iron and kept it low, under the tree, and the ball rolled up just short of the green, a pretty fair shot. Then I hit a good chip and a good putt, but the ball didn't go in. I took a bogey and went one over par.

A birdie on the next hole got me back to even, but then, on the sixteenth, I aimed a twenty-footer for a birdie, rolled it past the hole, missed coming back, and took a bogey. I bogeyed the next hole, too, and came in two-over at 72. Coody shot the same score, and Bies shot a 78.

I still think I can win this tournament.

June 13 Well, I got the suspense over with early today. I ruined my round in the first five holes. I took three bogeys, and I didn't exactly die, but my wounds were bleeding.

I came to the eighth tee three over par, and two things happened there to get my adrenaline flowing. First, some marshal wandered over to me and said, "Brewer just made nine on this hole." Can you imagine a guy saying anything more stupid? It reminded me of an incident in Michigan two years ago. I was just to the left of a par-five green in two, and a marshal looked at me, sort of giggled, and said, "Right from where you are, Weiskopf just shanked it into the lake." What idiots! I don't give a damn what Tom Weiskopf does, or Gay Brewer does. I'm only worried about Frank Beard's game. That guy really steamed me up.

Then Patty got me charged up, too. "Frank," she said, "if you don't start hitting the ball better, I'm going in and making plane reservations for Louisville tonight."

I got angry with her and told her she wasn't encouraging me the way she should, but then I realized she was giving me exactly what I needed. I was looking for sympathy. I wanted Patty to tell me I was playing great, but I was getting all the bad breaks. I wanted her to say, "Poor old Frank," and then I could've hung my head and staggered in with a 75 or a 76. Instead, she got me wanting to prove something to myself.

I birdied eight and nine to get back to one-over for the day, then parred the next four holes and came to the fourteenth, feeling I could get myself back in serious contention just by parring in. Then I put my approach shot into the lake. I just plain fanned it, a miserable, miserable shot. I took a double-bogey, fell back to three-over for the round and five-over for the tournament, and that's where I ended up, at 145. Charlie Coody shot a 68 to get in at 140, and Don Bies, with a 70 for 148, just made the cut.

It's hard to believe, but little Deane Beman is leading the U.S.

Open at 137, a stroke ahead of Murphy and Miller Barber. Deane is a terrific competitor and a fine golfer, but I think this course is going to catch up with him. If I had to pick a winner right now, I'd take George Knudson, who's at 140, or the Golden Bear. I said last week that there was no way Nicklaus could be a threat in this tournament, and he backed up my words with a 74 yesterday. But old Jack is something else. He went out and shot a 67 today and put himself just four strokes off the pace.

After my round, I saw Orville Moody, who's tied with Nicklaus at one-over. Orville came up to me and started moaning about his short putting, how he just couldn't sink a thing. Old Sarge has established himself as one of the better players out here, but he still has to learn that nobody else cares about his problems. We've all got our own.

All week long, people have been coming up to me around the clubhouse and on the course and introducing themselves and saying they're from Kentucky. I never get into conversations with them. In the first place, I don't have the time, and in the second, when they say they're from Kentucky, they could mean now or twenty years ago and they could mean from Lexington or from Harlan. I don't know why these people would think I'd care whether or not they were from Kentucky. As if I'd never seen anybody from Kentucky. Hell, I see people from Kentucky all the time.

I guess I'm jumpy. My nerves are frayed. This tournament is getting to me. Why couldn't they have just called it the Extra Special Houston Champions International, instead of the U.S. Open? Then maybe I'd be doing a little better.

June 14　　I can forget about the 1969 United States Open Championship. I'll show up tomorrow, but I might as well be in Alaska for all the good it's going to do me. I'm eight over par for the tournament now, eleven strokes behind Miller Barber, and even if I shoot a fantastic 67 tomorrow, I won't get up any higher than tenth place.

My round today's hardly worth mentioning. I bogeyed three of the first six holes, and I was through. I struggled through the rough and in the bunkers and came in with my second straight 73. The funny thing is that, after three rounds, I'm exactly even-par for the tournament if you only count the last eleven holes. I'm eight-over for the first seven holes.

The fellows I though might make their moves today fell apart even worse than I did. Nicklaus shot a 75, and Knudson took a 76. The Champions Golf Club finally got to Beman; Deane slumped to a 73, which dropped him back to third place at even-par for the tournament. Mr. X was Super X today, with a 68 to go four strokes under for the tournament. He's got a full three-stroke lead on the second-place man, Orville Moody; Sarge's putting must've picked up today because he shot a 68.

I saw Orville afterward, and he was laughing and kidding, just like he didn't have a care in the world. He's thirty-five years old and he's never won a PGA tournament, but, I'll tell you, if the wind blows up tomorrow, I'd put some money on the Sarge. If the weather stays calm, Miller's going to be hard to catch.

Either way, there ought to be a lot of excitement tomorrow for everybody except old Frank. The most exciting thing I'm going to do is get on a plane and go home to Louisville.

I've learned something here. I've learned you can never say, "I'm playing well." You can only say, "I played well." You never know what's going to happen to your game the next time you step on a golf course.

Frank Beard's Record

TOURNAMENT	1ST ROUND	2ND ROUND	3RD ROUND	4TH ROUND
Atlanta		DID NOT PLAY		
Memphis		DID NOT PLAY		
Western	66	71	70	74
U.S. Open	72	73	73	78

June 15   Miller Barber started today in first place, and I started in about thirty-fifth, and I played him even. But I guess that's no consolation for Miller. We both shot 78s. I fell into a tie for fiftieth, and Miller fell into a tie for sixth. I cost myself about two hundred dollars, and Miller cost himself half a million.

I could've told you who was going to win as soon as I saw the wind kicking up this morning. The more I think about it, there was no way old Sarge could've lost. He shot a 72 and finished the tournament at 281, one over par. Skippy Geiberger, with a 70; Bob Rosburg, with a 71; and Deane Beman, with a 72, ended up in a three-way tie for second place, a stroke behind Moody.

Orville is in a beautiful position now, just like Trevino was last year. He doesn't have any contracts with club or ball manufacturers, and now he can start negotiating out of the strength of being the Open champion. I don't care if Orville never wins another tournament the rest of his life; he is going to be financially secure. Actually, I expect Orville to be a great champion and have a great career; he keeps getting better and better.

I can't help thinking that last year I shot 280 on this same course, and the year before I shot 274, and if I'd matched either of those

TOTAL SCORE	FINISH	PRO-AM EARNINGS	INDIVIDUAL EARNINGS
281	3	—	$9,240.00
296	T 50	—	895.00

scores this week, I'd be the United States Open champion. I'd have all the prestige and all the money I ever dreamed about.

Instead, I'm still old what's-his-name, the man who hasn't won a tournament in more than two years.

7

I Can't Win
Anything
but Money

TOURNAMENT	SITE	PURSE	DATES
Kemper Open	Quail Hollow Country Club, Charlotte, North Carolina	$150,000	June 19–June 22
Cleveland Open	Aurora Country Club, Cleveland	110,000	June 26–June 29
Buick Open	Warwick Hills Country Club, Grand Blanc, Michigan	125,000	July 3–July 6
Minnesota Classic	Braemar Golf Club, Edina, Minnesota	100,000	July 10–July 13

June 22 / Cleveland   Every time I go home, Pro catches something I'm doing wrong. The man's a wonder, I played with him a few times this past week, and he noticed that I was standing too far from the ball, which was causing a flat swing. I moved in a little bit and started hitting the ball better right away. The last time I took off from the tour, Pro gave me a few tips and I went out and finished third in the Western Open. The time before that, he gave me a few tips and I went out and finished second in the Byron Nelson Classic. Maybe I ought to go home every other week.

Patty and I loaded up the station wagon again today, and I drove the family up to Cleveland and deposited them all in a motel. We're going to be on the road together for the next five weeks, if we can all stand it, but they won't be seeing me the next couple of days. I'm leaving tonight for a pro-am in Iowa City.

I've been following the scores in the Kemper Open the past few days without any pangs, any envy, and it's not just a regular $100,000 tournament. It's a $150,000 tournament I'm missing. Maybe

I'm getting sensible. Maybe I'm getting mature. Or maybe I'm just not upset because I know that in the next six weeks I'm going to be playing the richest stretch of the tour, playing for a total of $860,000 in prize money. All I need is one little streak of hot putting, and I could pick up fifty thousand dollars without batting an eye.

June 23 / Iowa City Professional golfers are supposed to follow the sun, but sometimes we get our schedules confused. I flew into Chicago last night, sat on the ground there for three hours, got into another plane, flew into Iowa City, and finally climbed into bed about two o'clock this morning. Then I got up at seven to have breakfast with my three partners in the Amana VIP pro-am. I can't usually face strangers that early, but Amana paid all my expenses and gave me a $750 fee to come here.

The first pro I ran into out at the golf course was Dale Douglass, who came here straight from winning the Kemper Open and thirty thousand dollars. Dale was floating. He won the Azalea Open earlier this year, but that had only a five-thousand-dollar first prize, so this was his first really important victory on the tour.

Dale's a classic example of how a fellow can develop late on the pro tour. He came out in 1963, the same year I did, and he didn't win a thousand dollars all year. In fact, his first five years on the tour, he didn't earn a total of fifty thousand. He didn't finish in the top three in a single tournament. He didn't even come close to breaking even. If it'd been me, I think I would've quit.

Then, last year, Dale suddenly found his touch. He earned fifty-seven thousand dollars in prize money, more than he'd won all five previous years put together. In the final month of the tour alone, he collected more than twenty thousand. He was leading the Sahara Invitational going into the final round, then lost in a play-off, the closest he'd ever come to a tour victory.

This year, he's been great. He's earned close to eighty thousand dollars, and he's among the top five money-winners. I remember just before the first tournament of the year, the Los Angeles Open, he walked up to me on the putting green and asked me about the possibility of hooking up with Hillerich & Bradsby. I told him I'd heard that H & B wasn't looking for any more pros. Dale seemed a little dejected; H & B ought to shoot me for not insisting they sign him.

Right after I left Dale, I spotted Charlie Coody. Charlie shot a 65 in the final round of the Kemper, came in second, and won himself about seventeen thousand dollars. Charlie got off to a real slow start this year—he won about fifteen thousand in the first four months—but now he's picked up thirty thousand in six weeks and he's climbed up among the top twenty-five money-winners. Charlie didn't mind finishing second in the Kemper; he'd passed about a dozen people with his final round.

"I'm gonna put that money to good use," Charlie told me.

Old Charlie'll probably put that money in some wallet he's got hidden away, and it'll be moth-eaten before it sees the light again.

The pro-am turned out fine. Besides my expenses and my fee, I won another thousand dollars for shooting a 70 and tying for third-low pro. A lot of companies are starting to hold affairs like this. They hire a dozen or two dozen pros and arrange a day with their customers. The customers are impressed, which makes the company happy, and the pros get an extra payday, which makes us happy. The only thing we lose is sleep. I've got to fly to Detroit tonight to put on the charm for Dow Chemical tomorrow.

June 24 / Detroit   The golf tour sure is glamorous. I left Iowa City about midnight, changed planes in Chicago, reached Detroit around three o'clock this morning, got to sleep half an hour later, and jumped up at seven. There was no prize money today, just a nice $1,500 fee, so I had a relaxed round with three top executives from Dow Chemical, General Motors, and Chrysler—enjoyable fellows to play with. These are important people, and maybe in three years or four or five, when I'm ready to quit the tour, one of them will remember me and say, "Hey, Frank, how'd you like to come work for us? We'll pay you fifty thousand a year to play golf with our customers." It would sure beat the hell out of a club job.

After the golf, there was the usual dinner, and the master of ceremonies, a local sportswriter, tore me up one side and down the other. Maybe he was trying to be funny, but he came off nasty as hell to me. He'd picked me to win the Open, he said, and I'd let him down, so he talked about how badly I'd played and how I'd choked, and he said he wondered how anybody could finish fiftieth and call himself a professional. I thought I was in front of Don Rickles, I was getting so cut up.

Then I stood up and jabbed back a little. I quoted Bill Hartack's line about how difficult it must be to write about something you don't know anything about, and the audience gave me a little standing ovation. Maybe business executives feel the same way as I do about some reporters.

June 25 / Cleveland   This life's getting a lot better. I only had to get on one plane this morning. The Dow Chemical people flew me on a private plane to Cleveland, so I was able to get to sleep by 2:30. I got up at seven, with thirteen hours of sleep in three nights, and went out for a nine-o'clock tee time in the Cleveland Open pro-am, and I'll tell you, when I got to the first tee, I knew my partners were in for a rough day. I mean, I was in no shape to be friendly old Frank Beard, and they were looking at me like I was something the good Lord had sent down.

I couldn't have inspired anybody today. I don't know whether it was my fault or what, but my partners struggled the whole round. They must've lost two dozen balls among them. One of the guys didn't finish a hole the entire day. If there was trouble to be found on any hole, he found it. I wasn't too red-hot, either. We not only didn't win anything; we didn't even turn in a score. I was glad to get finished and get back to my family. If I can survive these last three days and still win some money this week, I've got to be a helluva player.

I've got a few things on my side. This Aurora Country Club's a good course for my game, and I've got the kind of caddy I like, a sixteen-year-old boy who's got all the distances down right. If the weather stays decent and if I can just get my putter going, I ought to have a shot at some money. My putting has been atrocious the past two or three months, at least atrocious by my standards. With all my groaning about it, I'm beginning to sound like Palmer and Nicklaus and Casper and the rest of the big boys. The only thing I'm missing is their ability and their bank accounts.

Now that summer's here, the pros have brought out their families, and the swimming pool at the motel is just jammed with golfers' kids. Jimmy Colbert and his wife have their three children out, Deane Beman and his wife have their three, we've got our three, and even the Moose, Julius Boros, has most of his clan out. Old Boros has about seven children, and I've already seen four or five of them wandering around the motel. Julius looks like a big lapdog with all those kids following him around. It's kind of pleasant to have one of the superstars living with the people.

I saw Orville Moody today for the first time since he won the Open, and he's in an absolute stupor. I don't think Orville knows where he is these days. I tried to kid around with him a little, teasing him about the wind coming up the last day in Houston, and he didn't react at all. He usually laughs easily, but right now, instead of acting like a guy who just won a lifetime annuity, he's acting like a guy who's down to his last penny. I know he'll snap out of it, but this week the Sarge is in a fog.

Of course, I wouldn't mind being in that fog.

June 26   On the putting green this morning, I was chatting with Miller Barber, and naturally, the subject of his final round in the U.S. Open came up. "No sense thinking about it," Miller said. "What am I supposed to do, cut my throat? Hell, no. I'm just gonna go out and win the PGA this year."

Bert Yancey walked over. "I know how you feel, X," Bert said. "I've been there, too."

Bert was referring to his own finish in the Open last year; he went into the last round a stroke ahead of Trevino, blew all the way up to a 76, and finished third, six strokes back.

I was sort of surprised Bert brought up his own collapse. I thought he would've pushed it out of his mind by now, but I guess you can't forget something like that so easily. Bert just may have that thing preying on him every time he gets into contention in a major tournament. I wonder about that.

I played with Bert today, and even though he shot a 69, he wasn't thinking about the Cleveland Open at all. His mind's strictly on the British Open. He's going to England next week, and he's already burning to win that tournament. Bert wants a major title so bad, something he can put up next to his name.

Doug Sanders filled out our threesome, and I just about died when I saw Doug's outfit. He looked like the Good Humor man, wearing white bell-bottomed slacks with a red stripe and a red shirt. I guess I made kind of a face, and Doug said, "Hey, Beard, don't knock it. I make a million dollars a year on my clothing contracts."

I don't know. I don't know whether I want a million dollars bad enough to come out looking like that.

There couldn't be two people in the world more different than Sanders and me, but I really like Doug. He's been nice to me since the day I came out on the tour, and I hate to see the way his game is disappearing. He's not scoring too badly lately—he had a 70 today—but he just doesn't have his old zip, doesn't have the shots he used to have. I'm afraid he doesn't have much time left on the tour.

I played pretty poorly myself, but I managed to come in with a 69, scrambling, chipping up and one-putting a lot of holes. I know I'm a veteran when I can play like I played today and still get in one under par, only two strokes behind the leaders. Charlie Coody, Orville Moody, and young Jerry McGee shot 67s.

After my round, I decided to hit a few balls, and I rode to the practice tee with old Arnie. After I'd beaten him out of that Open exemption, he'd gone ahead and qualified, then went to Houston and tied for sixth place. If you finish in the top fifteen, you automatically qualify for the following year. "Well, Frank," Arnie said, "I guess I won't have to fight it out with you next year."

The king was cheerful, considering that he shot a 74 today after setting a course record with a 64 in the pro-am. I think Arnie's just about had it. I don't know why he keeps trying. He's won everything there is to win, he's got all the money he'll ever need, and now, each time he comes out on the course, the fans who don't know any better expect to see him charge. He can't. It must be as embarrassing as hell. If I were Arnie, I'd hang it up and forget it.

I bumped into Bobby Nichols, who'd shot a 74, too, but he was just about the happiest guy I've ever seen. "A bad round doesn't bother me at all anymore," Bobby said. "I'm damn glad I'm off the tour." Bobby took a full-time job this year at the Firestone Country Club in Akron, and from what I've heard, he's got a fabulous deal. I've known Bobby a long time—he's from Louisville and represents H & B—and he certainly didn't have to quit the tour. He's been exempt from qualifying for about ten years, he's won the PGA, he's finished second in the Masters, and he's won more than fifty thousand dollars each of the past five years.

Now, even though he's playing badly, Bobby's smiling. I get fed up with the tour even when I'm playing well. If I were playing badly, I'd probably slit my throat.

Maybe Bobby's got the right idea. Maybe I should just take a good job and get off this damn tour.

June 27   I played better today than I did yesterday, and I scored one stroke worse, a 70. I shot a 32 going out, which brought me within one stroke of the lead, and then, on the tenth hole, a par-four dogleg to the right, I pulled my drive into the left rough and wound up partly blocked by a tree. I could've played safe and just chipped out to the fairway, then tried to get up close and save my par. But I didn't.

"Well, Beard," I told myself, "you've reached the critical point in this round. Let's gamble and see how your luck's running."

I had a little tiny opening, and I tried to punch a seven-iron through, aiming for the green and hoping for a birdie. But I hit the tree and bounced back.

"What the hell happened?" Doug Sanders yelled.

"I just decided to see if this was my week to win," I said. "If I'd pulled that shot off, nobody could have beaten me."

Instead, I wound up making a double-bogey-six.

Actually, I wasn't too upset with a 70. I was happy to survive. The temperature was close to one hundred, and Doug's caddy got so dizzy he quit three times and came back twice. The last time, he was delirious from the heat. Doug picked a fellow out of the crowd to caddy the rest of the way for him, and the fellow's friends, who'd been drinking pretty good, razzed him all the way around. It was a little distracting, but not as distracting as it was wondering when Doug's first caddy was going to keel over.

Doug shot a 71, and Bert matched me with a 70. Bert and I are at 139, eight strokes behind the leader. Charlie Coody tied the course record with a 64, and he's got a four-stroke lead over the fellows who are tied for second, Bruce Crampton and John Schlee. John's the boy who quit the tour back in Miami after the National Airlines Open. That story about him not being able to break even made headlines in *The New York Times*, and some rich guy in the East saw it, called John, and offered him a good sponsorship deal. Now John's back on the tour, and he's won a couple of decent checks, nothing spectacular. As long as there are cases like Dale Douglass and Ken Still, fellows who couldn't make a living out here and then suddenly developed into outstanding players, a lot of young boys—and their sponsors—aren't going to give up their dreams easily.

June 28   Just before I left the putting green to go tee off today, Gardner Dickinson walked up to me. Gardner thinks I'm the best putter on the whole tour. "Hey, give me something quick," he said. "I got to go out there and play and I got the yips so bad I can't make a putt the length of my foot."

"Let me see you hit a few," I said.

I watched Gardner putt, and as far as I could tell, there was nothing wrong with his stroke. In fact, he's got one of the best strokes on the tour. But he just doesn't believe it.

Maybe, because Gardner hits every other shot so well, he's afraid that if he thought his putting was good, too, he'd either decide there was no more challenge and give up the game or he'd want to kill himself each time he didn't win. I don't know. But I knew I couldn't just tell Gardner he was putting well; that wouldn't help him any.

"You're a little wristy," I said. "Try to cut down the wrist a bit and come through with a stiff arm."

He'd been using hardly any wrist, anyway.

"I'll try it," he said.

Then Flip putted a few, turned to me, and said, "Man, that feels good. That's it. Thank you, Frank."

Gardner went out and played right in front of me, and I saw him sink some good putts. He shot a 68. I guess he thought I was a genius.

I teed off, pushed my drive into some trees, and by the time the smoke had cleared, I had a big, fat, triple-bogey-seven. In ten minutes, I'd gone from one-under for the tournament to two-over. I felt like just turning around and walking in.

I stayed out, and I'm glad I did. It was a struggle, but I got two of those strokes back and ended up with a 71. I played with Bob Charles, who shot a 68, and I'll tell you, there's nobody in the world I'd rather play with. The more I see of him, the more I'm impressed. If he ever developed a killer instinct, he'd win everything in sight.

Coody shot a 39 going out and looked like he might be blowing, but then he buckled down and shot a 32 coming in for a 71. He's still first, two strokes ahead of Crampton and four ahead of Schlee.

Nobody else is really close. I'm eight strokes back, and I'm tied for about tenth place. I could move up to some real money with a good round tomorrow.

The temperature hit one hundred today, and I'm beat. If anybody thinks the golf tour is all glamour, I'd like to show him my motel room. It is a thing of beauty. We've got everything we own in one room; it's one huge pile of dirty clothes, diapers, and children. We have trouble getting all the kids to sleep, we have trouble getting them dressed, and we have trouble getting them into restaurants. You start yelling at your wife, and she starts yelling at you, and you end up beating the kids. The only good thing you can say about the tour is that it pays well. Sometimes I wish it didn't pay so well; then, maybe, I could give it up. I know I can't do half as well at any other business, but the way I feel tonight, I think I'll pick up the want ads tomorrow and see if there's any gas stations for sale.

June 29 / Pittsburgh   Old Charlie Coody finally won a tournament today. After five years without a victory, he shot a 69 today, held his two-stroke lead over Bruce Crampton, and collected twenty-two thousand dollars. Outside of me, there's nobody I'd rather see win a tournament.

I can't complain about my own game, either. I sank a twenty-footer, a fifteen-footer, three ten-footers, and an eight-footer, came in with a 66, and moved up to a tie for fourth place, which was worth about five thousand dollars.

I clinched a place on the Ryder Cup team and I lowered my Vardon Trophy average. When I can get through a week like this, not hitting the ball well and still earning a big check, I feel like I'm stealing. Nothing builds up your confidence like playing badly and scoring well; you figure there's no way you can lose.

The fellow who's really playing badly is Jack Nicklaus, and he's scoring badly, too. He didn't even make the top fifty this week, and I've never heard so many fellows talking about how poorly Jack's playing. Bruce Devlin, Bob Murphy, and Tommy Aaron all mentioned it to me. I don't know what the hell's wrong with Jack, but something is. I won't say he's had it, but—

Of course, I retired Arnie the other day, and he finished 69-66-70 to tie for ninth place. You just can't trust the king.

Jack and Arnie and Cas and a bunch of the big boys are going to be gone the next two weeks. They're heading off for the British Open, taking Moody, Trevino, Archer, and Floyd with them, leaving the next two tournaments for us little unknowns. I won't miss them. I can't understand why anyone would go looking for prestige and pass up $225,000 worth of tournaments right here. Whether the big boys play or not, the checks from these tournaments won't bounce.

I got a big kick out of Jimmy Colbert today. He made that New Year's resolution not to get all involved in mechanics this year, and today, driving to the course, he gave me the longest dissertation I ever heard on hand position and hip position and shoulder position and all kinds of theories. He's back in as deep as ever, but he's playing good golf and he's locked up his place in the top sixty.

I had to drive over to Pittsburgh tonight—there's a Union Carbide pro-am tomorrow that I couldn't get out of—and if I'd shot a bad score today, it would've been a long, miserable ride. But, after a 66, the miles just flew by; even the crying of the children sounded good to me. You can tell almost exactly how a golfer did during a tournament by his mood on Sunday night.

July 1 / Grand Blanc   I dreaded going to that Union Carbide affair yesterday, but I've got to admit I had a good time. Harold Henning and I played bridge with a couple of the businessmen, Lionel Hebert demonstrated some of his trick shots, and we had an enjoyable dinner, without any sportswriters giving speeches. Then I went back to my motel, played with the children, got a good night's sleep, and spent most of today driving to Flint, Michigan, for the Buick Open.

After eight straight days of golf, I didn't even get near a course today, and I'm kind of grateful for the little layoff. I'll need all my strength to tackle the Warwick Hills Country Club, which is in Grand Blanc, just outside Flint. As far as I'm concerned, this is the toughest golf course on the tour, tougher than the Colonial or Akron. Nobody's broken 280 at Warwick Hills in three or four years, and even though I've finished pretty high here the last two years, I've got total respect for the course. I've got so much respect for the course that I was thinking seriously of skipping the Buick Open this year—until I got that free Buick out on the West Coast in January.

While I drove from Pittsburgh to Flint and Patty and the kids dozed off, a few things crossed my mind. I started thinking about my own game, and I realized that I've entered about twenty tournaments so far this year, and I've earned money in every one. I haven't missed a cut—in the Crosby, I made the team cut—and I've finished out of the top fifty only once, in the Phoenix Open, after I was in first place at the halfway mark. I've been steadier than ever. I've got a good chance to reach the $100,000 level for the third straight year.

Then I thought about the tour in general and about all the new faces, both the rookies and the new champions. So many guys have won the first tournament of their careers—I can think of nine: Lotz, Shaw, Still, Colbert, Henry, Douglass, Hinson, Beman, and Moody— but none of them is a rookie, and no outstanding candidate for rookie of the year has emerged. The boy I've heard the most about is Grier Jones, who won the intercollegiate championship last year, but I haven't seen him play; the boy I've personally been most impressed by is Jerry Abbott, but I'm not even positive he's a rookie. We have so many new faces popping up all the time I can't tell anymore who's a rookie and who isn't. A young fellow named John Levinson, who hadn't won five hundred dollars all year, jumped in and earned almost four thousand in Cleveland last week, and a lot of the guys thought sure he was a rookie. But John's been out here more than a year. Hardly anybody knows him except Yancey and me, because we've played a little bridge with him.

Looking back over the year, I was struck by the fact that there haven't been any triple-winners. Casper, Archer, Littler, and Douglass have each won two tournaments, and we've had about twenty different single winners. There's so much talent out here that pretty soon nobody'll win two tournaments in a year; a different man's going to finish first each week. Actually, I suppose that just by coincidence we'll have some repeat winners, but I'm convinced that the day is over when a superstar, or a small bunch of superstars, can dominate the tour. Casper won six tournaments last year, Nicklaus won five the year before, and Palmer won eight in 1963—nothing like that's going to happen again.

Cas'll be winning his share of the money for a few more years, but I think Palmer's definitely finished, and Nicklaus—the Jack Nicklaus we've known for most of the 1960s—is through. I don't think Jack's ever going to have another good year on the tour. Of course, I'm speaking relatively; a bad year for Jack is a great one for almost anyone else. But on sheer talent, on the ability to hit a golf ball far and straight and get it into the cup, Jack ought to win one out of every three tournaments; he's that good. But, like Arnie, Nick doesn't have any goals left; he has nothing to prove.

I think that over the next few years golf is going to be dominated by players like Coody and Hill and Moody and Archer and maybe me, solid players who won't win a lot of tournaments in any one year, but'll spend a lot of time going to the bank. The only fellow around who could become a superstar of the quality of Arnie or Jack is Tom Weiskopf. He's got both the equipment and the desire.

Actually, I'm hoping that a new superstar does come along, or that somebody like Nicklaus makes a tremendous comeback and wins a whole bunch of tournaments. My reasoning's purely selfish. We need a superstar, somebody colorful, to lift professional golf up to the next plateau, up to where the tournament minimum becomes $150,000 or $200,000, and I know damn well old Frank's not going to fill that bill.

July 2   Doug Ford and Phil Rodgers started razzing me this morning about the grip on my putter. I've had this putter about five years, and the grip's getting a little ragged.

"Hey, Beard," Rodgers said. "If you didn't have all those holes in your grip, you wouldn't know where to put your hands."

"You've won enough money this year, Frank," Doug said. "You can afford a new putter."

Let them kid me. I know my bad putting's better than most people's good putting, and as long as that's true, I'll keep using this grip till it falls off.

I went out and actually enjoyed myself again in the pro-am. I had three wonderful fellows—they were friendly, quick, and knew what they were doing—and we shot twelve-under as a team. That was worth a few dollars and my 70 on my own ball was worth a couple of hundred more.

My caddy's a pleasure, like all these schoolboys who turn out in the summer. They appreciate carrying your bag. It's as if you're doing them a favor, and they act like whatever you pay them is too much.

After my round, I saw Gene Littler, who told me he's ready to go home. "I'm taking my cash and running," Gene said. "You may not see me again till next year."

"Gonna leave a little money for the rest of us?" I said.

"You don't have to worry about me," Gene said. "I'm playing worse than I've ever played in my whole life."

I know Gene's not playing all that bad—he finished in the top twenty at Cleveland—but he's convinced himself that his game has gone to hell because he wants a good excuse to go home to his family and his cars. He's still top money-winner, the only man over $100,000, so if anybody can afford to get homesick, it's Gene.

I've got my own problem. I'm playing the worst bridge of my life. My golf game's picked up lately, and my card game's fallen apart. I lost some money today to Steve Reid, Deane Beman, and Dave Eichelberger. I'm going to start playing with the wives to get back in shape.

July 3   I'm at the point now where I should start playing my best golf, for a very simple reason. I've got no pressure on me at all. While a lot of fellows are struggling to make the top sixty, pressing, scrambling, trying to wish the ball into the hole, I'm just swinging away without a care in the world.

I've made the top sixty, I've made the Ryder Cup team, I'm high enough on the money list to qualify for all the big TV series, and I've reached the point where I really don't care whether I win much money or not. From here on in, most of it goes to the Internal Revenue Service, anyway. I'm not going to worry myself for them.

Warwick Hills played easier today than I can ever remember it playing, and I came in with a nice relaxed 70—two birdies and no bogeys. Every time I shoot a round without a bogey, I'm reminded of the streak I had in 1967. I went seventy-two straight holes at Hartford without a bogey, then parred the first twelve holes at the Westchester Classic to set a PGA tour record: eighty-four holes without a bogey. That's my kind of record, a record for not making mistakes.

The best part of my game today was my bunker play. I hit four bunkers, and each time I blasted out within three feet of the cup and sank the putt. I ought to give a percentage of my winnings this year to Dick Hart for finding me that old wedge.

I played with Jerry Barber, the former PGA champion, and he shot a 74, which is about par for him these days. I wonder what it is that drives him, that makes him keep playing when he knows the odds against him are so high. As far as I know, Jerry hasn't made a cut this year, and he's played in more than a dozen tournaments.

My other partner, Dan Sikes, shot a 72, and along the way he and I got to talking about the pressure of trying to win a tournament. Dan's a golfer's golfer, a real perfectionist, a fine stroker, and a fine putter, but he hasn't won a tournament in a year. He's been kidding about us maybe teaming up and playing best-ball so that we can at least win half a tournament each and break our streaks. "Frank," Dan said, "the trouble is that I want to win so badly that, when I get in a position to win, I try too hard. If I could just relax, just try to win a little money, then the tournament wins would come right along. I've been in position to win three times this year, and each time I thought about it so hard I couldn't function."

Dan's really burning for a victory. He won over $100,000 last year, and he's over fifty thousand so far this year, and he told me he'd give up winning $100,000 this year if he could have a victory instead.

I don't think I want a victory quite that bad.

July 4   Instead of fireworks, we celebrated with rain today. I was lucky. I had a late tee time, so I didn't even have to start. They called off play late this morning, with half the field on the course, and I ended up just taking it easy around the clubhouse.

At lunch, I got into a discussion with a few of the younger boys, fellows who haven't won much money on the tour, and they were steaming because, as far as they can tell, nothing has been done about the creation of a second tour. They've been campaigning for a satellite tour, kind of like a minor league which would enable the youngsters to build up their game before they had to go up against the Caspers and the Littlers and the Nicklauses. These guys are getting tired of showing up every Monday and finding about 150 or 175 golfers fighting for maybe ten or twenty qualifying spots. I tend to agree with them. Sooner or later, there's going to have to be a second tour.

As I was getting ready to leave the course, a reporter came up to me and asked if I had a few minutes. I broke my rule. I said yes. He started asking me about Nicklaus, and I told him exactly how I felt, how the old Jack Nicklaus didn't exist anymore. I wonder what I'll see in the paper tomorrow.

July 5   There it was, in italics: *"Frank Beard Says Jack Nicklaus Is Through."* I knew it. That newspaperman took my words right out of context and didn't bother to explain my feeling that Jack Nicklaus, when he's through, is better than most fellows at their peaks. I know that somehow or other, somebody's going to get a copy of that story to Jack, and when he gets back from England, he'll have something to say to me. When am I going to learn?

I played good golf again today—some more fantastic bunker shots—but I'll tell you, I got a little hot with some of the people in the gallery. Most people who come out to the golf course are pretty well behaved, but there are a few bad ones here. They carry booze and chicken bones, turn their transistors up high to listen to the Detroit baseball game, and don't know a thing about golf. One fellow today walked up to Dan Sikes after the sixteenth hole and said, "You three-under this round?"

Dan nodded.

"Hey," the man said. "That puts you ten-under for the whole tournament."

Dan was three-under for the day *and* the tournament. The man thought he was following R. H. Sikes, who'd shot a 65 to take the lead Thursday. The man spent sixteen holes walking with us and, all the time, thought he was watching somebody else.

Dan came in with a 69, and I shot a 68, which put me at 138. Lee Elder's leading at 135, Davy Hill's at 136, Larry Hinson's at 137, and there's a bunch of us at 138. We've got to play two rounds tomorrow, to satisfy the television commitment, so we're all in contention. Even Dan Sikes, at 141, isn't out of it. "If I didn't think I had a chance to win tomorrow," Dan said to me, "I'd pack up and leave. I wouldn't stay here just to try for a few thousand dollars."

Jerry Barber missed the cut again, with another 74, but I've got to give him credit. He plays to the utmost of the ability he's got left. He's one of the gutsiest fellows I've ever seen. He didn't have a chance today, but he tried every lick of the way. If half the players out here had his heart, they'd be fighting for every championship.

July 6   It was cold as blazes when I teed off at 7:12 this morning, and if anyone had told me I was going to play well, I'd have told him he was crazy. I knew I couldn't mess around with any cute shots in that weather, so I played conservatively and came in with a conservative 70.

Actually, I was pretty happy with a 70. The Warwick Hills course was playing tough today, and of a total of 142 rounds, shot by seventy-one professionals, only three were under 70. At the lunch break, Lee Elder was ten-under; Dave Hill was nine-under; Homero Blancas, Julius Boros, and I were eight-under; and Dan Sikes was six-under.

I played with Tom Weiskopf and Don Bies, both of whom started the day even with me, and I've never seen Tom play worse than he did this morning. He shot a 78, and he almost blew his top midway through the round. He had a tough little three-iron shot around some trees, and just as he drew his club back, a lady nearby aimed a camera at him and clicked it, a good loud click. Tom stopped in the middle of his backswing, glared at the lady, and turned purple from the neck up. "It's a good thing you're a woman," he said finally. "If you were a man, I'd have you thrown right off this golf course." Some of the fans here are unbelievable. Later in the day, some drunk kept cheering for me, "Helluva shot, Beard, way to go," and one time, as Tom brought back his driver, this drunk hollered, "Hit it, Weiskopf." I thought Tommy was going to hit *him* with the driver.

Tom was so disgusted with his morning round that, during the break, he decided he was going to leave the tour for a few weeks. "I'm not swinging right," he said. "I'm going off fishing, and I'm not coming back until I feel I can play again."

Bies had an entirely different problem. Right from the beginning, I could tell he had no thoughts of winning at all. He just wanted to make a decent check. Don's been a club pro out in Seattle for about ten years, playing in an occasional tournament and playing brilliantly, but this year, for the first time, he's playing the tour regularly. And he's struggling to make the top sixty. He can't shoot for the pin; he's shooting for the green. He's at the opposite extreme from the Palmers and the Nicklauses and, to some extent, the Weiskopfs, who care only about titles, not about checks. Don had a 76 this morning.

After lunch, the weather warmed up a little, and I felt pretty good about my chances. Then I bogeyed two of the first four holes and was just about to give up. But I guess there must be something inside me that won't let me flat quit. I buckled down and birdied five and seven, then parred the next four holes. When I went to the twelfth tee, I was eight-under, and I heard that Dave Hill, after eight holes, was twelve-under. Blancas was tied with me at eight-under, and Elder and Boros had shot themselves out of contention.

I knew that the twelfth through fourteenth holes were all good birdie holes, and I had to make my move. I watched Blancas, playing right in front of me, birdie two of them to go ten-under. I parred twelve, birdied thirteen, then dropped my approach shot on fourteen three feet from the cup. I went up and looked at my putt and almost cried. There was an old heel mark directly between my ball and the hole. I couldn't do a thing about it. I just told myself, "Well, Frank, I guess it's not your week to win, or that mark wouldn't be there." I putted the ball as straight as I could, and it hit the heel mark and veered off and missed the cup by a full six inches.

I was finished right there.

Homero birdied sixteen and drew even at eleven-under with Hill, who'd lost one stroke to par. They were both two strokes ahead of me. I parred in, and so did Hill, and when Homero bogeyed seventeen and double-bogeyed eighteen, I slipped in front of him and finished second for the third time in two months, for the sixth time since my last tournament victory. Dan Sikes finished fourth, a stroke behind Blancas, and won about six thousand dollars he wasn't really looking for.

All day long, I just never showed any confidence. I never told myself, "I'm going to win." The best I could manage was "I hope I'm going to win."

Dave Hill, playing behind me, was just brimming with confidence. He had his caddy, Junior, picking his clubs and lining up all his putts and nursing him home, and he said later he felt he had it all the way. That was the difference. Physically, Davy's no better a golfer than I am. But he had confidence, and I didn't. He won the championship and twenty-five thousand dollars, and now he's second behind Gene Littler on the money list and he's leading everybody in the Vardon Trophy averages.

I settled for winning $14,300, most of which goes to Uncle Sam. I finished with a score of 279. In either 1967 or 1968, that score would've won the Buick Open.

It's been so long since I've won a tournament that I don't know how I'd feel if it finally happened. I'd probably be so numb and surprised I wouldn't get any pleasure out of it.

I'm not dejected tonight. I'm more—I guess you'd say—lost. I went to the office today and did my job and did it well, but I didn't prove anything. I feel like I'm missing something, like I haven't proved I'm a man.

I can't win anything but money.

And—I never thought I'd say this—maybe money isn't enough.

July 7 / Edina   I got one of the touring caddies, a young Australian, to drive my car to Philadelphia today—we play in Philadelphia next week—and Patty and I and the kids flew from Flint to Minneapolis. I just couldn't see driving all the way up here and then trying to drive down to Philadelphia next weekend.

As we were coming off our plane, I practically ran into Steve Reid. I never saw anyone looking more dejected in my life. He'd been out trying to qualify today, and he'd failed, and now he was turning around and heading home. "I need a rest for a couple of weeks," he said.

Since Memphis, when he shot his 61 and won a big check, poor Steve hasn't done a thing. He missed the cut in the Western, missed the cut in the Kemper, missed the top fifty in Cleveland, shot an opening 83 and withdrew in Michigan, and then, today, failed to qualify.

"Frank," Steve said, "this is the worst damn golf course I've ever seen. You don't have a chance on it, not a chance, not the way you like to hit your irons. You try to spin 'em here, and you'll go crazy. If you were smart, you'd just turn around and get on a plane and go home for a week."

Patty was tired, the kids were screaming, and I was almost tempted to take Steve's advice. I've never had very good luck in Minnesota, and I got cut up in the press a few years ago when I had to withdraw during Patty's pregnancy. I don't know why I bothered coming out here.

July 8   I did everything I could this morning to postpone going out to the golf course. I got a haircut, took in the laundry, and bought some toys for the kids. I just didn't want to go play golf. I'm beginning to feel like I don't have to practice, like I can go out and shoot me a 68 or a 69 or a 70 without even trying.

Finally, about one o'clock, when I couldn't think of any more chores, I went to the Braemar Golf Club and registered and bumped into George Boutell, who's sometimes one of our bridge players.

"Congratulations, Frank," he said.

"What for?" I said. "I didn't win."

"Finishing second's not too bad," George said. "I figured it out the other day, and if you finish second in every tournament, you win $400,000."

I putted a little bit and then decided to play a practice round with Bunky Henry. Bunky hasn't done much since he won that National Airlines tournament, but he hasn't had to. With that one victory, he picked up forty thousand dollars and two years of exemptions, the rest of 1969 for winning a tournament and all of 1970 for making the top sixty. He's been living it up, going home whenever he feels like it, just enjoying life. Steve Reid would practically kill himself for two years of exemptions, for a chance to polish his game and concentrate on winning tournaments, and Bunky's taking it all in stride.

I played seven holes and quit. The course is easy and it's in poor shape. I don't feel much like playing this week, but they've put up $100,000, so I'll show up.

July 9   Homero Blancas rode out to the course with me this morning, and we talked a little about the Buick Open. His bogey-double-bogey finish cost him about $5,500, but he wasn't worrying about it. Homero's got a wonderful attitude. He's forgotten about last week, and he's only thinking about this week. He's a happy-go-lucky guy, and that's probably what keeps him from being one of the great players. But it also keeps him smiling.

I've mellowed completely on the pro-ams. I like everything about them now, from my partners to, especially, my scores. I shot a 68 today, which was worth a few hundred dollars, and got all my yardages and finished up early.

In the locker room, I found a letter from Joe Dey, the commissioner of the PGA, telling us that they've changed some of the tournament exemption rules, eliminating most of the British Ryder Cup players and cutting down the number of exemptions to be won in the PGA championship. They didn't do anything yet about those lifetime exemptions for PGA and U.S. Open champions, but I'll bet they make a change within a year or two. I'm really happy with Joe Dey. He became our commissioner early this year, and he's the best thing that ever happened to organized golf.

After my round today, I'm beginning to think I just may string together four 68s here and get that first victory in exactly two years; I won in Indianapolis two years ago today. I'd be happy to get it, very happy, but I've got to admit it would be a little less satisfying than getting it last week or a few weeks from now. The field here is really weak.

Out of the top twenty money-winners from last year, only four of us are here—Dan Sikes, Dave Stockton, Tommy Aaron, and me. Out of the field of 144, judging from the names I saw today, there are a hundred fellows you could line up in front of me and I wouldn't know one from another. Calling this a weak field is understatement. But a victory here would sure as hell beat no victory at all.

I spent most of the afternoon sitting around the pool at the motel with Homero and our wives. We all decided that when we got rich and retired, we'd spend our afternoons sitting around a pool and sipping Scotch, which was exactly what we were doing. I guess this tour life isn't as bad as I sometimes think it is.

Homero and I got to talking about Charlie Coody, who's been home for two weeks now, and we wondered what he was going to do with the twenty-two thousand dollars he won in Cleveland. We decided that Charlie's put the money in a can buried somewhere in his backyard, and it won't get back into circulation before the year 2000.

I might as well confess right now that I've given up on my diet. I don't know exactly what I weigh right now. Somewhere around two hundred pounds, I guess. I didn't realize how bad I look until I saw Bob McAllister today. Back in January, we both weighed 195, and he said he'd be damned if he was going to look like me anymore, he was going on a diet. Now Bob's down to a trim, husky 173, and me—I don't know anymore whether I walk or roll or bounce.

July 10   I'm a big star this week. Aaron, Sikes, Stockton, and I are the co-favorites to win the Minnesota Classic. We're the kings. We're the Palmer, Nicklaus, Casper, and Player of Minneapolis-St. Paul.

Still, when I woke up this morning, I didn't want to go to the golf course. I wanted to sleep or swim or do almost anything except play golf.

After four holes, I was two over par, and for the first time in a long, long time, I felt myself hoping that I'd miss the cut. I think if I'd picked up one more bogey on this easy course, I would have given up and just aimed for a 75 or something like that, the kind of score that would let me get out of here two days early.

But after I parred my fifth and sixth holes, I sank putts of fifteen, twenty-five, and fifteen feet to birdie my seventh, eighth, and ninth holes; and I made the turn one-under. I finished the day at 69, two-under. A couple of youngsters, John Lively and B. R. McLendon, shot 66s, and I'm tied for about tenth place with at least a dozen other people, including Mason Rudolph, one of my playing partners.

Except for those early bogeys and one three-putt green, I couldn't do anything wrong today. When I got in the rough, I found my ball sitting up on a nice fat lie. When I mis-hit a putt, the ball caught the lip and went in. The kind of things that happen when you're going to win a tournament were happening to me.

I even got a break off the course today. I came as close to being disqualified as I've ever come in my life. If you don't sign your scorecard, it's an automatic disqualification, and when I finished today, dripping sweat and feeling tired, I checked and rechecked my card, added it up and down and backward and forward, put it down on the scorer's table, and walked off without signing it. I got about fifty yards from the table, and suddenly, for some reason, I remembered. I sprinted back to the table, and one of the two women who were collecting the cards was staring at mine, not quite knowing what to do about a missing signature. She was about to hand it to a tournament official, and the rule is that once the scorecard reaches the hand of an official, it's final. I rushed up to the woman, asked her for the card, and signed it.

This tournament isn't the best in the world, and it doesn't offer the most prize money, but it sure does have one thing going for it. The sponsors provide a hospitality room, filled with hospitality hostesses, who do everything they can to make the golfers comfortable. The bachelors, particularly, love to play here.

I was sitting in the clubhouse this afternoon, eating lunch, and two of the hostesses happened to sit at the same table. One of them had the biggest lungs you ever saw, and she wasn't hiding them. All of a sudden, old Frank got pretty popular. Guys who hadn't said a word to me in three years were coming over and saying, "Hi, Frank, how you doing?" Standing next to me, with her sitting down, they had the perfect angle of vision.

I left the hostesses for the bachelors, but I'm exhausted tonight, anyway. I'm drained. I told Patty, "I don't know what a mental breakdown feels like, but I think I'm having one." I have absolutely no motivation. I don't want to play golf tomorrow.

July 11   Before I left the motel this morning, I turned to Patty and said, "Honey, if I get close to missing the cut, I'm gonna miss it. I really don't give a damn. I'm ready to take a couple of days off."

I teed off, and I'll tell you, I don't think I could've missed the cut if I'd tried. I couldn't play badly. Every time I stood on the tee, I knew I was going to hit the ball down the middle. Every time I got out on the fairway, I knew I was going to knock my iron shot next to the hole. Every time I lined up a putt, I knew I was going to make it.

I shot the easiest 67 I ever shot in my life—fourteen pars, four birdies, and no sweat. The course has improved a little day by day, and I'm spinning my irons fine. I missed only one green, and that time I blasted out of a trap about a foot from the hole. My bunker game has become incredible. One of these days I'm going to catch some of those boys who've been laughing at me for five or six years and get them into a bunker and take some money off them. They won't believe how much I've improved, thanks to hard work and a good wedge.

Dave Stockton's leading the tournament at 135, Dan Sikes and I are both at 136, and Tommy Aaron's at 139. So far, the big stars are holding up pretty well. The young boys who were leading yesterday, McLendon and Lively, shot up to a 75 and a 77 today.

Mason Rudolph, my partner, was moving along three under par today on the front nine, and then he started to three-putt and just lost all confidence in his putting. He ended up at even-par 71, so he's at 140 for the tournament. Mase is literally battling for his life. He was exempt for about ten years, really one of the top players on the tour, but for the past year and a half he hasn't been able to put two nickels together, much less win a tournament. I don't know exactly what he's earned this year, but I know it isn't much. If he misses the top sixty again—he missed last year—his career is basically finished, at the age of thirty-five.

It's strange, but seeing the trouble Mase's in kind of picked me up today. Here's a big-name player fighting for the top sixty like a scared rookie, and all I've got to worry about is whether or not I'm going to win a tournament. My problem's nothing compared to his. At the same time, I know that I could be in his situation with hardly any warning. It made me a little more determined. It made me want to play golf the rest of this week, to push back the day when I'll be going through exactly what Mason Rudolph's going through.

July 12   For the fifth day in a row, despite all my determination last night, I woke up not wanting to go to the golf course. I wasn't teeing off until 1:30, so I had plenty of time to sit by the pool with the kids and relax. I kept thinking how nice it'd be to spend the rest of the day sitting by the pool.

I didn't feel any pressure. I wasn't running scared the way I have been. It was almost like "Well, I've got to go play today, so the hell with it. I'll just go out and accept whatever happens."

What I needed was something to charge me up, and as soon as I reached the course, I got something. I had told a television man yesterday that I'd do a taping with him, but I'd gotten tied up with somebody else, and I'd never gotten back to the first guy. He walked up to me this afternoon and said, "I want to tell you, face to face, that was the rottenest trick anybody ever pulled on me. I waited for you for half an hour or an hour, and you didn't come back. You never intended to come back."

Well, that set me off. These newspaper and television reporters have been on us all week, complaining about how there aren't any big-name players here and how all the pros are bums because we won't patronize their tournament. Hell, there were only fourteen men in the world who earned $100,000 playing golf last year, and three of us—Sikes, Stockton, and me—are here, and that's not so damn bad. We may not be the biggest names in the world, but we deserve at least a little credit.

"Listen," I said, "you're going under the presumption I didn't intend to come back yesterday, and you don't know whether I was or I wasn't. I could give you an explanation, but you don't deserve it." I was hollering, and I guess the adrenaline started flowing, and that helped me all day.

Just before I teed off, Sikes came up to me and said, "Look, Frank, I hope you or I or Dave or Tom wins this thing just to shut these people up a little. If one of the young boys comes up from behind and beats us, the press is going to say they were right, there were no big-name players here, just a bunch of rabbits."

That gave me a little more determination.

I played with Stockton, and I shot one of the best rounds I've shot in a long time. I did miss an eighteen-inch putt on the sixteenth hole, but I wound up with my second straight 67. Dave shot a 69, and I moved into first place, a stroke ahead of him and two ahead of young Hale Irwin. Aaron's five strokes back, and Dan, who won his last championship here a year ago, blew to a 75. It's up to me and Dave to hold off the young boys tomorrow.

I had confidence in myself all day. It never even entered my mind that I might not be leading at the end of the round. "You know," Stockton said, "you looked like you were gonna play well, and you did. You didn't look like you were scared at all."

I'm in a familiar position—first place with one round to go for the fourth time this year. "I think I've got another second-place finish locked up," I told Patty tonight, but I wasn't serious. I'm not predicting I'm going to win tomorrow, but for a change, I feel that I'm not afraid of winning.

July 13   I don't have to look at the late-night news to know what happened today: Frank Beard is the champion of the 1969 Minnesota Classic. Old Frankie went out and played himself some golf, I don't mind telling you. I really made it happen. I shot a 66 and won the tournament by seven strokes.

It was almost anticlimactic. I knew all the way I was going to do it.

This morning, I wanted to go play golf, but when I woke up, the rain was coming down so hard I thought sure we'd get postponed. Instead, they just pushed the starting times back two hours—I didn't tee off until after three o'clock—and the sun came out and we played.

I was nervous most of the morning, nervous in a good way, the way I used to be back in the old days when I was winning my share of tournaments. I couldn't eat much breakfast. The kids irritated the hell out of me. I was on edge, and it's not the sort of thing you can manufacture. It either comes or it doesn't.

I went out to the golf course, thinking about what Dan had said yesterday about the press waiting to pounce on us, building up my determination, and when I got to the locker room, I realized I was out of golf balls and had to borrow some from R. H. Sikes.

Then I was off to the races. I birdied two of the first four holes and, on the fifth hole, faced the critical point of my round. I had a thirty-foot putt for a birdie, and as I got set to putt, a bug lit on my ball. I backed off, shooed him away, lined everything up again, drew my putter back, and moved it forward. An instant before impact, the bug flew back on the ball and startled the hell out of me. I left the putt six feet short. "Oh, God," I said to myself. "Here we go." I don't know what would've happened if I'd missed that six-footer. I know it would've broken whatever momentum I had. But I made it and doubled my momentum, and I was never in trouble again. I made the turn four-under for the day and fourteen-under for the tournament, and I had a five-shot lead over Hale Irwin, my playing partner, and six over Dave Stockton, and the suspense was over. I coasted in.

I had mixed feelings playing with Hale. He's a nice boy, with a wonderful wife, and I really like him, but I was pulling against him all day. What else could I do realistically? He was my closest pursuer for ten or eleven holes, and every time he hit a bad shot, I was jumping up and down inside. I like him, I wanted to see him do well—maybe finish second; he and his wife could use a good check—but I liked Larry Hinson, too, and that didn't help me any in New Orleans. I was caught in the middle; I guess I wasn't hoping for Hale to make double-bogeys. Just bogeys. But he ended up with a 74 and slipped right out of the top ten.

Stockton shot 73 and fell back into a tie for fourth, and Tommy Aaron came up with a 66 to tie a young South African named Hugh Inggs for second place. I was happy to see that Mason Rudolph finished with a 67 and won himself about two thousand dollars. Maybe Mase'll be able to fight his way into the top sixty.

The drought's over now, but I've got a little hollow feeling about this victory. Maybe I'm just tired, but I don't feel terribly excited. If the field had been a little stronger or if I hadn't been scoring so well the past few weeks or if the finish had been a little closer, the realization of winning might've been much more satisfying. The way it is, it's sort of a shallow victory; over in England, Tony Jacklin won the British Open yesterday, and he's the golf hero of the week, not me. Maybe I'll be happier tomorrow, but right now it just seems almost routine.

Patty didn't walk with me today; she had to baby-sit. So after I

Frank Beard's Record

TOURNAMENT	1ST ROUND	2ND ROUND	3RD ROUND	4TH ROUND
Kemper		DID NOT PLAY		
Cleveland	69	70	71	66
Buick	70	68	70	71
Minnesota	69	67	67	66

collected my trophy and the winner's check for twenty thousand dollars, I went back to the motel and picked up her and the kids and took them out to dinner for a big celebration of my first victory in two years and four days. We went to the corner Howard Johnson's and ate fillet of fish and chocolate-chip ice cream. The bill for the five of us came to six dollars.

TOTAL SCORE	FINISH	PRO-AM EARNINGS	INDIVIDUAL EARNINGS
276	T 4	—	$ 4,840.00
279	2	$235.48	14,300.00
269	1	268.75	20,000.00

8

The Biggest Pot
of All

TOURNAMENT	SITE	PURSE	DATES
Philadelphia Classic	Whitemarsh Valley Country Club Chestnut Hill, Pennsylvania	$150,000	July 17– July 20
American Golf Classic	Firestone Country Club, Akron	125,000	July 24– July 27
Westchester Classic	Westchester Country Club, Harrison, New York	250,000	July 31– August 3

July 14 / Philadelphia   That victory in the Minnesota Classic still feels a little shallow to me, but at least I'm glad I won by seven strokes. With that kind of margin, nobody can say for sure that, if all the big boys had been there, I wouldn't have won.

And the field wasn't all that bad. We did have four of the twelve members of the American Ryder Cup team—Douglass, Still, Sikes, and me; we did have eight of the thirty leading money-winners—us four, Aaron, Stockton, Bunky Henry, and Tom Shaw.

I didn't exactly beat amateurs, yet I've got to admit it was the poorest field we've had so far this year.

We stayed in Minneapolis last night and waited for a 2:30 flight today so that we could take advantage of family-plan rates. By flying after noon, Patty could go for half the normal fare and Danny and Randi could share a seat for one-third the normal fare. When we landed in Philadelphia, our car was waiting; the caddy had delivered it to the airport. But then I got lost looking for the turnpike exit to our motel, and it ended up taking us two hours to get from the airport to our room, almost as long as it took us to fly from Minneapolis to Philadelphia.

By the time we got settled—they didn't have a crib for us, so we had to put Danny and Randi in one bed—Patty was ready to cut my throat, I was ready to cut hers, and we were both about to hang the kids by their toes. "After a good night's sleep," Patty said, "we'll all feel better in the morning."

I hope so.

July 15   I got thinking today about the way I've been playing, and I realized I've never in my life had a streak quite like the one I'm on. In my last nine tournaments, I've finished in the top ten seven times, in the top four six times, second three times, and first once. I've won more than seventy thousand dollars in a little over two months.

In the last three weeks, I've played twelve competitive rounds, none higher than 71, seven of them in the 60s; if you count the pro-ams, nine of my last fifteen rounds have been in the 60s. My average official score since the U.S. Open has been 68.7. I can hardly believe how good I've been playing. I know I can't keep it up too long.

The streak has brought my earnings for the year up over ninety-five thousand dollars, and now I'm third on the money list, higher than I've ever been this late in the year. I'm first in Ryder Cup points, first on the money list for a U.S. Open exemption next year, and fourth in the Vardon Trophy standings.

With my check in Minnesota, I moved past Sam Snead and into eighth place on golf's all-time list of money-winners. Six of the seven in front of me—Palmer, Casper, Boros, Littler, Sanders, and Player—have been on the tour at least five years longer than me; the seventh, Nicklaus, has been playing one year longer than me.

Of course, that doesn't mean I'm the eighth-best golfer of all time. Ben Hogan and Byron Nelson aren't even in the top thirty. They were born about twenty years too soon. They used to get less for winning a tournament than I get for coming in fifteenth.

I didn't get to see Steve Reid today. He tried to qualify yesterday, and he failed again. Steve must be miserable. I heard that there were 230 golfers out yesterday competing for ten places in the Philadelphia Classic, and only scores of par or better made it. Steve had some good company; young Bert Greene, who's won a few decent checks lately, failed to qualify, too.

We'd better get that second tour soon. I've been talking to some of the young boys, and only a few of them are opposed to it. They just don't want to be labeled minor-leaguers. They've got sugar daddies paying their expenses, and they'd rather finish last among the big boys and win $150 and be able to say, "Oh, yeah, Arnie and I play in the same tournament every week," than win two thousand dollars for beating a bunch of unknowns and has-beens. The way things are going, I'm afraid we're just going to have to bruise a few egos. In the long run, a second tour'll produce better golfers and more excitement. The public will turn out to see a young kid coming up from the minors with a bit of a reputation; nobody ever wins a reputation as a rabbit.

July 16   The first person I saw at the course this morning was Charlie Sifford. "Charlie," I said, "after you won the L.A. Open, I figured you to win a hundred thousand this year."

Charlie Cigar's been having his problems. "Frank," he said. "I can't drive no more, and I can't make no putts. Nothing's working."

I feel sorry for Charlie. He hasn't done a thing since the L.A. Open, and I guess he's just gotten too old. He's forty-six now officially, maybe closer to fifty, and I don't think he'll ever get that shot at the Masters he's been dying for. Lee Elder'll probably be the first Negro to qualify for the Masters, and Charlie's worked so hard for it.

"If I can help," I told him, "I'll take a look at you. See if I can see anything."

"I don't know if anything can help Old Charlie," he said.

On the putting green, a few of us got to teasing Billy Casper's regular caddy, a fellow named Del. "We're bringing out bags of fertilizer, Del," we told him, "and spreading it all over the course."

Buffalo Billy's allergies have become something of a joke among the other pros; I know Billy, and I'm sure he's sincere, but the fact that his allergies never keep him out of the Masters or the U.S. Open or the PGA or the $250,000 Westchester Classic makes some of the fellows a little suspicious. They figure Billy ought to just play golf and forget about his allergies.

I had an uneventful pro-am round, then rushed back to the motel to lounge around the swimming pool, sip a little Scotch, and play some bridge. We played with the Bemans tonight, and I hadn't realized how much we'd been playing lately until little Danny, who doesn't know a deck of cards from a bag of Fritos, got tired of waiting to be tucked into bed and tugged on Patty's arm and said, "Mommy, aren't you dummy yet?"

July 17   After four holes today, I was three-over, and I probably would've given up if this hadn't been one of the Alcan tournaments. The Alcan Golfer of the Year tournament, with a first prize of fifty thousand dollars, is only open to about two dozen golfers, half of them Americans. We can qualify based on our performances in four separate tournaments—New Orleans, the Western, Philadelphia, and Hartford; we take our three best four-round scores from those tournaments, then add them together and the low dozen qualify. For the first two tournaments—New Orleans and the Western—I was low man. If I can just make the cut here, I'll clinch a place in the Alcan.

So I buckled down after the first four holes, birdied three of the par-fives, and came in even-par at 72. I was just happy to survive the heat today. The temperature was in the nineties, and the humidity was almost as high. Orville Moody passed out and had to be taken off the course in an ambulance; Chuck Courtney quit on the first tee. My last few holes, all I could think about was getting to the air-conditioned clubhouse and getting something cool to drink.

Soon as I got inside, I walked up to Lionel Hebert and said, "Liney, give me some of your tickets"—at most tournaments, you can't pay cash for anything; you have to buy food and beverage tickets—"so I can get something to drink. I'll pay you for 'em."

"You can't pay me," Lionel said. "I'm buying. I want to be able to say I bought a hundred-thousand-a-year man a drink."

I don't embarrass easily. "Okay," I said. "Buy me a drink."

Lionel got me a drink, and I sat down and looked at Dave Hill, who was sitting nearby, and said, "I couldn't beat you at Flint. You slipped past me."

"Beard, you couldn't beat me with a hammer," Davy said. "Hell, you had to go pick on the rabbits to win one."

I guess I'll never live that down—but the money spends just the same.

July 18   "Hey, Beardsie," Doug Sanders started yelling at me on the practice tee this morning, "aren't we splitting this year? Don't I get half that twenty thousand you won?"

"Okay, Doug," I said. "Let's split down the middle on everything —endorsements, clothing contracts, everything."

Sanders backed off on that. He just makes tipping money on the golf course.

I shot my second straight 72 today, and I'm somewhere in the top thirty, five strokes out of the lead. But I'll tell you, with a pair of 68s, I could win this tournament. I remember what happened here in Philadelphia last year. I started off with a 73 and a 72, and I figured I was going to miss the cut. I paid my caddy, checked out of the locker room, packed up my car, and then heard that my 145 made the cut. The last two days, I shot a 68 and a 65 and wound up tied for fourth place.

Tommy Jacobs has a two-stroke lead now at 139. Tommy came out here on the tour about ten years ago and looked like he was going to beat the world. He won a tournament his first or second year on the tour, finished second in the U.S. Open in 1964 and second in the Masters in 1966. Then, a flaw in his game—a loop at the top of his swing—caught up to him, and he just fell apart. He did nothing in 1967 and lost his exemption, did nothing in 1968 and nothing this year. A few months ago, he was talking seriously about quitting the tour and becoming a stockbroker.

There's something wild going on out here on the tour. Someone is sending phantom letters to the wives of some of the golfers, saying that their husbands are running around while they're at home. A few of the guys are upset because the letters are hitting too close to the mark, but even if you're pure as a lily, these letters can shake you up a little. If your wife gets one, whether you're guilty or innocent, she just might not believe you. I'll guarantee you this: I'll be checking my mail pretty close in the weeks to come.

July 19   Billy Maxwell came over to me on the putting green this morning and told me he was glad I'd won in Minnesota. "And I'm real happy you won by seven strokes, Frank," he said, " 'cause the one thing you're missing is a killer instinct. You just got to remember that these people out here are your friends every place except on the golf course. You got to go out and stomp on 'em. Beat 'em by seventy strokes, not just seven. When you're seven strokes ahead, you got to try to make it seventeen. If you don't, if you let up, if you get to thinking about anybody but yourself, you'll wind up second all the time."

I'd never heard Billy talk like that. I'd always thought of him as a pretty easygoing guy, despite his temper, and I'd always kind of laughed and kidded with him, never anything serious, and suddenly, I was seeing a whole different side of him. I realized that Billy's been out on the tour for fifteen years, a little fellow without great physical equipment, and all that time, he must've been burning to be one of the best. He has won eight tournaments, he has finished among the top twenty money-winners seven or eight times, but he's never won a major tournament and he's never won as much as thirty thousand dollars in a year. Now he's forty, and he's just about finished. He missed the cut yesterday, yet he was out practicing his putting today, and he was telling me to get it all while I could.

At the same time, Lee Trevino was on the putting green, laughing and smiling. Lee's been on the tour less than three years, and he's made a million dollars, and yesterday he took a double-bogey on the eighteenth or he would've tied Tommy Jacobs for the lead.

"Hey, Lee," somebody said, "I heard that when you came off the eighteenth, you were cussing in front of a bunch of kids."

"Hell," Lee said, "I didn't think these Philadelphia kids could understand Mexican."

Bob Murphy was standing near us, trying to get accustomed to a new putter. He left his car unlocked last night, and someone stole all his clubs. We must have four or five guys robbed every year on the tour; the professional thieves know when we're coming and keep a pretty good eye on us. I make it a point never to leave my clubs in my car. "I don't know what I'm going to do," Murph said. "I don't think I can play with any other sticks."

In the third round today, Grier Jones, a rookie who missed the cut in three of his last four tournaments, shot a 66 and tied Tommy Jacobs for first place. I'm pulling for Tommy tomorrow. I don't think he's got to worry too much about the rookie. I think he ought to worry more about Dave Hill, who's in third place, three strokes behind the leaders.

Maybe he ought to worry about old Frank, too. I shot a 70 today, and I'm in about thirteenth place, seven strokes back. But if I could shoot a 65 tomorrow, like I did in the final round last year, I just might sneak right in there and win this tournament.

July 20　On my way to the first tee today, I saw Dave Hill. "Davy," I said, "I think you're going to win this thing. But, I'll tell you, I'm going to give you a run for your money."

I got half of that right—and almost the other half. I had one of the most unusual rounds of my career. I shot nine birdies, three bogeys, and six pars for a 66, my third closing 66 in four weeks. I missed an eighteen-inch putt and took a bogey on the first hole— I must've set a PGA record for missed eighteen-inch putts this year—but the key was the thirteenth hole.

I reached the thirteenth all charged up, after birdies on three of the previous four holes. I was six-under for the tournament, and the leaders were nine-under, and I thought I just might catch them. The thirteenth is a drive-and-wedge hole, with the pin cut right in behind a bunker today. I hit a good drive, then told myself,

"This is it, Beard. This is where you find out whether or not you're going to win."

Then I took a little wedge and tried to push it just over the bunker, close to the pin. I missed by inches. I caught the lip of the bunker, rolled back in, blasted out five feet from the cup, and missed the putt. That was it. If I'd birdied instead of bogeyed, I'd have come in with a 64. If I'd parred, I'd have come in with a 65. A 64 would've won the tournament for me, and a 65 would've put me in a play-off with Hill, Jacobs, Gay Brewer, and R. H. Sikes, all of whom finished at nine under par. I was all by myself in fifth place.

Dave Hill won the play-off with a birdie on the first sudden-death hole and became the first triple-winner of the 1969 tour. He boosted his earnings up to $129,000 and moved past Gene Littler into first place. My $6,150 check kept me in third place and carried me over the $100,000 level for the third straight year. I clinched my spot in the Alcan tournament; after three qualifying tournaments, I don't think there's anyone within twenty strokes of me.

As I was leaving the locker room, I passed Lee Trevino, packing up his car, wearing his cowboy hat and his cowboy boots. I couldn't help but notice that he had a bigger crowd watching him load his car than I'd had watching me shoot a 66. He's got something I'll never have, a colorful circus air, an ability to have fun and let other people have fun watching him. The other day, I heard, he was on the practice tee, hitting a few seven-irons, and as he lofted one up, some lady said, "Oh, that's beautiful. Simply beautiful."

Lee whipped around and said, "Look, lady, I'm the U.S. Open champion. What the hell did you expect—ground balls?"

Lee laughed, the lady laughed, and the whole crowd laughed.

I could never act like that, but I'm glad Lee does. I'm not jealous. I'm grateful. He sure brings the people through the gate.

Davy Hill's closer to me than he is to Trevino. He doesn't clown around. He doesn't wear flashy clothes. He's never really been recognized for his ability and classified with the big boys. "When they see me leading the money list," Davy said today, after his victory, "why it's just gonna make some of them cats sick to their stomachs. They ain't gonna be happy about Dave Hill being on top."

It's difficult not to get a little bitter.

July 21   My wife must've been worrying that we had too much extra space in the station wagon because today, on the four-hundred-mile trip from Philadelphia to Akron, we brought along the Colberts' ice cooler. Jimmy and his wife flew, so we just jammed the wagon a little tighter.

We got to our motel early this afternoon, and I didn't bother going over to the course. I just sat around the swimming pool, watched the astronauts on the moon on television, and talked about anything but golf. I'm not even sure I'll go practice tomorrow.

My game's grooved—I don't have to mess with it at all—and I'm totally relaxed. I like this Firestone Country Club course, and it seems to like me, too. I tied for first place here last year, then lost in a play-off.

I've learned a good lesson the past couple of weeks. I was two-over after four holes at Minnesota and felt like quitting. I was three-over after four holes at Philadelphia and felt like quitting. After winning in Minnesota and finishing fifth in Philadelphia, I don't think I'll ever be tempted to quit again.

July 22   I went out to the course today mostly to start scrambling for passes. We're less than three hundred miles from Louisville, and the last time I was home, I played the big shot, promising everyone, "Come on over to Akron, and I'll get you passes." Now I've got ten or fifteen people rolling in here this weekend, all people I like having around, and I'd better find them tickets.

I saw Steve Reid for the first time in two weeks. "I told you when I saw you at the airport," he said, "that you shouldn't play that course in Minnesota. I told you it'd mess your game up."

We had a good laugh, then played a practice round against Dean Refram and Deane Beman. While we were walking down one of the fairways, Bobby Nichols, who's the home pro here, yelled to me, "Hey, Frank, I got something for you."

"What's that?" I said.

"A bank," Bobby said. "Something to put your money in."

I had a good laugh at that, too. I'll tell you, when you're winning, when you're playing well, you laugh at everything. I don't think there are two bad guys on the whole tour. I love them all.

The only thing wrong with playing well is the attention you get. You lose all your privacy. I can't eat a meal in a restaurant without getting interrupted anymore. It drives me crazy. I'm Frank Beard, but I don't care if nobody knows it except me and my family and my banker. After my round today, for instance, I stopped for a haircut in a little barber shop, tucked in a corner somewhere, and there were just a couple of old men in there listening to Arthur Godfrey or something. I figured I'd get a haircut, read a magazine, and relax for half an hour. The first thing the barber says is, "Hey, aren't you Frank Beard?" I ended up with four barbers around me, asking questions, talking golf, taking a whole hour to give me a good haircut. I'd prefer a worse haircut and less conversation.

When I got to the motel, we played a wild baseball game out back—Beman, Colbert, Hugh Royer, Fred Marti, myself, and about twenty of the golfers' kids. We were hitting and throwing and running, having more fun, and then, on one play, Jimmy Colbert and Deane Beman collided. Deane had to quit playing; he thought he'd pulled a rib muscle. We're all going to end up feeling that game tomorrow morning.

July 23   Patty's father called first thing this morning to tell us that Patty's mother died during the night. We'd been expecting the call for a long time, but still, it was a bit of a shock. Patty and I both realize that, in a way, after so many years of suffering, it's a blessing for her mother.

The funeral is going to be a quiet, simple, private affair, so Patty and I decided that she'd fly to Kansas City with Jennifer, and I'd stay here, play in the tournament, and take care of the two older children. There's nothing I can do to help in Kansas City. Patty left this morning, and I got a baby-sitter to come in.

This is my fifth straight tournament, the first time I've played five in a row since Florida, but I'm not feeling as tired as I thought I would. It just goes to prove that all the fatigue out here is mental fatigue. I know that if I'd played the last four weeks and never finished in the top ten, I'd be exhausted now.

I found out tonight that Deane Beman either cracked a rib or tore some cartilage in that collision with Jimmy Colbert. Deane may be out of action for a month or six weeks. He's got his place in the top sixty all locked up—he's thirteenth right now—but we all feel badly for him. Jimmy feels even worse than Deane does.

July 24   I got up this morning and found that one of my friends in the press had written another wonderful piece about me. I didn't even know the guy was interviewing me yesterday—we were just talking—but, of course, that's my own fault. I should've realized that reporters don't talk to pass the time of day.

He asked me about my putting, and I made the comment that, with my stroke, the way I can sink them from now to doomsday, it's like stealing out here on the tour, like daylight robbery. Well, the story today didn't even mention my putting. It said, "Frank Beard says that playing the tour is so easy, it's like stealing."

As soon as I got to the course, Frank Boynton ran up to me. "Beard," he said, "you ought to try playing with *my* swing sometime and see if that's stealing."

The monster—the Firestone course—got tamed today. In the old days, the middle 1960s, 68 would lead the tournament, 69 was unbelievable, par 70 was fantastic, and 72 was a good score. I came in with a 68 today—maybe the lowest round I've ever had here—and I'm in a ten-way tie for eighth place.

Two young boys, Terry Wilcox and Bobby Mitchell, shot 65s, Jack Nicklaus shot 66, and Steve Reid was in the group at 67. All of us owe a little debt to Dutch elm disease, which knocked out about five hundred trees here and a few strokes.

I made a good run for the lead myself. I was three-under after nine holes, but then some rain and some wind came in, and I shot one-over the second nine. I played with Bert Yancey, who's like a brother to me, and Bruce Crampton, and they both shot 72s. They'll probably have to shoot 72 or 73 to make the cut tomorrow, and not so long ago 144 was a helluva halfway score here.

I had a chat in the clubhouse with Larry Hinson, the boy who beat me in the play-off in New Orleans. Larry always seems a little embarrassed by the fact that he beat me, but he knows I was trying to cut his throat just like he was trying to cut mine. He wanted some advice today. He's been offered a contract by one of those big management agencies that handle a lot of athletes, from golfers to football players, and he wanted to know what I thought of it. I told him I'm opposed to those kinds of setups; I think most of them just rob the athletes blind, just take their percentage and run. "Larry," I said, "if you do it, don't get yourself locked into one of those long-term deals. 'Cause if you win a major tournament, you'll have so many offers you won't need anybody to look out for you. And if you don't win a major tournament, they're not going to do anything for you, anyway."

Art Wall walked over. "You gave him some good advice, Frank," Art said. "I've always stayed on my own, and maybe I've missed a few dollars that way, but I've made a lot of friends and I've never had anybody high-pressuring me."

I had to hustle home from the golf course to rescue the baby-sitter from the children. I'll tell you, the average housewife deserves the Congressional Medal of Honor for putting up with these ankle-biters all day. After three hours of it today, I was ready to dive in the pool and not come up. Patty'll be back tomorrow, and I'll sure be glad to see her.

July 25   Bruce Crampton has a great golf game, he may even have the ability to be the best on the tour, but he seems to think he's the unluckiest man in the world. If he hits a putt and it lips out, he'll say, "It couldn't have gone in. I putted it, didn't I?" Or if he hits a ball into a bunker, he'll say, "Well, that one's sure to be buried." Here's a fellow who's made a quarter of a million dollars in less than five years, he's got a wonderful family, and he's convinced that he never gets a break.

I got him upset today. On the second hole, I hit a shot that landed just short of the green, bounced over a bunker, and rolled up toward the cup. "That's the luckiest thing I've ever seen," Bruce said. "If that was my ball, it would have buried in the bunker."

Two holes later, I hit an iron out of the rough, and my ball bounced over another bunker up to the fringe of the green. Crampton threw his arms up. "That's it," he said. "That's it. I've never seen anybody so lucky in my life. I can't believe it. You better put a chapter in your book about how lucky you are."

A lot of the fellows know I'm keeping a dairy and kid me about it, but Crampton wasn't kidding. He's a strange guy. His attitude is costing him $100,000 a year. Why doesn't he just use what the Lord gave him—which is a helluva golf game—and stop moaning and crying? I moan too, but Bruce has got to realize that everybody gets some good breaks in this game and everybody gets some bad ones. He shot a 74 today and missed the cut. Bert Yancey made the cut with a 71.

I shot a "lucky" 67. I didn't even come close to a bogey all day. If my putter had just been warm—not even hot—from fifteen feet in, I could've had a 64, 65 easily.

It looks like I'll be playing in the final twosome tomorrow. I'm tied for third place at 135 with Raymond Floyd. Bobby Mitchell is second at 133, and the leader, with two straight 66s, is Jack Nicklaus. I guess that statement of mine about the Bear being through caught up to him and got him a little mad; he broke the thirty-six-hole record here. We'll probably be paired tomorrow. Jack's from Columbus, and we'll have half of Ohio following us.

When I got into the locker room, Orville Moody yelled, "Hey, Beard, what'd you shoot?"

"I'm five-under," I said.

"You're the playingest Jesse I ever saw in my life," Sarge said. "You're playing so good, it's unbelievable."

I'm averaging 68.8 for my last eighteen rounds, 67 for my last three. "Orville," I said, "I'll trade you all my rounds for that U.S. Open title you got."

"No deal," said Orville.

Old Sarge is a pretty smart fellow.

July 26   I woke up about six o'clock this morning with Randi
hitting me in the face with a shoe. Then the sun came in through the
window, and the baby started crying, and in the space of about ten
seconds, all the children were up and yelling. Mother and Dad
had checked into the motel, and so had my brother, Ralph, and
his wife, Betty, and their children; by nine o'clock, we had our
own three-ring circus going. Danny running after Pro and Randi
running for the pool and me trying to think about winning a golf
tournament. But I love it; it beats leaving them all at home.

The first person I ran into out at the course was young Ron
Cerrudo, and he said, "Looks like you're going to be stealing for
another week, Frank." The way that story came out the other day,
it sounded like I was saying I was the only guy out here who could
play worth a damn, and I'm taking a lot of kidding. And it isn't all
kidding. Down deep, some of the guys are saying, "Frank, we're
all out here trying to do our best. If we can't all be as good as you,
let us ride a little bit. Don't knock us." I'd like to get my hands on
that sportswriter.

Then, on the first tee, thanks to another writer, Nicklaus walked
over to me and said, "Hey, Frank, I see where you said I was
through."

"Jack," I said, "I did say that, but that wasn't all I said." I explained to him all I'd said about him having the potential to win
one out of every three tournaments and maybe $350,000 a year, but
that I didn't think he'd ever live up to his potential again. I didn't
think he was going to try that hard anymore.

"Frank," Jack said, "you were right. I don't have much motivation
left. What can I prove?"

He dropped the subject right there.

As we were walking down the first fairway, Jack said, "You leading the Ryder Cup list?"

"Yes."

"Good. You've been playing awfully well."

"I'm really happy about it," I said. "I've always wanted to play
on a Ryder Cup team."

Jack kind of smiled.

I guess something like playing on a Ryder Cup team couldn't get Jack all excited. He's already played on World Cup teams, Eisenhower Cup teams, and Walker Cup teams, always representing the United States. I've never represented my country, and I want to. For Jack, the Ryder Cup is just another week away from fishing.

The Bear still isn't playing well. He drove badly today. Of course, I wish my drives were as bad as his, but by his standards, his driving was atrocious. He shot a 71, and Ray Floyd and Bobby Mitchell both caught up to him and tied him for first place at 203. I shot a 72, and now I'm all alone in fourth place at 207, four strokes back. If I could shoot one of my regular Sunday 66s tomorrow, I might win the whole thing. That would really be like stealing, because my putting touch deserted me today for the first time in five weeks. I started off with two birdies, then on three consecutive holes missed three-footers. On the back nine I missed a four-footer and a six-footer.

My family and my friends followed me around, and they all looked a little shocked each time I missed a putt. I guess I've spoiled them the past few weeks; they think I can't miss any more. I didn't get upset. I've been getting more than my share of the breaks for a while, and if they start going against me now, I can't complain.

I'm not a machine. My hot streak can't last forever.

July 27   I never got into contention today. Nobody else did, either. Raymond Floyd just ran away from everyone. He shot a 65 and finished at 268, twelve under par, seven strokes under the tournament record. Bobby Mitchell slipped to a 73 and a tie for fourth place, and Jack Nicklaus slipped to a 75 and a tie for sixth.

For a long time, I thought I was going to finish in the top five. After fourteen holes, I was one-under for the day and four-under for the tournament, and if I'd parred in, I would've tied for fourth. The fifteenth hole is a long par-three, and I knew I couldn't reach it with a two-iron. I decided to hit my four-wood, my most troublesome club, and I just kind of shanked it. I tried to cut it in, but instead, I pushed it off and wound up under a little tree. The ball was up against the tree, and there was no way I could hit it right-handed.

I could've just tapped it out left-handed with a putter or a two-iron, then tried to put my third shot up close enough to get a bogey. But I decided to gamble. At the time, nobody was two-under or three-under, so I knew that a bogey or even a double-bogey wouldn't hurt me too badly. I also knew that a par would give me a shot at third place. "What the hell," I said. "Let's give it a run."

I took an eight-iron, turned it upside down, and got into a left-handed stance. I once saw Chi Chi Rodríguez hit a full upside-down eight-iron left-handed about eighty or ninety yards, and I thought maybe I could pull off a little miracle and get into par range. The TV cameras zeroed in on me—we were on national television—and I swung my upside-down eight-iron. And I whiffed. I missed completely.

That was enough gambling. I switched to a two-iron, turned it around, and chipped out from under the tree, then wedged up to the green and two-putted for a nice fat triple-bogey-six. Suddenly, I was only one-under for the tournament. I finished that way, with a 72 for the day and 279 for the tournament, good for a tie for eighth place—my fifth straight week in the top ten—and a check for about $3,500. A year ago, I tied for first place with 280; if anyone had suggested to me a week ago that anyone would shoot 268 on this course, I would've had the man committed. I can't get over Ray Floyd's score. He just played super golf.

My playing partner, Tom Weiskopf, shot a 30 coming in and, with a 66, moved into third place, behind Floyd and Bobby Nichols, who closed with a 67 on his home course. Both Tom and Bobby broke the tournament record, too.

I was glad to see Bobby do well. We've always had kind of a friendly Louisville rivalry, and at least as far as publicity's concerned, Bobby's usually come out ahead. He and Dean Eagle, the sports editor of the Louisville *Courier-Journal*, are very close; in fact, they worked together on a book. Dean tries to be impartial in reporting about both of us, but he doesn't always succeed.

Just the other day, after the first round in Akron, Dean called my folks—he does that once in a while when I have a good round— and my mother answered the phone. "Mrs. Beard?" Dean said.

My mother recognized his voice right away. "Yes, Dean?"

"Mrs. Beard," Dean said, "Bobby shot a 68 today—and so did Frank."

July 28 / Louisville   Homero Blancas' wife, Noel, and their little boy are staying with Patty and the kids this week while Homero and I go play in the Westchester Classic. The wives drove down early yesterday in the Blancas' car, and then Homero and I got here about three o'clock this morning.

As soon as I got up, I headed over to my bank to make a deposit. I was carrying around forty thousand dollars in checks last week, my winnings for the previous four weeks. Most pros do the same thing—get a tournament check and stick it in their wallets and kind of forget about it until they get home. I wouldn't mind having just the interest golfers lose carrying around checks from week to week.

I stepped out of the house on the way to the bank, and a neighbor spotted me. He didn't say hello or anything. He just said, "Not on *national television!*"

I knew what he was talking about. I'm probably going to end up getting more attention for that whiff in Akron than I got for winning in Minnesota.

"You got to watch that, Frank," my neighbor said. "You got friends watching. I was at the club, drunk, and you about made me sick."

Everywhere I went all day, I got reports on my beautiful performance on national television. Bill Boone told me not to worry, I probably didn't lose too many exhibitions. "It could've been worse," Bill said. "I mean, at least you hit it the second time."

I stayed up late tonight to watch the sports program to find out what happened in the Canadian Open. Tommy Aaron and Sam Snead tied for first place yesterday, and they had an eighteen-

hole play-off today. I guess most of the public must've been pulling
for the fifty-seven-year-old man, but I'll bet most of the pros were
pulling for Tommy. We all love listening to Sam, but we can't talk
to him. Sam doesn't listen to any stories except his own. We can talk
to Tommy all day, and he won't put in too many words of his own.

Tommy won. He beat Snead by two strokes in the play-off. Now
that he's finally won his first tournament, I bet he'll go on and win
a lot more.

July 29 / Harrison, New York   I arrived in New York today in
a driving rainstorm, so I didn't even bother going over to the Westchester Country Club. I just kind of took it easy and let a few
thoughts run through my mind.

I'm about to play in the richest tournament in the world. There's
a total of $250,000 in prize money, and the winner receives fifty
thousand dollars. With that much money at stake, the Westchester
Classic gets a fantastic field. It's by far the best field of the year,
stronger than the Open, stronger than the PGA, much stronger
than the Masters. The only golfer of any consequence in the whole
world who isn't here is Deane Beman, and he'd be here if his ribs
weren't cracked.

All these people are here for one reason: they want to win that
fifty-thousand-dollar first prize. So do I. But I'm not burning to win
it. I'm not telling myself, "I've got to win this Westchester Classic
or die." The furthest I'm willing to go is to think of a good score—
say 276, twelve under par—and aim at that. But I'm a businessman
before anything else, and if someone came to me tonight and said,
"Frank, I'll give you six thousand dollars if you'll withdraw from
the Westchester Classic," I'd take it. I play the odds, and the odds
say that I won't make six thousand dollars here. The odds say that
Jack Nicklaus won't make six thousand dollars here and Arnold
Palmer won't and Billy Casper won't. But each of those guys would
probably turn down flat an offer of six thousand dollars and say,
"Hell no, I'll take my chances on winning more." Not me. I go
with the odds.

My whole game is built around going with the odds. Suppose I
come to a hypothetical eighteenth hole, say a long par-five. Then

suppose I hit a pretty good drive, and I'm facing a creek in front of the green. I'm the last man on the course, and I'm ten-under, and the leader's in the clubhouse at twelve-under. I need an eagle to tie him. Suppose there are two guys in at ten-under and another two at nine-under and nobody else better than seven-under. Assume it's a regular $100,000 tournament, and first place is worth $20,000, second place $11,400, third place $7,100, fourth place $4,700, fifth place $4,100, and sixth place $3,600.

What do I do?

I know that maybe one time out of ten I can hit across that creek and get up on the green and have a putt for an eagle. Two times out of ten, I'll either get across the creek and miss the green or fail to reach the creek. Seven times out of ten, I'm going to land in the creek or in the woods or in some kind of trouble and be in real danger of taking a bogey or a double-bogey.

I also know that if I lay up short of the creek and hit a wedge to the green, I'll get close enough for a birdie one time out of three and get a par the other two times.

If I go for the eagle and make it—and then win a play-off—I'll collect twenty thousand dollars. If I go for the eagle and get a bogey and fall into a three-way tie for fourth place, I'll win $4,133. If I go for the eagle and get a double-bogey, I'll finish sixth and win $3,600. If I lay up, I'm either going to get a birdie, finish second, and win $11,400, or get a par, tie for second, and win $7,733.

What do I do?

I'll tell you right now, I'm going to lay up. I've got enough confidence in my game to think that I'll get the birdie and $11,400. But that's the limit of my confidence, and I'm not going to press beyond that limit.

Some people say that I'm not a gambler, but they're dead wrong. That's exactly what I am—a gambler—and like any good gambler, I play the odds.

I admit there are exceptional situations when I wouldn't lay up. If it were near the end of the tour and I needed twenty thousand dollars in prize money to make the top sixty, I'd go for it; I'd actually be shooting for a lot more than twenty thousand, at least double twenty thousand. Or if it were the Masters or the Open or the PGA— where the title is worth much more than the prize money—I'd go for it.

The rest of the time, I'd lay up. I can't feed my family titles.

As a matter of fact, if somebody offered me two thousand dollars for each tournament I sat out—with the exception, again, of the Masters, Open, and PGA—I wouldn't hesitate. I'd grab it.

A few sportswriters have said, even after my victory in Minnesota, that I don't want to win, that I'm afraid to win, that I play for second. Well, that's ridiculous. Purely as a businessman, I want to win. I know that first place pays more than second place.

If I'm going to be completely honest with myself, I've got to carry that reasoning one step further. If first place didn't pay more than second place—if you got no extra money for winning—then I'd be just about as happy finishing second.

And if the first ten finishers all received the same amount of money, I'd be just about as happy finishing tenth. I don't enjoy the pressure of leading, I don't like the feeling of being nervous, and I certainly don't want the notoriety of victory. Oh, I do like it the day after. I like reading in the papers about my victory, and I like accepting congratulations from my friends and from the other pros. But I hate the attention I get from strangers. I hate being known as "Frank Beard, the professional golfer."

I am absolutely sick and tired of having people ask me, "What's Arnie really like?"

Maybe I'm fooling myself. Maybe I really do want the attention. Maybe I really do want to be famous. Maybe I just keep telling myself I don't want attention because I get so little of it. I don't know. I'm no psychiatrist.

July 30   When I got to the Westchester Country Club today for the pro-am, I couldn't find the Titleist man, so I borrowed three golf balls from Phil Rodgers. "Old Moneybags is borrowing three golf balls from me," Rodgers announced to the entire locker room. "Old Beard owes me three golf balls."

I went out and had a pleasant pro-am round. I'd played with two of the three fellows before—nice, friendly guys—and I shot a 71, and we shot 62 as a team. It won't win us any prizes, but it did get me loosened up and ready for the tournament.

I didn't have to get my own distances today. The young Australian who'd driven my car to Philadelphia and had caddied for me there walked up to me today and handed me all the yardages, beautifully marked on a scorecard. He'd gone out and gotten them yesterday or the day before for Bruce Devlin. I knew they were perfect; he got the yardages for me in Philadelphia and didn't miss one.

When I got back to the clubhouse, I checked through the mail— we get deliveries at every tournament—and I saw a letter addressed to me in an obviously feminine handwriting. I thought it was probably for Patty; some of her friends write to her through me to save time. I opened up the letter, and I almost died.

Dear Frank,
I have been meaning to write for a long time. I enjoyed our flight over. I know that even though you act the role of a tough guy, you are sentimental. Every time I look at the music box you gave me, I think of you. I hope to see you again. I'm going to be in New York next week. If you get a chance, give me a call.

Cindy

It had to be a mistake. In the first place, I don't know any Cindy. In the second, I don't have any girl friends. And in the third, I never gave a music box to anybody.

Obviously, some guy had moosed this girl into believing he was Frank Beard. And, obviously, he'd done a lot better using the name than I ever had.

I was tempted to take the letter home and show it to Patty, but then I thought of those phantom letters that are going around, and I figured Patty might think I was using some kind of reverse psychology on her.

I didn't take any chances. I ripped it up and threw it away.

July 31 I walked in this morning with Phil Rodgers and Ray Floyd, and Phil kept saying, "When are you going to return those balls? What are you waiting for, Beard? To win a good check?"

We stopped by the bulletin board in the locker room and looked at all the lists posted, the money list, the Ryder Cup list, the official-money list, the all-time money list, all that stuff. Suddenly Rodgers let out a scream. "Well I'll be a sonuvabitch!" Phil said. "Floyd went by me. He passed me on the all-time money list." They were both somewhere around fortieth.

"Hell," Raymond said, "and you been out here at least six years longer than me."

"You ought to be ashamed of yourself," Rodgers said. "I've been in a six-year slump, and it took you this long to get by me."

"I don't know how it took me this long," Floyd said.

I don't know how it took him that long, either. Phil has been in a bad slump for about three years. But it never quiets him down.

Out on the practice tee, I ran into Al Balding, and he was moaning and groaning, swinging miserably and barely hitting the ball.

"What's the matter?" I said.

"Cracked my driver yesterday," Al said. "I'm trying out a new one."

"How long did you have the old one?"

"I'll tell you how long," Al said. "I got my wife and my children all together last night and told them there'd been a death in the family."

I had two wonderful fellows for partners today, Doug Ford and Roberto de Vicenzo. Doug was like a second father to me when I came out on the tour. He took me in, introduced me to people, and taught me a lot of things about golf I still use. As a former PGA champion, Doug's got a lifetime exemption, and he plays maybe twenty tournaments a year. He's independently wealthy by now, so he's not trying to earn a living out here. I love to see Doug and play with him, but in a way I wish he'd quit. He's forty-six, and he can't play his best anymore, and it just breaks my heart to see him messing up shots he used to handle with ease. Doug's one of the most respected people in golf, and it kills me to hear spectators saying, "What's that guy trying to prove?"

Roberto is also forty-six, but he's a big fellow, with a big swing, and he can still beat most of the younger guys. I'm a better-than-average driver, and he beats me by twenty yards off the tee almost every time. Roberto just may be the greatest stroker of the ball who ever lived. If he could only putt, he would've won everything in sight.

Roberto shot a 73 today, Doug shot a 77, and old Frank came in with a nice simple 69, fifteen pars and three birdies. I missed a four-footer for a birdie on the final hole, but I sank a thirty-footer for one of my birdies and a ten-footer for a par, and I didn't three-putt all day. If I can put together four 69s, I'll have that 276, twelve-under, I set as my goal.

As I came off the course, Gene Littler walked up to me and said, "C'mon, let's go."

"Where we going?" I said.

"Let's practice," Gene said.

"You've got to be kidding," I said. "As long as I've got that golden goose in my bag, I don't have to practice."

"I can putt like that, too," Gene said, "but I'm always one shot late getting to the green."

Gene had a 74 today.

After one round, the leader in the richest tournament in the world is a fifty-two-year-old man, Tommy Bolt. Tommy took only fourteen strokes more than his age.

August 1   I lost my concentration for a while today, partly because I started worrying about the wind—the guys who teed off early escaped the breeze—and partly because I started thinking about taxes. How ridiculous can I get? I was actually walking down the fairway and wondering, if I finished first, how much of the fifty thousand dollars I'd have to give the government.

I three-putted the second hole, and after eight holes, I was two-over for the round, only one-under for the tournament, and getting dangerously close to the cut. I knew that 145 would make the cut, but that anything worse than one-over would be out. I settled down, and on every single one of the last ten holes, I had putts of twenty feet or less for birdies. I missed eight of them, made two, and came in with a 72 for the day, 141 for the tournament.

Doug Ford shot a 75 and missed the cut by a mile. Roberto de

Vicenzo shot a 70, even though he couldn't make a putt. "If I stay here and keep putting like this," Roberto told me, in his Spanish accent, "I'll lose my brains."

Poor Roberto still has to put up with a lot because of that scorecard incident in the Masters. On the ninth hole today, while we were waiting for the threesome in front of us to hole out, Roberto happened to turn toward the gallery. Some idiot held up his hands, pretended to be writing on one palm, and shouted, "Roberto, don't forget to sign your card today!"

"They'll never leave you alone, will they?" I said.

"No," he said. "Every place I go."

When we finished, I handed Roberto his scorecard—I'd kept his, he'd kept Doug's, and Doug'd kept mine—and he looked it over carefully, then said, "Frank, you made a mistake." I had. I'd put down a five for the par-five fifth hole, and he'd made a six. If he'd signed the card with a score lower than he'd actually shot, he'd have been disqualified. (In the Masters, he'd signed a card with a higher score, which meant only that he had to take the higher score.) I made the correction, and Roberto sort of smiled and shrugged.

I'm going to need a 67 and a 68 the next two days to get that 276 I want. Right now, I'm five strokes behind the leader, Bert Greene, who failed to qualify just two weeks ago in Philadelphia. Bert's twenty-five; he's young enough to be Tommy Bolt's son. And Tommy's still hanging in, tied for second place, just one stroke behind.

August 2   I was standing on the putting green today, chatting with Bert Yancey, and Howard Cosell, the broadcaster, came strolling up. The first time I met Howard, I thought he was the most sarcastic and cynical loudmouth I'd ever seen. Now that I know him a little better, I think he's the most sarcastic and cynical loudmouth I've ever seen, but I like him. He must know more about sports than any man alive.

I started teasing him because he was wearing white tennis shoes, and before I knew what hit me, he counterattacked. "Ah," he said, "there is the colorless, anonymous, ineffectual Frank Beard, whose name shall live in golfing annals because of his colossal failure under crisis conditions in a sudden-death play-off in New Orleans against the renowned Larry Hinson." For Howard, that was a short sentence, but I didn't have any comeback.

Then I went out and played with Bobby Nichols as my partner, the two of us competing for low Louisvillian in the Westchester Classic. I parred the first eight holes, then sank a six-footer for a birdie on nine, a five-footer for a birdie on ten, a fifteen-footer for a birdie on twelve, a ten-footer for a birdie on sixteen, and a ten-footer for a birdie on eighteen. Without a bogey, I shot a 67—eight strokes lower than Bobby Nichols—and moved into second place. I'm tied with four other guys, but we're all four strokes behind Bert Greene. I saw some IBM statistics after the round today, and Bert has taken only eighty putts in the first fifty-four holes, an average of less than a putt and a half a hole.

When I played with Bert at the Doral Open in Florida, he was unbelievably wild. Evidently, he's straightened himself out, because this Westchester course really punishes wildness. Bert's a dedicated, hard-working boy, and no matter what happens tomorrow, he's got a place locked up in the top sixty. He's going to be exempt from qualifying next year for the first time in his career. Of course, he could start being exempt tomorrow if he holds on to his lead. Four strokes are an awful lot for the rest of us to overcome; the best thing we've got going for us is the pressure on a boy who's never been in a position like this before.

As I went to my car in the parking lot outside the clubhouse, Bob Lunn congratulated me on my 67. "If you shoot exactly the same score tomorrow, you'll take all the marbles," Bob said. "I think you're going to do it."

Some friends of mine took me to see *Oh! Calcutta!* tonight. I wanted to keep my mind off golf, but that was ridiculous. I'd never been to the theater in New York before—I think the only show I'd ever seen was *Brigadoon* in Dallas—but I'll tell you, if *Oh! Calcutta!* is typical, I haven't been missing a thing. You sure don't come out humming the tunes. The whole cast ran around nude, and the show was miserable. It wasn't sexy. It wasn't funny. It wasn't even interesting. It was so dull that, even with all those naked people strutting around, my mind kept drifting back to golf.

On the way back to my room from the theater, I stopped and picked up a copy of the New York *Daily News* and read that five men were tied for second place in the Westchester Classic—Tommy Bolt, Lee Trevino, Dan Sikes, Harold Henning, and *Ralph* Beard. All the older sportswriters seem to remember my brother better than they remember me; half of them call me Ralph to my face.

At least they got the last name right.

August 3   I went to Mass this morning at St. Patrick's Cathedral, something I'd always wanted to do. It was one of the few churches I'd been in in a long time that really had a traditional feeling to it. I felt good there. I felt relaxed.

And then I went to the Stage Delicatessen for breakfast. I don't suppose there are too many people, not even native New Yorkers, who can say they went to *Oh! Calcutta!* and St. Patrick's and the Stage Delicatessen all in the space of fifteen hours.

I began feeling nervous, almost nauseous, on the way to the golf course. I wasn't too confident. If someone right then had offered me third-place money—$17,750 in a $250,000 tournament—to drop out of the final round, I'd have accepted in a second. I was still playing the odds, and I knew that the odds were against me catching Bert Greene and against me beating all four of the men I was tied with.

When I got to the course around one o'clock, I had almost two hours to kill before my tee time. I spent half an hour in the locker room chatting with a few reporters. Sometimes, I've got to admit they can be pleasant. I disagree with a lot of the things they write, but I've got to keep reminding myself that they're just trying to make a living, too.

On the practice tee, I hit the ball terribly. I was too nervous to do anything right. I wanted to get into the ball game and get going.

On the putting green, Dan Sikes walked over to me. "Bert's a good golfer," Dan sad, "but I don't think he's going to win this tournament. I think the winner's going to be one of us at eight-under. I wouldn't mind making this one my first victory in more than a year." Dan had a twinkle in his eye, like he was figuring I was the one he had to beat.

Sikes and Bruce Crampton teed off two groups in front of me. Then came Tommy Bolt and Al Mengert, the fellow who'd played all by himself in the Western Open, then Harold Henning and me. Bert Greene and Lee Trevino were the final twosome; I figured Lee's chatter would either keep Bert relaxed or drive him crazy.

I couldn't have asked for a better partner than Harry the Horse. He's my friend. He's not loud. He's quick. He doesn't agonize lining up each one of his shots. My game plan was simple. I wasn't really thinking about catching Greene, but I wanted to do as well as possible to beat Sikes, Henning, Bolt, and Trevino. I especially wanted to get through the first four holes at even-par, because I knew that if I picked up a bogey or two there, I'd start aiming for a 70 or a 71 or a 72 and give up any chance at the first three places, the big-money places. I wasn't looking for any birdies on the first four holes.

The first hole, a 190-yard par-three, called for a four-iron shot, but I took a five-iron. I didn't care if I was a bit short. I just knew that if I went over the green, I'd never get my par. I knocked the five-iron on the green, about twenty feet short of the pin, and two-putted for my par.

I played the second hole, a short par-four, just as conservatively. I used a three-wood off the tee, giving up some distance so that I wouldn't miss the fairway, then hit my second shot eight feet from the cup. My first putt curled off at the hole, and I made another par.

On the third hole, I hit a super drive, then an eight-iron, then two putts from twenty feet for my third par.

On the fourth, a long par-four, I used a three-wood off the tee anyway, sacrificing distance for accuracy again. But I pushed my shot into the right-hand rough. As I walked down the fairway, I said to myself, "Okay, Beard. Here's where we find out how this round is going to go."

The rough had been brutal all week, but when I reached my ball, it was sitting up absolutely perfect. "Things just might be coming my way today," I thought. I hit a seven-iron, and my ball landed short of the green and rolled up ten feet from the cup. I thought my first putt was going to be a little short, but it kept right on going and dropped into the hole for a birdie-three.

I walked over to a friend of mine in the gallery and I said, "I'm going to win this tournament." My heart was up in my throat. The combination of the good lie in the rough, the roll on the iron shot, and the birdie putt was just too good to believe. I was one-under after the first four holes.

On the fifth hole, I lipped out an eight-foot birdie putt.

On the sixth hole, I lipped out a twelve-foot birdie putt.

I wasn't bothered. I knew they'd start dropping.

On the seventh hole, I knocked in a three-foot birdie putt, and when I came off the green, I heard that Greene had lost a stroke to par. He was now eleven-under for the tournament, and I was ten-under.

Dark clouds rolled in over the course, and after I hit a good drive on the eighth hole, a dogleg to the left, rain started sprinkling down. I turned to Henning. "God, I hope it doesn't keep raining," I said.

From the fourth hole on, I'd been worrying about rain. I could feel that I was playing my best game and I knew that I couldn't possibly do it two days in a row. This was my day, and I had to get my round in, or I wouldn't stand a chance. I got angry just thinking about the possibility of a rain-out. "I've got my momentum going," I told myself, "I've got a real chance to win this tournament and make my whole year and what happens? A rainstorm!"

I got hot. I groaned and I didn't concentrate and I didn't stop to think that everyone else was playing in the same rain, and I just plain psyched myself into hitting a poor four-iron shot. The ball skipped off the right side of the green and up a little hill and stopped near some rocks. My lie wasn't bad—another good sign—but I had to assume the damnedest position to make the chip. I knew I was a dumb ass for letting the rain get to me. I knew, too, that if I made a bogey, my momentum would disappear. This was my first real crisis of the day. I hit a pretty good chip, but the ball ran about eight feet past the hole. I faced an uphill putt, breaking to the right, for my par. I rolled it in.

Right then, I knew that, unless someone got hot and shot out to Mars somewhere, I was going to win the Westchester Classic and win its fifty-thousand-dollar first prize.

On the ninth hole, a par-five, I tried to cut my second shot, a four-wood, my weak club, into the green, but I didn't make it. I caught a bunker twenty yards short of the pin and thirty yards to the left of it. I went down in that trap, and with the old wedge

Dick Hart gave me, with the hours and hours of practice paying off, I blasted out seven feet from the hole. I knew I'd make the putt. I knew it. I stroked it right in the cup.

I made the turn three-under for the day, eleven-under for the tournament, all even with Bert Greene, who was coming up the ninth fairway behind me. Then I looked at the scoreboard. I could've strangled Dan Sikes. He was thirteen-under, two strokes in front of me; he'd eagled the ninth hole and birdied the tenth. He had eight holes to play and a two-stroke lead and a burning desire for victory and a fantastic record on this course. He'd finished second in the Weschester Classic in 1967 and 1968, both times with a score of 273, fifteen under par; in 1967, he'd set a course record with a 62.

On the tenth hole, I sank a fifteen-footer for a birdie, to go twelve-under, and I could feel the adrenaline surging through me. I didn't care what Dan Sikes did. I was going to win.

On the eleventh hole, I was so charged up I didn't dare use a driver or I might land in a creek about 270 yards out. I hit a three-wood instead, then a five-iron, then two putts from twenty feet.

On the twelfth, a par-five, a good birdie hole, I got greedy. I tried to blast my drive five hundred yards and, instead, hooked it into a fairway bunker. I got out with an eight-iron, pitched up, and two-putted for my par. After I parred the thirteenth, I heard that Sikes had bogeyed the same hole to fall back to twelve-under, even with me. But I also heard that Greene, who wasn't folding, had birdied both nine and twelve to go thirteen-under. On the fourteenth, a short par-three, I hit an eight-iron six feet from the cup. I sprang off that tee like a peacock, positive I had the whole tournament in my hip pocket.

Harold Henning had the same putt I had for a birdie, only longer. It looked as if it would break to the left. I watched Harold putt, watched him play for a break to the left, and watched the ball fail to break. I played my putt almost straight in, and the ball broke, caught the left edge of the cup, and lipped out. I almost couldn't believe it. I'd already chalked up my birdie.

But I didn't lose my momentum. On the fifteenth, all charged up, I hit a super drive, leaving myself only a four-iron to the green on the toughest hole on the course. I mis-hit the shot. I came off the four-iron and left it in the bunker on the right of the green. Then I blasted out fifteen feet from the pin, and, suddenly, I'd reached the second critical point in my round. If I missed, I was out of it.

I lined up my putt, a fifteen-footer, breaking left, into the "tiger teeth," into the grain. The green was kind of spiked up. The putt was tricky. I hit it and watched it and said to myself, "It's not going to break enough." Then the ball rolled up toward the hole, veered left, and dove in.

I knew that the Westchester Classic was mine. Greene was still thirteen-under, Sikes twelve-under, and I twelve-under. Yet I knew I had to win; too many breaks had gone my way.

On the sixteenth, normally a three-iron, I was so pumped up I hit a four-iron within twenty feet of the pin, then lipped out my birdie putt. Behind me, Bert Greene bogeyed the fifteenth; he, Sikes, and I were all even at twelve-under—twelve-under, the target score I'd set before the tournament began. Henning was in fourth place at nine-under.

I missed the fairway on the seventeenth, reached the green from the rough, and two-putted for a par. I went to the eighteenth tee, a long par-five, demanding about a 270-yard drive to clear the dogleg, bending left up to the green guarded by fairway bunkers. "Now just keep it smooth," I told myself. "Don't jump. Don't lurch. Just get any kind of drive out there so you can lay it up short of the bunkers on your second shot."

I hit a great drive, long and straight, and when I reached my ball, Sikes was on the green, less than twenty feet from the pin set in one of the dips on an undulating green. Sikes missed his birdie putt, leaving himself three or four feet from the hole, then lined up his second putt carefully. Three times he backed away from the putt. I watched him, knowing how badly he wanted to win. Finally, he putted. He missed. He took a bogey and slipped to eleven under par.

Right then, I did something I'd never done before. On the course, I stopped and prayed to God for victory. "If You let me win this tournament," I said, "I'll give five thousand of the fifty thousand to some needy children, to people who haven't been nearly as privileged as I am."

"Go, Frank, go," I heard people yelling. "Go, go."

I never for a moment considered trying for the green. I knew I couldn't get across those fairway bunkers with a rifle. I knew my only chance for a birdie was to lay up, then knock a wedge in close and make the putt. I took a four-iron and hit the ball just where I wanted it, ten yards short of the traps.

My ball was perched up on a fluffy lie, perfect for a pitch-and-run shot, just the kind of shot I wanted. I didn't have to use any tricks, anything special; all I had to do was make contact with the ball. "Stay down, Beard," I told myself. "Stay down. Just hit it good and solid."

I hit the shot perfectly. The ball rolled up two feet from the pin. I marked my ball. Harold sank a ten-footer for a birdie to finish ten-under, alone in fourth place. Then I hit my putt, a slight break to the right, and it ran into the cup. I had a birdie. As far as I was concerned, it was all over. It never for a moment entered my mind that Bert Greene might birdie the last hole, too.

Bert hit a big drive. A year ago, Bob Murphy came to the same hole needing a birdie to tie Julius Boros; Murph played short of the bunkers, wedged up, and missed his birdie putt, and a lot of people criticized him for playing too conservatively. I thought he made the right move.

But now Bert took out a four-wood to go for the green, and as big a hitter as he is, as charged up as he had to be, I knew he couldn't make it. He didn't. Instead, he caught one of the fairway bunkers. He blasted out fifteen feet short of the hole, an excellent recovery considering the circumstances, and then missed his putt.

I was champion of the Westchester Classic.

I went on national television, and all of a sudden, the rein I'd always held on my emotions gave way. I felt tears trickling down my checks. I knew that millions of people were watching, and I didn't care. I thanked Patty and the children, thanked Pro and my mother, and quietly, I thanked God.

I decided I'd send the five-thousand-dollar check I'd promised Him to needy children in Dallas, where my sister is a nun.

As I came off the eighteenth green, after the television interview, Dan Sikes walked over to me. "Frank," he said, "you don't know how hard I was pulling for you to make that last putt." I knew what Dan meant. If I'd come in at twelve-under, instead of thirteen-under, he might've killed himself for missing that short putt on eighteen. Now, he could tell himself, "Well, my putt didn't cost me the tournament, just a little money."

Bert Greene didn't seem to feel too badly. He hadn't lost the tournament; I'd won it. He'd shot a par 72 on the final round, a tremendous performance by a young fellow under pressure, but I'd shot a 67. I'd finished at 275, one stroke lower than the goal I'd set for myself at the start of the week.

The only sour note of the day was struck by my caddy, an older fellow, a regular caddy at the Westchester Country Club. He'd shagged about two hundred balls all week, carried my bag for five rounds, and kept my clubs and balls clean. That was it. He never gave me a single distance; I checked him once, and he was twenty yards off. He never lined up a single putt. He never offered a single word of encouragement. He was quiet, polite, and punctual, and nothing more. He did no more or less than he would've done if I'd come in fiftieth. I decided that, even though he'd done nothing special, I ought to give him $750, more than I'd ever paid a caddie before. I handed him a check, and he looked at it with complete disdain. "Are you kidding?" he said. He was bitter. He said he thought he deserved twice that much. I couldn't believe it.

He couldn't spoil my day. I was floating. I'd defeated the toughest field of the whole year, a field so tough that the two leading money-winners going into the tournament, Dave Hill and Gene Littler,

Frank Beard's Record

TOURNAMENT	1ST ROUND	2ND ROUND	3RD ROUND	4TH ROUND
Philadelphia	72	72	70	66
American	68	67	72	72
Westchester	69	72	67	67

both missed the cut; in fact, eight of the top thirty money-winners missed the cut. Billy Casper finished eight strokes behind me. Jack Nicklaus finished eight strokes behind me. Arnie Palmer finished fourteen strokes behind me. The Masters champion, George Archer, finished nine strokes behind me. The Open champion, Orville Moody, and the British Open champion, Tony Jacklin, both missed the cut.

By a margin of twenty-five thousand dollars, I was the leading money-winner on the professional tour. I'd won $155,000, far more than I'd ever won in a full year.

I was champion of the richest tournament in the whole world.

August 4 / Louisville   The telephone kept ringing off the wall all day. Radio and television reporters and newspapermen wanted to interview me from morning to night. Telegrams came in from everywhere, and our house was upside down.

Patty looked at me this evening and smiled. "Next time," she said, with a wink, "see if you can finish second. That'll be good enough."

I used to feel that way myself.

TOTAL SCORE	FINISH	PRO-AM EARNINGS	INDIVIDUAL EARNINGS
280	5	—	$ 6,150.00
279	T 8	—	3,530.00
275	1	—	50,000.00

One of the Big Boys

August 11 / Dayton   Everybody's treating me like a king. Everybody's picking me to win the PGA championship. Johnny Pott walked up to me today and said, "How 'bout a loan, Frank?" Jack Nicklaus said, "Turn around, Frank. I've always wanted to see what a number-one money-winner looks like."

I played a practice round with a friend of mine, a club pro named Johnny Cook, and when we teed off, a couple of hundred people followed us down the fairway. I'd never had a gallery that big for a practice round. I looked around to see if Arnie had joined us.

August 12   Patty turned to me tonight and said, "I just can't take it."

"What do you mean?" I said.

"Everyone's saying to me, 'How does it feel to be rich?' I don't feel any different. I don't think we're any different."

"Of course we're not, honey," I said.

"Well, I wish they'd stop this stuff about being number one," Patty said. "I'm beginning to wish you were number one hundred."

August 13   I'm becoming self-conscious about everything I do. I was sitting out on the porch of my motel room this afternoon, and suddenly, I found myself thinking, "I'd better get down by the pool, because if I don't, people are going to look around and say, 'Well, Frank Beard is number one on the money list now, so he just stands off like some kind of god.'"

August 14   I gave a reporter an interview the other day and told him that I found a lot of the tour to be drudgery, that the golf part was like being in a pressure-cooker, and that I hated it when my family wasn't with me. The story came out saying flatly, "Frank Beard hates the tour."

"If you don't like the tour," Dave Hill said to me today, "why don't you get off it and become a milkman?"

August 15   My streak ended today. After twenty-five straight rounds of 72 or better, I shot a 75 in the second round of the PGA championship.

August 16   Patty's still upset. Some of our friends—not our close ones, but some of the others—seem to be ignoring us. I don't know whether they're jealous or what. Patty can't figure out why they won't accept us as they always did. We haven't changed. I'll tell you, if our life's going to continue like this, I'd just as soon drop back and be number ten again.

August 17   With closing rounds of 69 and 68, I managed to come in tenth in the PGA championship. I've finished in the top ten in seven straight tournaments, with fifteen of twenty-eight rounds in the 60s. In two months, I've earned about $105,000.

August 18 / Louisville   I think I understand now what happens to the superstars. The pressure is unbelievable when you're on top. I don't mean on the golf course. I mean from the press, from the public, even from your friends. I won't have to put up with it for long—I'm just a temporary hero—but if I were a superstar, I guess I'd buy a private plane and stay in private homes and keep away from everyone else as much as possible. I've been a little harsh on Jack and Arnie and Cas. I'm getting a taste of what they go through, and I don't envy them at all.

August 20   Arnie had to withdraw from the PGA tournament the other day with an inflamed hip. Nobody's got more determination or more spirit, but this time I really think he's finished.

August 27 / Hartford   When I was a bachelor on the tour, I used to spend some nights taking care of Frank Boynton's son, Sandy. When I saw Frank today, for the first time since the Westchester Classic, he said, "Well, I'm glad to see that my old babysitter finally made good."

August 30   I was paired with Davy Hill the past two days, and I'm going to make a statement: right now, I'd take Dave Hill against any golfer in the world. There is absolutely nothing he can't do, from driving to putting. He's got his nerves and his temper under control, and it's going to be some job to stay ahead of him on the money list the rest of the year.

August 31   I finally finished out of the top ten, way out. I just stumbled through the Greater Hartford Open and ended up tied for forty-second place. I won $297.50, not even enough to pay expenses.

I wasn't too unhappy to see Bob Lunn beat Dave Hill in a play-off for the championship. Davy shot 68-68-66-66, then lost the play-off on the fourth sudden-death hole. He still collected $11,400, and now I'm only fifteen thousand dollars ahead of him in the money race.

September 12 / Washington   I met President Nixon today. He came out on the White House Lawn to greet the American Ryder Cup team, and we all putted for a while on the little green that President Eisenhower had built during his term in office. When it got to Trevino's turn to putt, Lee whipped out a five-dollar bill and said, "Hey, Mr. President, want to bet me on this putt?"

September 13   Gene Littler took me aside today, before we left for England, and said, "Frank, are you going to make golf your career?"

"Sure," I said.

"Well, you're going to have to lose some weight," Gene said. "That's all there is to it."

Gene's always been kind of an idol of mine, and he'd never said anything like that to me before.

I took a vow right then that I'd definitely straighten out.

September 20 / Southport, England   Well, I played in my first Ryder Cup Match, and I didn't do too much for the United States. I lost my only singles match, and in team play, paired with

Billy Casper, I won once, lost once, and drew once. The match wound up even, sixteen points for the United States and sixteen for Britain, and we retained the cup.

October 18 / Las Vegas   Orville Moody, who just came back from winning the World Cup with Lee Trevino, came up to me in the locker room today and said something that made me feel good. "Back in April, Frank," Sarge said, "somebody told me you'd put on your tapes that I was going to be one of the best players on the tour. I'd always had a lot of respect for your ability and your judgment, and when I heard that, I said to myself, 'If Frank Beard thinks that about me, maybe I *can* be a good player.' From then on, I started thinking like a good player and playing like one."

October 19   I went into the final round of the Sahara Invitational today with a one-stroke lead and a good chance to win my third championship of the year. Instead, I finished second. The Bear, Jack Nicklaus, stormed past me with a 65 in the final round.

Dave Hill finished right behind me, so now, with five tournaments to go, I've got a twenty-thousand-dollar lead.

November 2 / Napa   Jack Nicklaus won his second straight tournament today and moved up into fourth place on the money list. I'm fifty thousand dollars ahead of him and twenty thousand ahead of Hill with three tournaments to play.

November 9 / Honolulu   I was right. Jack Nicklaus is through. He only finished second today, giving him a total of $62,300 in prize money in his last three tournaments.

November 30 / Louisville   Jack Nicklaus slumped all the way to sixth place in the final round of the Heritage Classic in South Carolina today.

I stayed home and skipped the tournament—the fourth tournament I've skipped since the Westchester Classic—but a bunch of my friends had a good week. Dick Hart, who gave me my wedge, tied for ninth and won $2,400. Homero Blancas, whose family stayed with mine during the Westchester Classic, finished fifth and won $4,100. Doug Ford, who I thought ought to quit at forty-six, finished fourth and won $4,700. Dick Crawford, who's been fantastic the second half of the year, tied for second and won $9,250.

And the championship went to my old friend Arnie.

Maybe the king's not dead, either.

December 7 / Hollywood, Florida   Arnie won his second in a row today. He won the Danny Thomas–Diplomat Classic, the final event of the 1969 tour, and he won in style, with a charge, a closing 65 that enabled him to come from six strokes in back of Gay Brewer.

I think he may stay on the tour next year.

December 10 / Louisville   Finally, and officially, I wound up first on the money list, at $175,223.93, almost $19,000 in front of Dave Hill and $35,000 in front of Jack Nicklaus. This was the first time since 1962, in his rookie season, that Jack didn't finish either first or second on the money list. And it was the first time since 1959 that the leading money-winner on the PGA tour wasn't Arnie (three years) or Jack (three years) or Billy (two years) or Gary (one year).

A lot of big names didn't make the top sixty. Doug Sanders missed. Al Geiberger missed. So did Mason Rudolph, Billy Maxwell, and Kermit Zarley. Marty Fleckman didn't make five thousand dollars for the whole year; he finished 154th on the list. Jack Montgomery's rib operation kept him out of the top sixty; he missed by a couple of thousand dollars.

Dick Crawford won back his exemption by finishing forty-sixth. And, by the margin of a few hundred dollars, by finishing fifty-eighth among the official money-winners, Steve Reid won a year off from qualifying.

I saw that Charlie Coody ended the year nineteenth on the money list with earnings of $79,996.26. That's an awful lot of money to take completely out of circulation.

December 28   I'm getting ready to leave for the 1970 tour. It's a brand-new year, except for a few things.

Patty's pregnant, and I weigh 205 pounds.

Frank Beard's 1969 Record

TOURNAMENT	SCORE	FINISH	PRO-AM EARNINGS	UNOFFICIAL EARNINGS	OFFICIAL EARNINGS	TOTAL EARNINGS
SOUTHERN CAL*	139	T 6	$ —	$ 800.00	—	$ 800.00
LOS ANGELES	WD	—	187.50	—	—	187.50
KAISER*†	141	T 25	—	414.97	—	414.97
BING CROSBY*	MC	—	1,100.00	—	—	1,100.00
ANDY WILLIAMS	289	T 9	2,475.00	—	$ 3,325.00	3,325.00
BOB HOPE*	351	T 5	—	3,175.00	—	5,650.00
PHOENIX	278	T 52	—	—	142.86	142.86
TUCSON	283	T 11	200.00	—	2,200.00	2,400.00
DORAL	289	T 43	30.00	—	442.50	472.50
CITRUS	285	T 18	—	—	1,207.77	1,207.77
MONSANTO			DID NOT PLAY			
JACKSONVILLE	284	T 17	—	—	1,450.00	1,450.00
NATIONAL AIRLINES	289	T 46	89.29	—	480.00	569.29
GREENSBORO	283	T 31	—	—	819.20	819.20
MASTERS	290	T 19	—	—	2,100.00	2,100.00
CHAMPIONS			DID NOT PLAY			
BYRON NELSON	278	T 2	641.67	—	9,250.00	9,891.67
NEW ORLEANS	275	2	462.50	—	11,400.00	11,862.50
TEXAS	284	T 24	—	—	810.00	810.00
COLONIAL	284	10	200.00	—	3,125.00	3,325.00
ATLANTA			DID NOT PLAY			
MEMPHIS			DID NOT PLAY			
WESTERN	281	3	—	—	9,240.00	9,240.00
U.S. OPEN	296	T 50	—	—	895.00	895.00

Tournament	Score	Place			
KEMPER	276	T 4	DID NOT PLAY	4,840.00	4,840.00
CLEVELAND	279	2	235.48	14,300.00	14,535.48
BUICK	269	1	268.75	20,000.00	20,268.75
MINNESOTA	280	5	—	6,150.00	6,150.00
PHILADELPHIA	279	T 8	—	3,530.00	3,530.00
AMERICAN	275	1	—	50,000.00	50,000.00
WESTCHESTER			DID NOT PLAY		
MILWAUKEE			DID NOT PLAY		
PGA	282	10	—	4,375.00	4,375.00
AVCO			DID NOT PLAY		
HARTFORD	281	T 42	—	297.50	297.50
MICHIGAN			DID NOT PLAY		
ALCAN*	278	3	7,500.00	—	7,500.00
SAHARA	276	2	578.33	11,400.00	11,978.33
SAN FRANCISCO	275	T 14	308.33	1,600.00	1,908.33
KAISER‡	282	T 31	—	828.34	828.34
HAWAIIAN	289	T 44	50.00	291.66	341.66
HERITAGE			DID NOT PLAY		
DANNY THOMAS	288	T 49	100.00	207.28	307.28

* Unofficial
† First Kaiser of year
‡ Second Kaiser of year

TOTALS

Tournaments Entered	34
Official Tournaments Entered	29
Average Strokes Per Official Round	70.527 (112 rounds)
Pro-Am Earnings	$ 6,926.85
Other Unofficial Earnings	11,889.97
Total Earnings	183,523.93

The Top Sixty Money-Winners

TOTAL MONEY* 1969

1.	Frank Beard	$175,223.93	31.	Homero Blancas	59,454.64
2.	Dave Hill	156,423.30	32.	Bob Murphy	56,525.97
3.	Jack Nicklaus	140,167.42	33.	Juan Rodríguez	56,312.95
4.	Gary Player	123,897.69	34.	Bunky Henry	56,020.90
5.	Bruce Crampton	118,955.80	35.	R. H. Sikes	54,934.72
6.	Gene Littler	112,737.27	36.	Larry Hinson	54,267.02
7.	Lee Trevino	112,417.51	37.	G. Dickinson	53,978.97
8.	Ray Floyd	109,956.63	38.	Lee Elder	53,678.67
9.	Arnold Palmer	105,128.42	39.	Howie Johnson	52,602.95
10.	Billy Casper	104,689.46	40.	Julius Boros	50,403.63
11.	George Archer	102,707.46	41.	Jim Colbert	43,693.12
12.	Dale Douglass	91,553.53	42.	Harold Henning	43,118.47
13.	Tommy Aaron	91,462.41	43.	George Knudson	42,964.34
14.	Miller Barber	90,107.38	44.	Jim Wiechers	40,100.90
15.	Dan Sikes	89,103.68	45.	Charles Sifford	39,864.30
16.	Tom Shaw	83,332.01	46.	Dick Crawford	39,376.56
17.	Bert Yancey	83,111.29	47.	Terry Dill	38,681.54
18.	Tom Weiskopf	81,593.79	48.	Dick Lotz	38,210.29
19.	Charles Coody	79,996.26	49.	Bob Dickson**	37,798.77
20.	Deane Beman	79,846.98	50.	Grier Jones	37,193.79
21.	Orville Moody	79,176.47	51.	Bobby Nichols	36,793.60
22.	Bruce Devlin	77,962.54	52.	Ron Cerrudo**	35,861.25
23.	Bert Greene	76,181.47	53.	Bob Goalby	35,521.98
24.	Bob Lunn	73,606.17	54.	Johnny Pott	35,252.12
25.	Ken Still	72,514.21	55.	Fred Marti	34,945.98
26.	Dave Stockton	70,707.43	56.	Bobby Mitchell	34,155.31
27.	Don January	65,630.93	57.	B. R. McLendon	34,074.86
28.	Gay Brewer	64,315.80	58.	Don Bies	33,340.68
29.	Larry Ziegler	59,804.12	59.	Rod Funseth**	33,111.13
30.	Bob Charles	59,734.11	60.	Tony Jacklin**	33,036.66

* Excludes Southern California Open and Alcan, but includes pro-ams and unofficial events such as Bing Crosby and Bob Hope tournaments.
** Did not make top sixty among official money-winners; were replaced by Bob Stanton, Phil Rodgers, Steve Spray, and Steve Reid.

Vardon Trophy Standings

1969

	ROUNDS	STROKES	AVERAGE
1. Dave Hill	90	6331	70.344
2. Frank Beard	112	7899	70.527
3. Tommy Aaron	112	7921	70.723
4. Don January	83	5883	70.880
5. Dan Sikes	98	6951	70.929
6. Lee Trevino	106	7520	70.943
7. Arnold Palmer	89	6318	70.989
8. Jack Nicklaus	80	5683	71.038
9. Miller Barber	111	7904	71.207
10. Dale Douglass	126	8981	71.278

(A minimum of eighty rounds is required to be eligible for the Vardon Trophy.)

Modern Era Official Money Leaders

(*Through 1969*)

1.	Arnold Palmer	$ 1,121,566.17
2.	Jack Nicklaus	996,524.17
3.	Billy Casper	981,924.48
4.	Julius Boros	761,732.06
5.	Gene Littler	637,159.11
6.	Gary Player	592,623.22
7.	Doug Sanders	549,087.70
8.	Frank Beard	514,402.59
9.	Dan Sikes	453,775.40
10.	Don January	441,012.62
11.	Bruce Crampton	431,086.74
12.	Sam Snead	422,214.70
13.	Gardner Dickinson	413,445.66
14.	Bob Goalby	402,808.84
15.	Al Geiberger	399,412.04
16.	Gay Brewer	397,500.82
17.	Bobby Nichols	393,584.21
18.	Doug Ford	392,912.63
19.	Art Wall	378,521.58
20.	George Archer	371,943.79
21.	Dow Finsterwald	365,111.91
22.	Miller Barber	352,342.66
23.	Tony Lema	352,095.09
24.	Dave Hill	344,514.69
25.	Tommy Aaron	339,818.11

About the Author

FRANK BEARD began playing the tour long before he became a professional golfer. He was born in Texas on May 1, 1939, then attended high school in Kentucky and college in Florida. In his seven years on the pro golf tour, he has won eight tournaments and more than half a million dollars in prize money. He and his wife, Pat, and their three children, Danny, Randi, and Jennifer, live in Louisville, Kentucky.

About the Editor

DICK SCHAAP, former city editor and syndicated columnist for the New York *Herald Tribune*, collaborated with Jerry Kramer on *Instant Replay* and *Farewell to Football* and with Joe Namath on *I Can't Wait Until Tomorrow . . . 'Cause I Get Better-Looking Every Day*. He is the author of *R.F.K.* and *Turned On: The Friede-Crenshaw Case*. He and his wife, Madeleine, and their son, Jeremy, reside in New York City.